M000201845

Many Christians know *what th[ey believe]* [about these] issues, but not *why*, and are left [...] us to engage these topics with [...] right tactics to the tough conversations.

—JOHN STONESTREET, president, Colson Center; host, *BreakPoint*

Koukl answers the critic's toughest challenges—and maybe even the believer's own doubts—but then adds the specific tactical questions necessary to help believers navigate difficult conversations safely, graciously, and effectively. Of great value for practical apologetics and evangelism.

—WILLIAM LANE CRAIG, author, *Reasonable Faith*

Greg Koukl has a gift for clarifying complex issues. This book provides guidance on how we can maneuver in tough conversations to impact culture for Christ. You'll be amazed at your ability to engage your critics in a winsome and attractive way.

—DAVID LIMBAUGH, *New York Times* bestselling author, *The True Jesus* and *Jesus on Trial*

Greg Koukl is my go-to source for guidance on navigating tough conversations about Christianity. In *Street Smarts*, Greg raises the bar. This book will take your Christian conversations to a new level.

—J. WARNER WALLACE, *Dateline*-featured cold-case detective; author, *Person of Interest* and *The Truth about True Crime*

Filled with practical advice, *Street Smarts* is the perfect book for those who want to walk with others through the intellectual and existential challenges of our cultural moment.

—DR. STEPHEN C. MEYER, author, *Return of the God Hypothesis*

Street Smarts is Greg's best work. It is a fun, engaging read that exhibits street savvy—a real understanding of the culture in which we live and breathe and have our being.

—J. P. MORELAND, distinguished professor of philosophy, Talbot School of Theology, Biola University

The wisdom in this book comes from a lifetime of engaging people on the street. Greg will teach you the skill of using questions in your interactions with skeptics and build your confidence to carry them out with grace and truth.

—SEAN McDOWELL, associate professor of apologetics,
Biola University; coauthor, *Set Adrift*

Street Smarts is the book I wish I'd had when I first set out to learn to defend my faith. An indispensable guide for any Christian navigating difficult conversations in today's hostile culture.

—NATASHA CRAIN, author, *Faithfully Different* and
Keeping Your Kids on God's Side

This book offers effective tools to equip believers, who, by God's grace, can help unbelievers move closer to considering and embracing the gospel.

—PAUL COPAN, Pledger Family Chair of Philosophy
and Ethics, Palm Beach Atlantic University

On full display in *Street Smarts* are Greg's many gifts, including his uncanny ability to engage his critics with both charity and rigor. Even if you find yourself, as I do, not agreeing with every single point that Greg makes, he gives you the blueprint on how to move forward and think through the many contested issues that bedevil our age.

—FRANCIS J. BECKWITH, professor of philosophy, Baylor University

Street Smarts addresses the topics necessary to help us dialogue effectively with our friends who desperately need the truth.

—DAN KIMBALL, author, *How (Not) to Read the Bible*

Greg Koukl is well-known for his Socratic-questioning approach—a more appealing way to use apologetic arguments in our case for Christianity. *Street Smarts* goes farther, providing application to philosophic positions and particular challenges. Well written, highly recommended.

—GARY HABERMAS, distinguished research professor, Liberty University

On every page of this book you'll learn what to say and how to say it, even when dealing with today's thorniest issues.

—JEFF MYERS, PhD, president, Summit Ministries

If you liked Greg Koukl's earlier book, *Tactics*—and who didn't?—then you're going to love this new work.

—MARK MITTELBERG, author, *Contagious Faith* and *Confident Faith*; executive director, Lee Strobel Center for Evangelism and Applied Apologetics at Colorado Christian University

Koukl's crisp, clear, and careful writing style make this book an absolute joy to read. I could not recommend it more highly to thoughtful Christians and apologists of every stripe.

—CRAIG HAZEN, director, Graduate Program in Christian Apologetics, Biola University

Street Smarts gives you the philosophical framework as well as the practical dialogues needed to defend Christian beliefs and practices.

—DR. CHRISTOPHER YUAN, author, *Holy Sexuality and the Gospel*; producer, The Holy Sexuality Project video series (for parents and their teens)

Street Smarts puts one of the sharpest Christian apologists in the country in your back pocket. It provides blueprints on a variety of timely topics to help us with the conversations we all need to have in a post-Christian world.

—SCOTT KLUSENDORF, president, Life Training Institute; author, *The Case for Life*

STREET
SMARTS

STREET SMARTS

USING QUESTIONS TO ANSWER CHRISTIANITY'S TOUGHEST CHALLENGES

GREGORY KOUKL

ZONDERVAN
REFLECTIVE

ZONDERVAN REFLECTIVE

Street Smarts
Copyright © 2023 by Gregory Koukl

Requests for information should be addressed to:
Zondervan, *3900 Sparks Dr. SE, Grand Rapids, Michigan 49546*

Zondervan titles may be purchased in bulk for educational, business, fundraising, or sales promotional use. For information, please email SpecialMarkets@Zondervan.com.

ISBN 978-0-310-13915-7 (audio)

Library of Congress Cataloging-in-Publication Data

Names: Koukl, Gregory, 1950- author.
Title: Street smarts : using questions to answer Christianity's toughest challenges / Greg Koukl.
Description: Grand Rapids : Zondervan, 2023.
Identifiers: LCCN 2022061341 (print) | LCCN 2022061342 (ebook) | ISBN 9780310139133 (paperback) | ISBN 9780310139140 (ebook)
Subjects: LCSH: Apologetics. | Evangelistic work. | Witness bearing (Christianity) | BISAC: RELIGION / Christian Ministry / Evangelism | RELIGION / Christian Living / Social Issues
Classification: LCC BT1103 .K679 2023 (print) | LCC BT1103 (ebook) | DDC 239—dc23/ eng/20230419
LC record available at https://lccn.loc.gov/2022061341
LC ebook record available at https://lccn.loc.gov/2022061342

Italics in Scripture quotations are the author's own for emphasis.

Scripture quotations, unless otherwise indicated, are taken from the New American Standard Bible® (NASB®). Copyright © 1960, 1971, 1977, 1995 by The Lockman Foundation. Used by permission. All rights reserved. www.lockman.org.

Scripture quotations marked NIV are taken from the Holy Bible, New International Version®, NIV®. Copyright © 1973, 1978, 1984, 2011 by Biblica, Inc.® Used by permission of Zondervan. All rights reserved worldwide. www.zondervan.com. The "NIV" and "New International Version" are trademarks registered in the United States Patent and Trademark Office by Biblica, Inc.®

Any internet addresses (websites, blogs, etc.) and telephone numbers in this book are offered as a resource. They are not intended in any way to be or imply an endorsement by Zondervan, nor does Zondervan vouch for the content of these sites and numbers for the life of this book.

All rights reserved. No part of this publication may be reproduced, stored in a retrieval system, or transmitted in any form or by any means—electronic, mechanical, photocopy, recording, or any other—except for brief quotations in printed reviews, without the prior permission of the publisher.

Published in association with the literary agency of Mark Sweeney & Associates, Chicago, Illinois 60611.

Cover design and art: Brian Bobel
Interior design: Denise Froehlich

Printed in the United States of America

23 24 25 26 27 TRM 5 4 3 2 1

To Steese Annie
My chosen, my beloved
Bone of my bone, flesh of my flesh
To have and to hold
To love and to cherish
In sickness and in health
For better or for worse
As long as we both shall live

CONTENTS

FOREWORD

Conversations with murderers are always challenging, but they're even more awkward when following a booking. A shared meal can make all the difference.

I first started eating meals with my arrestees the year I became a Christian. As I read through the Scriptures for the first time, I observed that some of God's most important conversations happened over a meal. There's something utterly disarming about eating with someone, even if one of you has just been arrested.

One suspect, Cal, seemed uncomfortable at first. He watched me suspiciously as I finished setting the small table with paper plates and plastic utensils. I doubt he expected any of this, especially in a sparsely furnished interview room. His attitude softened slightly as I opened the boxes of Chinese food, however. I knew from prior interviews with friends that chow mein was his favorite dish.

Over the next ninety minutes, I asked Cal about his childhood, his hobbies, and his kids.

We eventually finished the Chinese food and circled around to the subject of his marriage. I limited my line of inquiry and spent more time listening than speaking. I did my best to let him talk, although I did ask several clarification questions designed to expose the truth. We eventually discussed the disappearance of his wife. Although we were quite friendly by that point in our conversation, Cal never confessed to killing her.

But Cal did demonstrate his mastery as a storyteller.

As I was interviewing Cal, I knew a confession would have been a home run of sorts, but I knew I didn't need to swing for the fences to drive in a run. Like any winning baseball strategy, singles, doubles, and triples will get the job done.

Cal didn't confess that night, but everything Cal did say helped convince the jury of his murderous character, even if unintentionally. He calmly lied about nearly every detail of his marriage and unemotionally described his wife's disappearance. We captured every mistruth—every single, double, and triple—on video. It was enough to help the jury detect the lies, and our mealtime conversation became an important part of the cumulative case against him.

I was alone with Cal that night in the interview room, but I wish Greg Koukl had been my partner.

I first started listening to Greg's radio show before I became a Christian. I knew from his interaction with callers he was a first-rate interviewer. I loved listening to him as he talked to people who were just like me: skeptics who mistakenly thought Christians were irrational "blind believers."

I resonated with Greg's approach. He listened. He asked good questions, collected key data, and spotted the inconsistencies. He also understood the value, in baseball terms, of simply making contact with the ball. He kept hitting singles, doubles, and triples and resisted the temptation to swing for the fences. Greg was street smart.

After I became a Christian, I got to meet Greg. I now consider him one of my dearest friends. He's also my mentor. He'll be your mentor too if you listen carefully to what he teaches in this book. Cops understand the value of street smarts, but I know of only two books accurately illustrating for Christians how to navigate spiritual conversations smartly. Both are written by Greg Koukl.

Consider this book a ride-along opportunity. Sit in the passenger seat and glean wisdom from a master investigator and interviewer. Pay attention to everything Greg is about to teach you. When you're done, you'll know how to spot a lie and make a solid case for the truth.

—J. WARNER WALLACE, *Dateline*-featured
cold-case detective; senior fellow, the Colson
Center for Christian Worldview; author,
Cold-Case Christianity and *Person of Interest*

PART 1

STREET MAP

CHAPTER 1

MAKING A HARD JOB EASIER

I have a confession to make: evangelism is hard for me.

Surprising for a person in my shoes, I suspect. I have spent nearly half a century defending Christianity, making the case that the smart money is on Jesus—frequently one on one, often before university audiences, sometimes on television and radio, and regularly opposed by hostile witnesses.

Nevertheless, there it is. Evangelism is a challenge. I have friends who relish gospel engagements as the sweetest activity of their lives. I'm glad for them, but that is not me. I do a good bit of evangelism, but it still makes me uncomfortable, and I suspect I'm not alone. You may be much like me.

There are few things that cause more nagging guilt for Christians than sharing their faith. They feel guilt because they don't witness enough. They don't witness enough because they're scared. And they're scared for good reason. Sharing the gospel and defending it—apologetics—often feels like navigating a minefield these days. For most of us, engaging others on spiritual matters does not come easy, especially when people are hostile.

It's one of the reasons we often stay off "the street," so to speak, when it comes to spiritual matters. We avoid environments where we don't feel safe. Most of us wouldn't wander into the local atheist club meeting or mingle with the marchers in an LGBTQ parade. It's too scary. We simply don't know how to handle ourselves.

If that's you, take comfort. Not only is there a clear path through those minefields (more on that in a moment), but I want you to know your apprehension is understandable. Would it surprise you that the great apostle Paul shared your trepidation? Listen to this: "And the Lord said to Paul in the night by a vision, 'Do not be afraid any longer, but go on speaking and do not be silent; for I am with you, and no man will attack you in order to harm you, for I have many people in this city.'"[1]

Would it surprise you to know that when Jesus sent his disciples out on their first short-term missions trip, he told them "Do not fear" three times inside of seven sentences?[2] Why did he do this? Because Jesus understood there were reasons to be anxious. He understood the obstacles. He wasn't chastising his followers. He was encouraging them.

Confrontations awaited them, no question, but Jesus said they shouldn't worry about how they would respond when trapped in a tight spot. Yes, they'd face daunting obstacles, Jesus admitted, but they had a reliable ally—the Holy Spirit.[3]

Good advice, to be sure, but easily misunderstood since there was another detail many miss about the disciples' situation. Jesus gave this assurance not at the beginning of his ministry but well into it. When he first called Simon and Andrew, for example, he made a different kind of promise: "Follow Me, and I will make you fishers of men."[4]

Yes, the Spirit would be with them, helping them, speaking through them in the tough times. Still, there was something else the disciples needed. There was work to be done before these novices could cast their nets for the kingdom. Jesus was going to train them. He was going to instruct them, equip them, prepare them. He would put them through their paces in private so they'd be ready to face the heat when they encountered it on the street.

That is the rationale behind *Street Smarts*. Following Jesus' example—and with God's help—I want to teach you how to be more effective "fishers of men" by equipping you in a specific way to address the challenges to your Christian convictions that you face.

Where Is the Street?

In general, "the street" is anywhere you feel vulnerable, out of your element, exposed to danger. Opposition lurks in the shadows, so you stay safely in the light, keeping your distance from threats you don't think you can handle. There is wisdom in this approach, of course, when navigating perilous physical environments.

What we sometimes forget as Christians, though, is that in the spiritual arena, we are the light that's meant to penetrate the darkness. Yet we hesitate. Like the Hebrew spies of old encountering giants in the land of promise, we've become "like grasshoppers in our *own* sight."[5] The challenges seem bigger than they are, and we seem smaller.

A word about those giants. The giants are real, but they're not as big as you think.

I want you to consider something that intimidates many Christians yet actually works in favor of Christianity in a way believers do not realize: when you think about it, there are many ways to show Christianity to be false.

I'm sure that's something you did not expect me to say, but it's true. For example, our story starts, "In the beginning God. . . ." If there is no God, though, then there is no story. End of issue.

Christians are disciples of Jesus. If Jesus never existed—or was not anything like the man we discover in the ancient historical records known as Matthew, Mark, Luke, and John—then our project never gets off the ground.

If there is no soul that survives the death of our physical bodies, when we perish we stay in the ground. No one goes to heaven or hell, so what's the point of the so-called good news? And if right and wrong are merely matters of personal opinion, as moral relativists suppose, there can be no real sin—nor the personal guilt that goes with it—so judgment in a place like hell makes no sense, anyway.

The resurrection is another point of exposure. Even Paul admits that if Jesus didn't rise from the dead—if we are trusting in a Christ who turned to dust in the grave—then people should feel sorry for us. "We are of all men most to be pitied," he says bluntly.[6]

These challenges—and there are more like them frequently encountered on the street—are certain routes to Christianity's demise if they succeed. They represent what might be called the "soft underbelly" of Christianity. They are convictions we hold that make us vulnerable because, at least in principle, they could be mistaken. Another way of saying this is that Christianity is falsifiable.

As daunting as that may sound, think of this. The possibility that Christianity can be debunked—disproved, discredited, and invalidated—is not a bad thing. Oddly enough, it's a good thing. If a view is falsifiable—able to be shown to be false—then it is verifiable—able to be shown to be true.

And that's exactly what Christians can do. Simply put, those challenges don't destroy Christianity, for a good reason. Those challenges don't succeed. Quite the contrary, we have the evidence and we have the answers, answers you will find in this book. *Street Smarts* will give you the tools you need to face and defeat those ideological strongholds raised up against the knowledge of God.[7]

Get Smart

I have begun to make a case for why you should be serious about reading *Street Smarts* carefully and learning from it. I started with a negative observation—the task of engagement can be daunting—because I want you to be sober-minded about the enterprise, but I don't want you to be overwhelmed by it. That would be a mistake.

Here is the positive side. There is a better way: get street smart. That is what I will help you do in this book.

The first thing I want you to think about is that it's natural to *feel* vulnerable when you *are* vulnerable in some measure. Jesus anticipated it, and he warned us in advance. Paul experienced it—just like you and I do—and he overcame it. You can overcome it, too, with a helping hand.

The helping hand is the second thing that makes all the difference. Let me introduce that point with a question. Do you like taking tests? Most people don't. Tests are trying. We may falter, even fail, and no one likes to take a fall.

Now let me ask you another question. Do you mind taking tests when you know the answers? That changes things, doesn't it?

The unknown is frightening while it remains unknown. The giants shrink, though, when you learn how to deal with them. That takes information. It takes knowledge. It's part of the training Jesus gave his own team—carefully preparing them for the tests ahead of them—and it's the kind of training you will find in this book. With that training under your belt, the Holy Spirit then works in you and through you, helping you effectively employ the things you have learned.

Street Smarts trades on a basic approach I explain in detail in an earlier work called *Tactics: A Game Plan for Discussing Your Christian Convictions*.[8] That plan is a formidable tool to keep you in the driver's seat of otherwise difficult or discomfiting conversations with skeptics and challengers—yet in a safe, genial, and amazingly effective way. The tactical approach has transformed my ability to make a difference for Christ.[9]

In chapter 4 of *Street Smarts*, I will revisit that basic game plan with you, bringing you up to speed on how it works and how you can put it into play quickly and successfully. Consequently, though reading *Tactics* first will be tremendously helpful, *Street Smarts* will still serve you well as a stand-alone guide to answering common challenges effectively, even if you are a newcomer to the tactical approach. It's easier than you think if you simply follow the steps.

Street Smarts takes the next step. It moves us beyond the basic game plan by significantly expanding on the third part of that plan: using questions to expose a weakness or a flaw in another's errant view about God or God's world.

> The goal, of course, is to help nonbelievers see what's true so they can move closer to embracing Christ and the forgiveness only he can provide.

In *Tactics*, I address common objections to Christianity in order to illustrate how to use the third step of the game plan to respond to them. In *Street Smarts*, I focus on the larger issues themselves—atheism, the problem of evil, abortion, science and Christianity, and so on—giving you insight on how those challenges falter and supplying you with the questions you can use to point out those liabilities.

The training, then, consists of two parts. First, there is the content. In order to use questions to answer challenges, you must know the answers to the challenges. You must be able to see where the weaknesses lie. When you begin to recognize the flaws in some of the toughest opposition you will face as a Christian, the giants begin to shrink.

Second, there is more to making your case with nonbelievers than seeing flaws and noting weaknesses. You also need to know how to leverage the knowledge you have. That is the next part of the training—learning how to tactfully expose the weaknesses you've discovered by using questions in a precise and particular manner. Jesus said to be shrewd, but gentle. That is exactly what's needed on the street.

Thus, for each challenge, I will supply appropriate initial questions to help you smoothly and amicably join the conversation. I'll then expand those initial questions into sample dialogues to guide your steps forward according to the game plan, productively bringing those weaknesses to light in a gracious, disarming way.

These mini dialogues will not be complete, of course, since it's hard to know how any individual conversation is going to play out in the long run. They will be adequate, though, to get you going and move you in a constructive direction. Once you're in the driver's seat of the conversation—and that is a key advantage of the game plan—you'll begin to gain momentum, making the rest of the dialogue much easier and more productive.

Remember, these sample conversations are model exchanges, not scripts you'll need to memorize. Of course, it's a good idea to internalize the key questions and have a clear grasp of the basic direction you want to go with them, but you don't want to come across as robotic.

Also, since I have condensed and compacted these exchanges for brevity's sake, they might seem a bit curt at first reading. In practice, though, I'm careful not to be pushy. Take the core ideas I offer and weave them into your conversations in a friendly way that fits your personality.

The street smarts approach has proven itself over the decades I've been using it in a host of hostile encounters. It has also proven itself in the lives of thousands of others I've taught over the years, allowing them to maneuver almost effortlessly and with complete safety when talking with others, even in the most challenging conversations.

Simply put, I want to make a hard job easier for you—much easier. I am going to show you how to maneuver effectively and comfortably in conversations using questions to answer the challenges you face as a Christian. I will give you both the content you need and the plan necessary to employ it. By confronting the giants one by one, I will shrink them down to size for you. I will show you how to make the case that the Christian view of reality is true.

No Silver Bullets

A word of warning. The answers I provide in this book to the array of objections you will face on the street are good ones. They are gleaned from years of sitting at the feet of others much smarter and more experienced than me. The answers have stood the test of time and fierce opposition. Also, the tactical game plan is sound, honed over thousands of hours of engagement with challengers and critics.

Even so, there are no silver bullets. Accurate information and clever maneuvering do not guarantee results. On their own, no information, no matter how sound, and no technique, no matter how shrewd, will ensure that an objector, skeptic, or critic will come to his senses,[10] acknowledge his error, and turn to Christ.

A host of factors shape beliefs. Some are reasonable, but others have nothing to do with sound thinking. Emotions and prejudices play a huge part in forming people's opinions—especially with moral and spiritual concerns. Authentic conversions—as opposed to emotion-driven "decisions"—generally take a serious evaluation of the ideas, an honest, soul-searching moral self-assessment,[11] and lots of time.

The process is rarely tidy, partly because life itself is not tidy. Some conversations seem almost magical. Other attempts go nowhere and quickly die a natural death. No matter.

Consider this. Though your thoughtful, gracious, tactically sound presentation of the truth initially appears to bear no fruit, though your conversation is messy, disorderly, and herky-jerky, do not despair. The long-term impact of your moments of faithfulness can be profound. Trust me. I've seen it happen, and it has happened in my own life. God knows; we don't.

> People come to Christ only because the Father enables them: "No one can come to Me," Jesus said, "unless the Father who sent Me draws him."[12] Even *Jesus'* preaching, then, was ineffectual without the special work of God.

So, here is my advice. Your task is to present the truth as clearly, as graciously, as persuasively, and as faithfully as you can. That part is 100 percent your responsibility. This is where *Street Smarts* will help you. All the rest is up to God—100 percent. You do the talking; God does the persuading. Simple.

Once you realize the results are ultimately not in your hands, but in his, your conversations will be more relaxed, and your outcomes will be more rewarding. If your goal is to win people, you will frequently be disappointed. If your goal is to use your street smarts to be faithful in the moment before your audience of one, then you can be successful in every encounter.

Being effective on the street these days, though, requires a change in our understanding about personal engagement concerning the gospel. In my opinion, we need to revise our thinking about witnessing and revamp our approach to evangelism. Instead of pressing for a quick harvest, we need to settle in for some extended gardening.

CHAPTER 2

HARVESTER OR GARDENER?

I ended my last chapter with what might have sounded like an odd recommendation. I suggested we might be approaching evangelism in a manner unsuited for our time. I'd now like to give you a clearer idea of what I had in mind when I wrote that.

Let me start by making an admission that might surprise you. It may even shock you. Then I would like to show you how this surprising—even shocking—admission is connected to an insight that could revolutionize your approach to evangelism.

If this insight impacts you the same way it did me, then talking with others about Christ will likely become easier, safer, and more effective for you than you ever thought possible. The adjustment I am going to suggest, though, is controversial.

Here is my confession. I haven't prayed with anyone to receive Christ in more than thirty years. Though I have been a Christian nearly half a century, have spoken on more than eighty university campuses, have publicly defended Christianity on six continents, I have not "led" anyone to Christ in decades.

I know that sounds unbelievable, even borderline pathetic—but from a biblical perspective, it makes perfect sense. I have stumbled upon something I wish I had seen years earlier, since the Gospels and the book of Acts are thick with it. Because of this discovery,

I have been much more effective for the cause of Christ than any time before.

I want to tell you why I've been, by one measure, such a spiritual "loser." I also want to show you how what I learned may radically improve your effectiveness as a voice for the gospel. I want to show you how you can be more fruitful than you ever imagined you could be as a witness for Christ, even without logging "decisions."

First, though, the backstory.

Simple Times, Simple Gospel

I became a Christian in Southern California during the Jesus movement in the early '70s. Evangelism back then was fairly uncomplicated. Share the simple gospel, answer a few questions, invite a person to receive Christ, then pray. And many did. Not too tricky.

Would that were still the case.

Times have changed. The gospel is not "simple" anymore, nor are the questions people ask or the challenges people present. The gospel is still the gospel, of course. That hasn't changed—or rather, it shouldn't change, although many who consider themselves "broad-minded" fiddle with it, hoping to tickle contemporary ears.[1]

No, the truth is still the truth and always will be. It needs no renewal, no revision, and no restoration. The way people hear the truth, though, has changed dramatically because the cultural conversation has changed dramatically. Our task is to make the unchanging message—and the foundational ideas that frame it— more intelligible to contemporary ears.

In the '70s, Christian words and Christian doctrines made sense to people, more or less, even if folks didn't believe them or, if believing, didn't live them out. It was clear that the doorkeepers of culture back then were increasingly post-Christian in their views, but for the most part, they had not become anti-Christian. Those days are gone.

Worse, the hostility nowadays is not just against the gospel proper—which has always been a stumbling block—but against virtually every detail of the biblical view of reality, including what it means to be human, what it means to be gendered, what it means to be moral, even what it means for something to be "true."

Bestseller lists frequently feature rhetorically powerful offerings challenging virtually every aspect of the Christian worldview. Consequently—at least in the minds of the rank and file—the smart crowd has weighed in and found Christianity wanting both rationally and morally, so they have no reason to give our message a second thought.

Surprisingly for many, the words of hope we offer are often taken as words of veiled hostility and even hatred of outsiders—bigotry toward those who don't hold our spiritual views or respect our moral convictions.

The culture has moved on. Unfortunately, our methods have not. They've remained largely static. We continue to be dedicated to outdated devices, often laced with Christian language that is largely unintelligible to nonbelievers. People don't understand our ideas, so they don't understand our message—which to them seems obsolete, antiquated, and irrelevant.

That confusion can be spiritually lethal, as Jesus points out.

Roadkill

In Matthew 13, Jesus relates the famous parable of the sower. The first seeds sown, he says, fall beside the road, and birds swoop down and carry them away. No mystery here. Hard ground, no growth. Some people just won't listen. Not too complicated. But there is more to Jesus' point.

In his clarification to his disciples, he explains what he meant. "When anyone hears the word of the kingdom," he says, *"and does not understand it*, the evil one comes and snatches away what has been sown in his heart. This is the one on whom seed was sown beside the road" (v. 19).

The seed is sown, true enough. The seed lands "in his heart," according to Jesus. It's not bouncing off tough turf. The message is internalized at some level. Yet something critical is missing. Jesus tells us what that is. He says that the word sown in the hearer's heart is not understood. When people are spiritually puzzled, they become easy prey. The word of life is quickly snatched away by the devil.

By contrast, Jesus tells the disciples, "The one on whom seed was sown on the good soil, this is the man who hears the word *and understands it*; who indeed bears fruit and brings forth, some a hundredfold, some sixty, and some thirty" (v. 23).

So here is the question. According to Jesus, what is the chief difference between the first group and the last group—between the faithless and the faithful, between the ones who bear nothing and the ones who bear an abundance? The difference is this: The second group *understands* the message. The first does not. They become roadkill.

This insight is central, I think, to Paul's exhortation in Colossians 4:5–6: "Conduct yourselves with wisdom toward outsiders, making the most of the opportunity. Let your speech always be with grace, as though seasoned with salt, so that you will know how you should respond to each person."

Vital to my point is Paul's last phrase. Circumstances are unique and people are individuals. They sit at different places along the continuum between total rejection of God and complete surrender to Christ. If our personal evangelistic game plan emphasizes only the end of that journey—the harvest—then we are not following Paul's directions since we are not crafting our communication uniquely to each person.

The cookie-cutter approach that was adequate to the task fifty years ago now leaves listeners mystified, dumbfounded, confused—in a word, without understanding—so the seeds that are scattered are easily snatched away. The evil one steals the word we have sown because the message itself is incoherent to many who hear it. It is not intelligible to them given the unique cultural circumstances we find ourselves in.

I'd like to offer an antidote based on an insight that suggests a more productive approach.

Spadework

I want you to think about an aphorism—a pithy, insightful maxim—that's not especially profound in itself but has profound implications for our approach to sharing the gospel. It's a truism that has transformed how I personally do evangelism. Here it is: before there can be any harvest, there has to be a season of gardening.

Fruitful harvest, in other words, is dependent on diligent spadework: sowing, watering, weeding, nurturing. Here is how I put the point in the past: "Before someone ever comes to Christ, there is always a period of time—a season, if you will—when they are thinking about the gospel, mulling it over, wondering whether it might be true. They may be putting out little probes by asking questions. They might even be fighting back a bit. But still, they're wondering—maybe praying secretly, *God, are you real?* When this happens in someone's life, it's an opportunity for you and me to do some spadework, what Francis Schaeffer called 'pre-evangelism.'"[2]

That's what was happening to me as a college student at UCLA in 1973. I was testing the waters, asking questions, pushing back, and—eventually—listening.

The night I finally trusted the Lord—a Friday night, September 28, 1973—my younger brother Mark had come to my apartment for a visit, intent on continuing his efforts to bring me to Christ. When he launched into the gospel—yet again—I cut him short.

"Mark," I said, "you don't have to tell me about Jesus anymore. I've already decided I want to become a Christian."

It took me a few minutes to peel him off the ceiling, then I bowed my head, confessed my need, pleaded for mercy, turned my life over to Christ, and began my journey with him.

There is something in this exchange I do not want you to miss. When I was ready, I responded—no fuss, no pushback, no hesitancy. That's the way it is with ripe fruit. Fruit that's ready is easy to pick. All it takes is a little bump, and it falls into the basket. The gardening came first; that was the hard part. In evangelism, when the spadework is done well, the harvest pretty much takes care of itself. The first makes the second possible.

> I don't know of a single case in the book of Acts where somebody actually "prayed to receive Christ." Nor is there evidence of "altar calls" in the early church. Neither is wrong, mind you; they're just not a biblically necessary part of evangelism.[3]

This last point, of course, is the controversial part. Many think that every gospel encounter should include some sort of invitation, some nudge toward a decision, some attempt to close the deal (more on that in a moment). My own conviction on this, though, is grounded in Jesus' comments in a familiar gospel text.

Two Seasons, Two Workers, One Team

Consider Jesus' words in John 4—a passage well known for Christ's remarkable conversation with a woman in Samaria at Jacob's well. In this case, though, I want you to notice something Jesus says after that famous conversation. His instruction to the disciples teaches an important lesson that is not so well known.

The twelve arrive on the scene just as the Samaritan woman leaves for Sychar to tell others about the amazing man she's met at the well. Here is what Jesus then says to the twelve: "Do you not say, 'There are yet four months, and then comes the harvest'? Behold, I say to you, lift up your eyes and look on the fields, that they are white for harvest. Already he who reaps is receiving wages and is gathering fruit for life eternal; so that he who sows and he who reaps may rejoice together. For in this case the saying is true, 'One sows and another reaps.' I sent you to reap that for which you have not labored; others have labored and you have entered into their labor" (vv. 35–38).

I read this passage for years without noticing a critical calculus of evangelism embedded in that conversation. In this exchange, Jesus identifies one field—Sychar, in this case—but distinguishes between two different seasons—sowing and reaping, or what I refer to as gardening and harvesting. He identifies one team—God's people—but distinguishes between two types of workers: those who sow and those who reap, those who garden and those who harvest.

For Sychar, the reaping season was at hand. Someone else had done the heavy lifting, but the disciples now had the light labor. They were going to gather the low-hanging fruit, the easy pickin's. Again, the harvest is easy when the crop is ready.

Go for the Gold?

Some Christians are convinced we should try to get to the gospel in every encounter. Go for the gold. Press for the decision. Close the deal. I think the impulse is right-hearted, of course, but it's wrongheaded; there are problems with this approach.

One problem I've already alluded to. I suspect we are not

spending time listening to people long enough to learn their cultural language. If we do not first listen to understand their views, how will we be able to communicate in such a way that they will understand ours? If we speak words of truth, but they fall on uncomprehending ears, there will be no understanding. Those precious gospel seeds will get whisked away and, in that conversation at least, the devil will have the day.

There's another problem. What happens when a massive number of Christians gifted as gardeners rather than as harvesters are presented with a harvesting model of evangelism that's inconsistent with their spiritual temperament? I'll tell you. They sit on the bench, inactive, out of play. The idea of pressing someone for a decision—especially in today's hostile environment—is simply too unsettling, too disconcerting, and, frankly, too frightening.

I sympathize completely. The fact is, most of us are not good closers. Consequently, we never get into the game. And when gardeners don't garden for whatever reason, the harvest suffers. Remember the sluggard from Proverbs. He did not plow after autumn, so he reaped nothing when harvest time came 'round.[4]

Please do not misunderstand me. Harvesting is critical. There would be no kingdom expansion without it. Yet without the spadework—the plowing, the planting, the cultivating—there's no kingdom growth, either. There is no good harvest without good gardening. Remember, one sows, then the other reaps. Consequently, I do not feel compelled to shoehorn the gospel into my conversations in an odd or artificial way, pushing toward the finish line if the circumstances don't warrant it.

The good news should never get the short shrift, of course. Remember, though, that the good news has little weight without the bad news. Most people don't care about insulin, for example, unless they have diabetes. Indeed, Jesus himself didn't get to the good news in every conversation. In fact, his most famous moral discourse—the Sermon on the Mount in Matthew 5—was almost entirely bad news, not good. He closed his comments with "Therefore you are to be perfect, as your heavenly Father is perfect" (v. 48). Moral perfection? Hardly encouraging tidings.

No, I do not swing for the fences in my spiritual conversations with others. Instead, I have a different goal, a more modest one.

Lower the Bar, Raise the Impact

When I'm in a conversation that I hope will lead to spiritual matters, I never have it as an immediate goal to lead that person to Christ. I make no effort to get them to sign on the dotted line. I don't try to close the deal. I don't even have it as a goal to get to the gospel, though I may end up there.

Do I want that person to come to Christ? Of course I do. Is the gospel necessary for that? Again, of course. It's "the power of God for salvation to everyone who believes."[5]

Getting to the gospel is not the issue, though. Returning for a moment to the parable of the sower, the problem is the ground the seed falls on. There's no understanding. The hard ground needs tilling first before the seed has any chance of taking root.

I have adopted, therefore, a more modest goal when I engage others in conversation. It's one I communicate clearly at the outset of virtually every talk I give to a secular audience. Here is what I tell them: "I'm here tonight because my life has been deeply changed by an ancient teacher. His name is Jesus of Nazareth. Decades ago, while I was a student at UCLA, I began to think more carefully about the claims Jesus made about himself, the claims he made about the nature of reality, and the claim he made on my own life. After thinking hard on the issues, asking a lot of questions, and doing a lot of arguing, I finally concluded that Jesus got it right, that he saw the world the way it really was. I realized the smart money was on Jesus, so I decided to follow him."[6]

Then I say something they do not expect to hear. I tell them

I'm not there to convert them. "I have a more modest goal," I say. "I just want to put a stone in your shoe. I just want to annoy you a little bit, but in a good way. When you leave this auditorium, I want something I said to be poking at you, getting you thinking, because I think Jesus of Nazareth is worth thinking about."

Then I move forward with my talk, whatever it happens to be. I've made it clear to them, though, that I'm not in harvest mode. Instead, I'm gardening.

At this point you may be wondering, *Does this guy ever get to the gospel?* The answer is simple: of course I do. Then the next question: *When do you get to the gospel?* Here's my answer: I get to the gospel whenever I want.

I know that may sound cheeky, but there's a point here. I do not feel forced to squeeze the gospel into a conversation in an artificial way simply because someone told me I was supposed to. Rather, I get to the gospel when I think I can position it in a meaningful way, when it fits the natural flow of the discussion I'm having.

Jesus understood this. He took his time. He paced himself. He carefully weighed his words to be sensitive to his audience and to the unique circumstances he faced.

Often, he went only halfway, letting the bad news—the unbearable burden and impossible obligation of flawless goodness—weigh upon his listeners. Only later, after they were exhausted from shouldering the crushing weight of their own sin, would he say, "Come to Me, all who are weary and heavy-laden, and I will give you rest."[7]

Rest from what? Rest from the burden of the bad news; rest from the hopeless load of striving to be justified by law, a burden Christ was willing and able to lift from their shoulders. That's gospel. Yes, he got to the good news, eventually. But first he gardened.

In the many years I have taught this concept publicly in front of audiences, I've watched carefully when telling them about the importance of gardening before harvesting. I can see in their eyes something slowly beginning to dawn on them.

Here is what the expression on their faces tells me that they're thinking, *I can do this*. And they are right, of course. They can. Yes, I've lowered the bar a bit for them. But a lower bar gets them off the bench and into the garden, and that means a bigger harvest in the long run.

Who's in Your Garden?

All of this brings me back to my original confession, the one that made me sound like a pathetic Christian, an evangelism loser.

Years ago, I realized I was not a harvester but a gardener. My efforts for decades—on radio and at public events, speaking in churches and at universities, writing books and articles—have all been, largely, to serve a single end: gardening.

The reason I haven't personally prayed with someone to receive Christ in more than three decades is that I haven't really tried. I'm not in harvesting mode because I'm not a harvester; I'm a gardener. And so, I suspect, are most Christians. They just haven't thought of themselves that way since the option was never really open to them.

There's something else you need to know, though. You need to know who's been in my garden.

Does the name J. Warner Wallace sound familiar to you? He's the legendary cold-case detective who, as an atheist, applied his considerable investigative skills[8] to the alleged eyewitness reports found in the Gospels. In the process he became a believer, then an apologist, and then a bestselling author. You might have read his books, which include *Cold-Case Christianity*, *God's Crime Scene*, *Forensic Faith*, and *Person of Interest*.

You may know of J. Warner Wallace, but here's something you probably don't know about him: he was in my garden. When J. Warner Wallace was still an atheist, he was listening to Stand to Reason's radio broadcast. And I've met many other Christians who have told me they were just like him.

Do you realize what happened? I was patiently—and unknowingly—doing spadework on Jim Wallace, and countless others, when somebody went into *my* garden and harvested *my* crop. Do you think I care? Of course not. Remember Jesus' words "that he who sows and he who reaps may rejoice together." One field, one team, but two different seasons, and two different kinds of workers.

In the body of Christ, different people have different gifts.[9] When it comes to working the field, some sow and some reap—as Jesus taught.

Bringing in the Sheaves

If what I have written so far really bothers you—if you think I'm letting people off too easily, if you think I should be pushing them harder to get to the meat of the matter in spiritual conversations—I suspect that you are a harvester. And I'm glad you are. We need you.

If, on the other hand, what I've said encourages you, if you're thinking, *I can do this*, then you are probably a gardener. That would be most Christians, I expect, and we need you, too.

If that's the case, if it's beginning to dawn on you that you might be a gardener like me, then make it your modest goal to try to put a stone in an unbeliever's shoe. Focus your efforts on giving him just one thing to think about. That's plenty good for starters. Don't worry about the endgame. Instead, get busy doing some spadework.

Remember, you don't have to swing for the fences. You don't even have to get on base, in my view. All you have to do is get into the batter's box, then let the Lord take things from there. That's the secret—and the beauty—of gardening.

If you do that—if you get off the bench and get into play in simple ways that are friendly, yet moderately challenging, I think you're going to see a dramatic difference in your impact for the kingdom. Don't ever forget, the more gardeners we have, the bigger the harvest is going to be. Then both "he who sows and he who reaps may rejoice together" in the bountiful result.

Once you're off the bench, off the sidelines, and out on the street, it really helps if you have a game plan. And that is what I will give you in the next two chapters.

CHAPTER 3

HOW QUESTIONS KEEP YOU SAFE

Having a plan is a huge benefit when you navigate what might at first appear to be choppy waters in conversations with others about Christ. Indeed, it's hard to even get launched if you don't know which direction is best.

It's one of the reasons so many Christians have difficulty engaging the world that Jesus has sent them into as ambassadors. The cultural waters seem stormy, and many believers simply stay tied to their mooring for fear of being swamped by the tempest just beyond their anchorage.

There is a way out, though, a fairly simple approach to get you through the breakers and out into open water—a navigational game plan that is extremely safe, surprisingly straightforward, and amazingly effective.[1] Briefly put, the key to navigating effectively with others in rough spiritual waters is to use questions. Carefully placed queries are the core of the tactical game plan that will keep you from capsizing.

Why questions? There are a number of good reasons, but the simplest is this: questions keep you safe. They keep you out of harm's way, yet still allow you to make amazing progress even though—at least initially—you're not exposing yourself to attack by revealing your own thoughts on a matter.

Let me tell you where I first got this idea.

Taking a Tip from a Bumbling Detective

I call the plan itself "Columbo" after the iconic Lieutenant Columbo—the cagey TV detective of a bygone era who had an amazingly successful method of capturing criminals.

Cloaked in a rumpled trench coat, a stub of cigar wedged between his fingers, Columbo always seemed a bit confused as he poked around the crime scene muttering to himself. His polite yet bumbling manner was thoroughly disarming. No threat here. Columbo was harmless. Or so it seemed.

Lieutenant Columbo's opening salvo always appeared innocuous, but it was the key to his effectiveness. He'd simply say, "Do you mind if I ask you a question?"

The initial queries were innocent enough, each answer yielding just a small bit of information—which usually prompted another question. Then another, and another. Each answer provided an additional part to the puzzle that the clever lieutenant was quietly piecing together in his mind until he showed his hand and solved the crime.

Asking questions was second nature to Columbo—a habit, he admitted. Make it your habit, too. The key to Columbo—the heart of the game plan itself—is that the Christian takes the initiative in a disarming manner with specific questions chosen to move the dialogue forward in a safe, relaxed, but productive way.

> Lieutenant Columbo wasn't alone. Jesus used questions constantly, with more than three hundred of them recorded in the Gospels. Plato's mentor, the ancient philosopher Socrates, constantly questioned his students, using what we now call the "Socratic method."

Why questions? Because questions provide advantages that mere assertions—even sound ones—cannot supply. Remember, assertions make you vulnerable; questions keep you safe. Here are four ways questions can increase your margin of safety while still providing a great opportunity for you to make a difference.

Questions Get You Going

Most people find that starting a spiritual conversation is a bit awkward. Using a well-placed question, though, is a safe way for more timid types—and bolder types, too—to get off the bench and into active conversation. It helps ease you into the game, so to speak, in a genial, non-threatening way, especially when your questions show an interest in the other person and his ideas.

I once had a fun conversation with a witch in Wisconsin that started when I asked about her necklace—a five-pointed star called a pentagram often associated with the occult. "Does that jewelry have spiritual significance?" was all I said. Yes, it did. She was "a pagan" and happy to talk about the particulars. More questions followed as I probed for detail on her views. I was relaxed, and so was she. It was painless.[2]

Sometimes simple questions trigger a longer chat you never intended to have that bears unexpected spiritual fruit. Let me tell you about an inconvenient conversation I had one morning with a Seattle waitress that's a perfect case in point.

First, though, you need to know something about me: I'm not a morning person. Before my first cup of coffee, I have little spiritual conviction at all. To complicate matters in this case, I had worked events Friday night and all day Saturday and had another one first thing that Sunday morning.

I had no interest in talking with anyone about Jesus at that ghastly hour. In fact, I had no interest in talking at all. I just wanted to be left alone to enjoy my coffee and a bit of egg and toast quietly at the hotel cafe before heading off to my early assignment at a local church. My waitress, though, had a different outlook.

"So, what brings you to Seattle this beautiful morning?" she gushed—far too buoyant and talkative for my temperament at that hour.

I scrambled for a line to fend her off and escape this early morning annoyance. "I'm going to preach at a church this morning," I said. *That will send her scurrying*, I thought. I was mistaken.

"Oh, that's great!" she responded.

Her reply confused me. What was "great" about my giving a sermon? *Maybe she's a believer*, I thought. So I asked her, "Are you a Christian?"

"No, I'm not. I used to be, but not anymore. Now the universe takes care of me."

The first thought that came into my mind at that moment was, *Huh? What can she possibly mean?* Her perplexing comment was enough to rouse me a bit from my post-dawn stupor. I still was not in the mood for conversation—especially a spiritual one—but I couldn't help myself. As my inner "Columbo" began to take over, another question tumbled out.

"I'm confused. How can the universe take care of you? Is the universe a person?"

"Oh no," she said confidently.

"Then how can the universe take care of you?"

My question caught her off guard. "Well," she stammered, "uh, I guess I mean that *God* takes care of me."

Well, that makes more sense, I thought, until she added, "God *is* the universe." Inside my head the same question popped up again. *Huh?*

"Is the universe a person?" I had to ask.

"No."

"Then how could God *be* the universe?"

Now, I promise you, I wasn't trying to trap her. I wasn't even trying to witness to her—too early for me for something that complicated. All I was trying to do was make sense of what she was saying.

I went a couple more rounds with her, fielding more odd statements and making more futile attempts at getting clarity before she finally took my order and drifted off to another table. I breathed a sigh of relief, turned my attention to my coffee, and reflected on our short chat.

Amazingly, none of my questions seemed to trouble her. Nothing I'd said caused her the least bit of distress. She exited our brief conversation supremely confident in the soundness of the confusing view of reality that she'd traded Christianity for.

Or so it seemed. Later, though, when she dropped my check on the table, she paused and said something I did not expect to hear.

"You know, no one has ever asked me questions about my views before," she said, then added, "and it got me thinking."

Notice what had happened. There I was, lost in my early morning lethargy with no intention of talking to anyone. Yet by using simple questions with the waitress, I effortlessly initiated a conversation that God used to put a stone in her shoe even when I wasn't trying.

> There's a reason questions make the initial stages of a conversation so much easier. Once you ask, it's the other person's turn to answer. All you need do is listen. It's simple. Once you're rolling, the conversation almost always gets easier as opportunities for more questions present themselves.

I had no more time for talk since my church appointment loomed, so I looked for a quick exit. "Well," I answered with a smile, "if we had more time, I could ask you more questions, and then you could do more thinking." It was all I had a chance to say.

Fortunately, I had a copy of *The Story of Reality* in my bag.[3] I grabbed it quickly and offered it to her before I left, and she received it with the same energy she had greeted me with earlier.

Questions Get You Valuable "Intel"

Talking with others about controversial, volatile topics like the gospel can be scary. Sometimes there are landmines out there. It's always safer if you find them in advance. Questions help you do that.

Once, on a flight out of LAX, I chatted amiably with a thirty-something passenger sitting next to me. As I gently drew him out with questions, I learned he was not a Christian, though he used to be. In fact, he said, he used to be a preacher's kid. What had happened to his preacher dad? "Oh, he's still alive. He's just not a preacher anymore. He's not a Christian anymore, either."

Valuable intel? You bet. As I listened more to his story, the outlines of his spiritual topography came into focus. It wasn't a pretty picture. If I'd jumped into the conversation leading with the gospel, I'm sure I would have hit a trip wire. In situations like this one, questions often reveal obstacles in your path you can carefully maneuver around once you know where they are.

Questions Protect You from Having to Defend Your Own View

The reason for this benefit of using questions is pretty obvious. If you're asking questions, you're not making statements. Since the burden of proof is on the person making the claim (more on that later), you're in the clear. If you stick with questions, you'll have nothing to defend, so you're in a safe place, not vulnerable to counterattack.

Holding back a bit before showing your hand can rescue you

from what might be a premature and awkward conflict of ideas. For example, in some cases you may not think you have the liberty to express your beliefs as freely as you'd like. Maybe the person you're chatting with is more interested in doing the talking than doing the listening.

No problem. In those situations, here's how to make your job easier. First, ask questions and listen, a lot. Second, after listening, don't swing for the fences. Instead, just try to make one good point stick.

Let me give you an example of how that basic approach worked for me on a forty-seven-minute flight from Los Angeles to San Jose. I'd settled in for the short hop, expecting to get some work done, when a middle-aged gentleman sat down next to me.

Stuart, a world-traveling frequent flier, was in an expansive mood and clearly wanted to talk. He had strong opinions about religion, ideas he advanced without reservation. I tossed up a quick "Lord, help me" prayer. Then I listened, asking simple clarification questions here and there, waiting for an opportunity.

We talked the whole flight. Or I should say, Stuart talked the whole flight. I listened, mostly, because Stuart had a lot to say. His extensive travels and survey of world religions had convinced him that, despite his Catholic upbringing, the teaching of every religion ultimately boiled down to the same thing. The common core? Love—peaceful coexistence, people getting along.

By contrast, those folks who thought their *own* religion was the right one were the problem. The word "hate" slipped in at this point, along with the word "racket," describing religion's passion for passing the hat.

My three-word prayer went off again in my mind. Still, I continued listening. Every sentence I heard contained details I disagreed with, but simply contradicting Stuart wouldn't have helped, so I held my tongue and waited.

I did express concern that he might have missed the main point of these different religions, and I mentioned that the existence of racketeers in religion doesn't make all religion a racket (he agreed). Other than that, I said almost nothing. I let him talk. Eventually, Stuart asked what my religion was.

"I'm a Christian," I said.

He grunted. "So you're saying 90 percent of the people in the world are wrong and going to hell?"

"Well, I didn't say that," I responded, carefully choosing my battlefield. "I just don't think they can all be right."

Unruffled, Stuart glanced sideways at me and smiled. He was clearly impressed with his own musings. "So, do you think I've done a good job thinking this through?" he asked.

"Well, since you asked . . . no, I don't think you have, Stuart." A startled look replaced his smile, but he didn't get angry because I was answering him, not attacking him.

"I certainly don't say that with any animosity," I continued, "and you *have* done a lot of thinking about it. But no, I don't think you've thought through this issue well.

"For example, you've considered what seem like similarities in religion, right?" I shrugged. "Look, when you think about it, Islam is not about love, but submission. Christianity is not about love, but forgiveness. Buddhism is not about love, but escaping suffering. Hinduism is not about love, but escaping the illusion of the world. Love may be significant in each, but it's not the central message of each.

"And what of the differences?" I continued. "Why think a modest similarity is more important than the massive dissimilarities?"

I paused as he absorbed the point. "As to your comment about 90 percent being wrong, I don't see how anyone can avoid that, no matter how much love they have for people. Look, maybe my religion is mistaken. Maybe all religions are mistaken. But even if one group gets it right—pick any one, it doesn't matter which—that means all the rest, 75–90 percent of the people on the planet, got it wrong. It's not hate; it's just simple math."

When we landed in San Jose, our chat came to a friendly close. I shook Stuart's hand, wished him all the best, and then quietly entrusted him to God.

> Even for those tutored somewhat in refuting challenges and objections to Christianity, questions provide a vital element that may be missing for them—a bridge from the content they already know to the interaction they are trying to initiate. It's a shrewd way of spanning that gap and managing conversations.

Two things stood out for me about this encounter that I don't want you to miss.

First, I waited a long time before jumping in with both feet. Instead of sounding off the first time I heard something I disagreed with, I waited for the right moment. As long as I wasn't making my own case, I had nothing to defend. Simple clarification questions got me going. Since, initially, I wasn't sure of the best way to maneuver, I chose silence and attentive listening.

Second, when my opportunity arrived, I was genial but direct, giving Stuart one main thing to think about, one "stone in his shoe." Though I did take a moment to question his shallow summary of world religions, the central idea I wanted him to be clear on was that his statement that all religions were true just didn't add up. We could all be wrong, but we can't all be right.

So here's my advice. When you're afraid a conversation may get awkward, first, shoot up a quick prayer for help. Then, be patient and listen—a lot. Ask plenty of clarification questions. Wait for the right opportunity before weighing in. Finally, take what God gives you, even if it's less than you hoped for. Don't swing for the stands. Just make one good point.

Questions Make Exiting Easier, So Entering Is Easier, Too

Flying home after nearly two weeks of grueling work in Paraguay, I had a midnight layover in São Paulo, Brazil. I was tired and didn't want to talk. I was also hungry, but I didn't trust the airport restaurants, having had a bad experience in Uganda a month earlier.

I saw a young American chatting in Portuguese with a waitress, so I asked for his advice. He gave the restaurant a thumbs up. It was late at night and we were the only patrons, so I suggested we sit together to enjoy our meal.

I learned quickly why this young Yank spoke Portuguese so well; he was an LDS missionary. Now I was at loggerheads with myself.

It was a great opportunity to witness, of course, but I did not want to endure an evening of evangelism with a Mormon missionary at midnight in Brazil after two weeks of talks. Like I said, I was tired.

Then it dawned on me. I didn't have to mentally commit myself on the front end to a lengthy bout with a nonbeliever. If I was willing to simply start with a few questions about this Mormon's beliefs, I could easily exit the spiritual side of the exchange whenever I ran out of gas. Plus, asking about his views was a lot simpler than preaching about my own.

When I realized that opening the conversation by asking a few questions of the LDS missionary did not commit me to a late-night match of spiritual haggling, my entire attitude changed. That insight gave me the sense of safety I needed to step out in a comfortable, relaxed way during that midnight meal in the airport of São Paulo, Brazil.

In the same way, when you realize that if things become uncomfortable for you for some reason, you can stop the conversation by stopping the questions, there's no hindrance to starting. Easy out, easy in.

You may be wondering whether I make a difference for the gospel by focusing principally on questions. I do. And you will, too. Questions will help you ease into conversations, they'll give you valuable intel, they'll allow you to sidestep the burden of proof until you're in a solid position to defend your view, and they'll make it easy to exit when it's time to go.

Put simply, questions keep you safe.

What I want to show you next is how questions can form the foundation for an easy-to-use, three-step game plan to get you smoothly and effectively into meaningful spiritual conversations.

CHAPTER 4

THE GAME PLAN

Our focus in *Street Smarts* is on answering challenges, objections, and attempted defeaters to our views as Christians—and also, to some degree, on making a positive case for Christianity.

I have already mentioned that the technique I'm teaching you to help you successfully navigate those conversations involves using questions. It's a shrewd way of managing your interactions and keeping you comfortably in the driver's seat in otherwise awkward situations.

The tactical game plan is your guide to using those questions well. It equips you with a set of objectives and corresponding queries to help you move forward in discussions with others about Christianity— especially with critics and challengers of your Christian faith.[1]

I will offer more detail in a moment, but let me start by giving you a quick sketch of that plan.

My first questions (Columbo #1) are designed to give me *valuable information* that sets the stage for what follows. Further inquiries probe the *rationale* for a person's beliefs or objections (Columbo #2). The key to street smarts, though, is using carefully selected questions to make a point—specifically to *expose the flaws* in a critic's objections and thus neutralize his challenge (Columbo #3).

During encounters like these, your tactical maneuvers are

meant to provide safety for you in conversation while encouraging the objector to think more carefully about his complaints or consider problems with his views he may not have been aware of.

The first two steps of the three-step plan are simplicity itself, providing you with a kind of roadmap you can use to navigate the initial stages of your interactions. These steps offer critical insight into the other's views before you attempt the slightly more advanced third step.

The initial moves are gentle and nonconfrontational, motivated by a genuine curiosity and a desire to understand. They allow you to make tremendous headway in a conversation even when you have zero insight into the challenges you're facing and no skill at verbal maneuvering.

The third step of the game plan, though, is a little trickier. This last phase is where verbal sparring is more likely to happen since you'll be taking the initiative—in a careful, clever way—to make a point, either offering a contrary opinion or uncovering a weakness or a liability in the other's view. That's where you'll encounter a modest speed bump that this book will help you navigate.

> One university professor told me that the tactical approach has kept her safe in the hostile environment of the academy while still allowing her to make progress using questions to gently—yet effectively—challenge her colleagues' views.

I have two broad goals here. The first, strangely enough, has nothing at all to do with evangelism.

I know that the toughest critic you will ever face is yourself. Every Christian has doubts at one time or another. That's natural. In *Street Smarts*, I want to fortify your confidence that your biblical worldview provides solid answers to your own concerns. I want to give you the assurance you need to provide confidence regarding legitimate questions that arise in your own mind. I want to shrink those "giants" down to size for you.

Second, I want to show you how to persuasively put that knowledge into play, leveraging the power of these truths by using specific questions—not statements—to help you navigate in shrewd ways and gain a substantial tactical advantage in conversations. I want you to be able to give others something concrete and meaningful to think about regarding Jesus and the world he made.

Street Smarts will help you successfully navigate both of these difficulties—your own doubts and also the challenges you'll face from critics. Your key to success, though, is understanding how the Columbo game plan works.

Columbo Step One

Here is your first, vital step. When you're involved in a conversation with someone who has confronted you with an objection or a challenge, I want you first to focus on one thing and one thing only. Your initial goal is not to answer the objection, anticipate other challenges, give evidence for Christianity, or even launch into the gospel. That would be premature. Taking that tack might get you backed into a corner with no productive place to go, especially if your challenger is aggressive.

In fact, I do not want you to be thinking about anything at all that you might face further down the road in your chat together. Those concerns will only distract you at this stage—and might even intimidate you into silence.

Instead, what I want you to do at this point is merely to get the lay of the land. You need a clear picture of exactly what you're up against—the complaint, objection, or challenge your friend is offering.

Simply put, you need intel. Consequently, at the outset of any conversation, I want you to focus on a single task: gathering information. That's all. Gathering information is remarkably easy. All you have to do is ask simple clarification questions in a gentle, curious, probing way. To do that, you need a model question to help you get going. Here it is: What do you mean by that?

Remember, this is a *model* question. You can use it as is, of course, but it's best to modify it slightly to make your opening queries sound softer and more conversational.

You might say, for example, "I'm a little confused by what you said. What exactly did you mean by that?" or, "I'm not sure I understand you. Can you clear this up for me?" or, "Help me out here. What specifically are you getting at?" or, "How so? Can you give me more detail?" or, "Are you saying . . . ?" then fill in in the blanks, as appropriate. Or you can simply say, "Tell me more."

> My conversation with the Seattle waitress mentioned in the last chapter consisted completely of clarification questions. All I was trying to do—somewhat reflexively— was get clear on her views. Note that even without my going any further in the game plan than Columbo #1, God still was able to use that first, uncomplicated move.

This initial Columbo question has several virtues. First, when you have some form of this query at the ready, it gives you a simple, safe entry point into what might seem to be a daunting discussion. Opening in this way quickly and effortlessly produces momentum for your side of the interaction. Because you asked the question, you are now in the driver's seat of the conversation.

Second, offering this question immediately tosses the ball back into your challenger's court, giving you a bit of a breather and buying you some time to sort out your own thoughts on the matter.

There's a third benefit to this approach, though, that might catch you pleasantly by surprise. When you ask your first clarification question, you will frequently face something you never expected: silence. I admit this sounds strange, but I've encountered it many times. Critics enter a conversation with their sails filled with bluster, but when asked for even a modest explanation, those sails often go slack since they have no idea how to respond.

The fact is, many people you'll encounter simply do not know what they mean by the objections they offer since they've never thought the issues through for themselves. Instead, they've been socialized by others to offer certain stock challenges that have effectively stonewalled Christians because those believers never asked for clarification.

One more point. It's critical that when you ask for clarification, you listen carefully to the response. This practice is important for three reasons.

First, it's common courtesy to pay attention. Politeness is not only a required virtue for Christians, it also increases your persuasiveness. Second, if you're not clear on your friend's view, you might misrepresent it when you respond. Refuting a distortion is not only bad manners, it's bad thinking.[2] Finally, your friend's response to your question may uncover more ambiguities you'll need to clarify to understand him accurately (e.g., "I get the first part of your point, but this other thing you mentioned isn't quite clear to me. What did you mean by *that*?").

So, the first step of our tactual game plan—Columbo #1—is simply to gather the kind of information you need to understand the other person's objection or challenge.

Columbo Step Two

The next step of your game plan builds on the information you gathered with the first step. Once you have a clear picture of what a person believes, you'll then want to understand why he believes it. You'll want to find out the reasons—if he has any, and if he can articulate them—for the contrary view he's advancing.

I call this step "reversing the burden of proof." The burden of proof is the responsibility ("burden") someone in the conversation has to give reasons ("proof") for his view.

Here is the basic burden of proof rule: the one who makes the claim bears the burden. If a critic says something is true, then it's his obligation to provide reasons why anyone should take his claim seriously—especially if his point is controversial.

I say "reversing" because it's common for a challenger to make a contentious claim (e.g., "God doesn't exist") and then assume that the responsibility to refute him is on the Christian theist. That's backward. Initially, the burden of proof is on the atheist—the one who made the claim—to offer reasons why his denial of God is reasonable.

If we allow a challenger to sidestep his responsibility here and instead push the burden back on us (i.e., "Prove me wrong"), then we've essentially given him a free ride, relieving him of any responsibility to make his case.

So here's our rule for Columbo #2: No more free rides. Every time someone makes a contentious claim—and after you get clarification on what he means by his assertion (Columbo #1)—you are going to ask your second Columbo question, some form of the query, "How did you come to that conclusion?"

Again, this is a model question. Use it as is, or mix it up with variations: "I'm curious, what are your reasons for that?" or "What gives you confidence your view is true?" or, "How exactly does that work?" or, "Why do you think that's the way it happened?"

Do not be surprised if your question generates another "dead air" moment: silence. You've graciously assumed your friend has actually come to a conclusion—that he's considered the evidence and settled on a view he thinks is sound. Frequently, this is not the case. If he's mute in response to your probing, simply wait him out a bit and let him think. The silence works in your favor.

Notice that at this stage of the game plan you haven't taken on any risk since you haven't advanced your own view in any way. You've simply been using questions to ease into the shallow end of the pool, so to speak. No pressure; no worries. So far, so good.

These first two steps form the initial road map you can use to navigate the street. The moves are gentle and nonconfrontational, compelled by genuine curiosity and a desire to understand. Step three, though, is a bit more advanced.

Columbo Step Three

Now you're at a crossroads. Time to decide which direction to go next. You already have some idea of what the other person's view is and why he thinks it's reasonable. Now it's time to move in a different direction.

The final step of the game plan is the more challenging one since you will not be using questions passively to gather information (either about your friend's ideas or his reasons for them). Instead, you will be using questions actively to *give* information of a specific kind—in this case, pointing out a weakness or a flaw in the other person's view.

Which brings us to the speed bump. Your final maneuver of the tactical approach requires three things you may not have: (1) awareness of the weakness or flaw, (2) insight into what questions you might use to expose that liability, and (3) a basic blueprint in your mind of how you will direct the initial moves of the unfolding conversation—your opening queries, your friend's likely responses, and your next couple of moves.

This final phase takes you into the deeper end of the pool, and the rest of this book is dedicated to detailing each of those three steps on a variety of common challenges you'll face to help you successfully navigate those waters.

In a moment, I'll outline the basic approach of Columbo #3. Let's say for the sake of argument, though, that you have no insight into the flaw or any sense of how your friend's view is compromised, so you have no idea what questions to ask next. Now what?

If at this point in a conversation you realize you have nothing more to say—not unusual for younger Christians or those new to the tactical approach—no matter. Employing just the first two steps of the game plan as a gardening tool still provides an opportunity for God to use those simple queries in amazing ways. It happens all the time.

If nothing else, you've gained an education about another's views along with some practice having a relaxed discussion so that future conversations like this will be easier for you. I often suggest that beginners commit themselves simply to being students of others' views for a season, using their first two Columbo questions as a guide. Wade into deeper water when you're ready.

> Just asking questions and listening carefully to the answers will teach you two important lessons. First, non-Christians are not as scary as you thought. They won't loom as large for you once you've talked a bit while showing a genuine interest in their views. Second, challengers are not as smart as you thought, either. The objections—once your critics are pressed to clarify them—are frequently less ominous than you feared.

Your first task with Columbo #3, then, is to identify for yourself the flaw or weakness in the other person's challenge or point of view. That's the target your questions will now be aimed at.

Let's say, for example, someone claims there is no God. I know that a powerful evidence for God's existence is that the universe had a beginning.[3] My plan, then, will be to leverage the scientific evidence for the genesis of the universe and argue that God is the most reasonable cause. That's my target.

Once I have my target—the point I want to make—clearly in

view, I then have to think about the steps I need to take to get to my conclusion. I need to quickly strategize how I can use questions to make my point.

For example, suppose someone says, "Abortion is health care," and then, based on that assertion, begins making the case for adequate health care—including abortion—for women, especially those who are poor.

Now, I happen to know—and so do you, once you think about it—that killing unborn children has nothing to do with health care. My target, then, is to show that abortion does not serve the health needs of anyone, mother or child. Consequently, my questions are going to move the discussion in that direction. Here's what a sample dialogue might look like (I've put the key questions in bold):

"Abortion shouldn't be illegal. It's health care."

> **"Let me ask you a question. What is health care?"** [Columbo #1]

"It's care that's provided to make someone healthier, obviously."

> "Good. I agree.[4] But now I have another question. **Is pregnancy an illness?"** [Here I'm beginning Columbo #3.]

"Of course not."

> "So, when a woman is pregnant, she's not sick, right?"

"Right."

> **"Maybe I'm missing something here, but how can abortion be health care for the mother if the mother is not sick?"**

"But pregnancy is a health care concern."

> "I agree, but in the case of abortion, you're not helping a woman have a healthy pregnancy; you're

helping her end it, so the woman's health is not an issue, is it?"

"Right."

"What about the fetus? What does abortion do to the fetus?"

"It kills it. That's the point, isn't it?"

"Right, but then how is abortion health care for the fetus?"

Notice what I've done. I've identified a flaw, quickly strategized steps I needed to take to reveal the flaw, then employed a series of questions to expose the flaw.

There's something else you may not have noticed, though. By using questions, I subtly enlisted my challenger as a willing—though unwitting—partner helping me unpack the problems with his view.

This dialogue could easily have been a monologue. For example:

Health care helps sick people get better. But pregnancy isn't a sickness, so abortion can't be health care for the mother. Abortion doesn't sustain her health in pregnancy, either. It terminates her pregnancy by killing the baby, so abortion isn't health care for the baby. Therefore, abortion isn't health care.

All the elements of the earlier conversation are still in place; all of the same reasons remain that lead to the same conclusion. But notice the difference. The monologue is a series of assertions that invite resistance or negation at virtually every point. Consider this:

"Health care helps sick people get better."
"Not always. Sometimes it keeps them from getting sick."
"But pregnancy isn't a sickness, so abortion can't be health care for the mother."
"Yes, it can be."

"Abortion doesn't sustain her health in pregnancy, either."

"It does if she doesn't want to be pregnant."

"It terminates her pregnancy by killing the baby, so abortion isn't health care for the baby."

"It's not a baby. It's a blob of tissue."

"Therefore, abortion is not health care."

"Yes, it is."

By using the tactical approach, though, I'm able to employ questions instead of assertions, inviting my challenger to provide the same information he might otherwise have reflexively disputed. He then becomes my accomplice by affirming the very points that eventually undermine his own view.

> Every time you ask a question, it's the other person's turn to respond. Using questions, then, generates dialogues instead of monologues or "preachimonies."

This shrewd element of Columbo #3 will often catch your friend by surprise, leaving him speechless when he realizes the corner that his own admissions have backed him into. Your method, though, has not been unkind, unfair, or deceptive. You have merely connected the dots for him—dots he has provided with his responses to your questions—and gently guided him to consider problems he may not have countenanced if you had just preached at him.

First Time's the Charm

Consider the experience of one of my radio callers the very first time she attempted to put the Columbo tactic into action. Here is Katie's account, as she related it to me on the air:

I had just read your book, *Tactics*. Soon after, I went into a bookstore and asked if they had a Christian section, so the salesperson walked me over to that aisle.

"I don't know much about this section," she admitted. "I used to believe in Jesus, but I don't anymore." Then she started to walk away.

"Oh, really? What happened?" I asked. [Columbo #1]

"I was raised in a church," she said, "but my father eventually talked me out of all that. I decided I believe in the universe, and I'm good with that."

"Wow, that must have been a really interesting journey to go on. By the way, what do you mean by 'the universe'?" [Columbo #1]

As she answered my question, I began to have this thought: *Don't push it. She's actually, somewhere in there, wanting to talk about this. I can feel it.*

I thanked her for helping me find the section I wanted. She began walking away, then turned around and came back to talk with me more.

It was so much easier focusing on gardening instead of trying to close the deal all the time, knowing that if God wanted to do something, he was going to do it. I simply kept asking more "What do you mean by that?" questions and eventually she admitted something surprising.

"I know God got me out of many tough situations in my life," she confided, "like drug addiction. I know it was God, even though I called him 'the universe.' I guess I don't believe that Jesus was the Son of God, though. He taught a lot of good things, but I don't believe he was the Son of God."

"Why not?" I asked. [Columbo #2] After we talked awhile, she admitted again—tearfully, now—that she believed in God and he'd helped her immensely.

"If you believe that God was able to save you from a jail

cell, what about the eternal jail cell you might end up in if you're wrong?" I asked.

"You had to go and say that, didn't you?" she said.

"Look," I said gently, "I'm not here to convert you. I just wonder why, when you're so convinced God was the one who saved you from drug addiction and jail, God wouldn't be able to save you from hell. Is that something you're worried about? If that's a possibility in the back of your mind, wouldn't you want to know?"

"Can I have your phone number?" she asked. "Because I really want to think about this. Can I call you with questions?"

We've texted back and forth together since then, and she's told me, "I've been thinking a lot about this, and I can't wait to talk to you."

A few observations: First, this conversation started with simple questions meant to gather information—Columbo #1. That's all. Second, Katie's style was not confrontational or pushy, but warm and curious. Her friendly questions were all that were needed to move the conversation forward without making the salesperson defensive. Third, Katie eventually got to the issue of the gospel—both the bad news and the good[5]—but only after she built a bit of trust, which didn't take long. Finally, Katie made a new friend who was interested in staying in touch so they could talk more about spiritual matters.

One more thing. This was Katie's very first attempt at using the game plan. She started in the shallow end of the pool, then got bolder as her confidence grew and the salesperson responded positively to her questions. God clearly used Katie's baby steps to begin to make a difference in her new friend's life.

For the moment, think about getting into a few modest, relaxed conversations using the first two steps of the Columbo game plan to help you start gardening effectively. As you move through the rest of these chapters, you'll also learn how to apply the third step of the plan creatively, persuasively, and productively.

You will discover how solid the Christian worldview is. You'll also discover the flaws and liabilities of challengers and how to be more effective exposing their mistakes—always using questions.

First, though, you'll need some intel on what you're up against on the street. Though many of our current challenges have a novel ring to them, the basic problems are not new. They've arisen out of age-old schemes that originated in the invisible realm and trade on a foundational lie that goes back to the very beginning.

CHAPTER 5

THE STREET'S INVISIBLE BATTLEFIELD

Before we begin answering challenges, it's critical we know exactly what we are up against on the street. In military terms this is called "intel." Good intel guards us from blundering into perilous conflicts we didn't see coming or opposition we were not prepared for and, thus, not equipped to handle. It gives us the lay of the land before we venture forward.

The intel I am talking about now is strategic, not tactical—the big picture, not the individual maneuvers. To navigate the street effectively, we need to know the spiritual topography, the contours of the terrain we'll be traversing in our conversations. What exactly are we up against?

In the next two chapters, I will supply two important pieces of intel to guide you. The first will help you understand the chief spiritual obstacle you will encounter. The second will help you understand the chief ideological obstacle you will face. The two are connected, since the ideological obstacle is a deadly spiritual scheme that originated in an invisible realm.

The Unseen Realm

We live in a world made by an invisible Being, and this world is thick with invisible things. They are "all around us," in a sense, but not immediately obvious since the visible realm is so much more imposing.

In 2 Kings 6:15–17, the prophet Elisha's attendant saw something in the visible world that overwhelmed him—the Syrian army encircling their city with horses and chariots. "Alas, my master!" he said. "What shall we do?" Elisha, though, was not shaken. He saw a deeper reality in the unseen world. "'Do not fear, for those who are with us are more than those who are with them.' Then Elisha prayed and said, 'O Lord, I pray, open his eyes that he may see.' And the Lord opened the servant's eyes and he saw; and behold, the mountain was full of horses and chariots of fire all around Elisha."

Elisha saw something his servant did not see: the enemies of God surrounding the city were themselves surrounded by a massive invisible force arrayed for Elisha's protection. The prophet was able to see the unseen.

I want you to consider a familiar passage that talks about that unseen world and contains an insight you may not have thought about before. Here is that passage: "Put on the full armor of God, so that you will be able to stand firm against the schemes of the devil. For our struggle is not against flesh and blood, but against the rulers, against the powers, against the world forces of this darkness, against the spiritual forces of wickedness in the heavenly places. Therefore, take up the full armor of God, so that you will be able to resist in the evil day, and having done everything, to stand firm" (Eph. 6:11–13).

In this text, Paul tells us we are at war. He acknowledges the reality of opposition in the visible world ("flesh and blood") but instructs us that the more fundamental conflict is a deeper one in the invisible realm ("the heavenly places"). This, you already know.

Here is what you may not have seen before. Paul also tips us off that the enemy operates according to specific "schemes"—battle plans, of sorts—that inform the devil's maneuvers. Paul counsels that being clothed with the proper armor allows us to "stand firm" against these battle plans, resisting the devil's subterfuge.

Weapon One

I want you to consider a quartet of verses that add up to a sobering truth alerting us to the principal way Satan advances his army in the spiritual battle.

- "We know that we are of God, and that *the whole world lies in the power of the evil one*" (1 John 5:19).
- "And the great dragon was thrown down, the serpent of old who is called the devil and Satan, *who deceives the whole world*" (Rev. 12:9).
- "And even if our gospel is veiled, it is veiled to those who are perishing, in whose case *the god of this world has blinded the minds of the unbelieving* so that they might not see the light of the gospel of the glory of Christ" (2 Cor. 4:3–4).
- "The Lord's bond-servant must not be quarrelsome, but . . . patient when wronged, with gentleness correcting those who are in opposition, if perhaps God may grant them repentance leading to the *knowledge of the truth*, and they may *come to their senses* and escape from *the snare of the devil*, having been *held captive by him to do his will*" (2 Tim. 2:24–26).[1]

It may not have occurred to you how complete the enemy's penetration into the minds of men has been, but these passages make it unmistakable. According to the New Testament, the entire world is in the devil's deathly grip. He holds people captive to do his bidding by trickery and deceit, blinding the minds of those who are perishing, keeping them from coming to their senses and seeing the world the way it really is.

Not surprising, then, that the very first step in arming ourselves for battle against the devil is to gird our loins with truth (Eph. 6:14). When we fight with God's weapons of warfare that "are not of the flesh, but divinely powerful for the destruction of fortresses," we attack those lies and lay waste to them, "destroying speculations and every lofty thing raised up against the knowledge of God" (2 Cor. 10:4–5).

The principal weapon at the enemy's disposal allowing him to gain ground in the spiritual conflict, then, is not power but deception. If the basic strategy for Satan's spiritual assault is spreading lies, then our most potent countermeasure in the battle against him is its opposite: spreading truth. The response to lies—the answer to deception, the antidote to deceit—is truth.[2]

Seeing the Unseen

We are at war battling otherworldly forces in the unseen realm with weapons that are effective to oppose the spiritual strategies and demonic plans in play against us. Our job is to resist those schemes by exposing them, doing everything we can to stand firm by countering lies with truth.

There is another angle, though, a key insight you must not miss, a clue that will allow you to unveil the unseen schemes, making them visible to you.

A person who can see will not easily stumble into a ditch, even a small one. He'll walk around it. A blind person, on the other hand, will walk off a cliff because no matter how deep or wide the abyss, he will not know it is there. In the same way, Satan can foist a very big lie on the world—one so obvious that thoughtful Christians easily see through it—yet the world at large will be oblivious to it because they have been blinded.

And here is the clue, the "tell," the giveaway that reveals the scheme and helps inform our own counteroffensive against it in battle. Look for the big spiritual lie that seems completely transparent, the obvious ploy that appears ridiculously ham-handed, the massive ditch that can't be missed but the world doesn't seem to see, the abyss the blind masses fall into without giving it a second thought. Find that, and you will find the scheme.

If you wonder why anyone would buy into such an obvious spiritual error, if the gullibility of the multitude perplexes you, if you catch yourself saying, "This makes no sense," then you have probably stumbled onto a scheme. You have identified a maneuver in the battle since the only explanation for such lack of spiritual perception is spiritual blindness—and we now know who is responsible for that.

Let me give you a pair of examples.

Two Schemes

The first scheme is easily revealed by answering this question: What single religion in our culture has the suffix *phobia* attached to it to protect it from criticism? Is it "Hindu-phobia"? "Jew-phobia"? "Buddha-phobia"? "Christian-phobia"? Hardly. It's "Islamophobia." The word has become a fixture in the social lexicon, showing up not only in Wikipedia and Urban Dictionary but also in *Merriam-Webster*, the *Oxford English Dictionary*, and the *Cambridge English Dictionary*, to name just a few.

Why is this significant? Because Islam is arguably the most dangerous religion currently in the world. On September 11, 2001, 2,977 lives were snuffed out by Muslim terrorists. Yet within a few short months, Islam somehow achieved most-favored-religion status in the West. Muslims—following a tradition clearly taught in the Qur'an, the Hadith, and the Sunna and acknowledged by a host of respected Muslim scholars and clerics—make headlines weekly with acts of murder, mayhem, and mutilation all over the globe. Yet any public criticism of that faith is labeled bigotry.

To be clear, multitudes of kind, generous, peaceful Muslims—especially those you'll likely meet at work, at school, or in your community—reject this doctrine. Nevertheless, hundreds of millions affirm it. The cultural pressure in the West, then, to characterize Islam as basically peaceful is misleading, even though many individual Muslims abhor Islamic violence.

Factions of Islam also violently oppose Judaism and Christianity. Maybe I have an overactive imagination, but does anyone else see a scheme slipping past the eyes of the spiritually blind?

The second scheme—one I will cover in depth in the next chapter—has been around for a long time, but people continue to be taken in by it despite its obvious absurdity. This con has gone through a number of iterations over the years, but it still boils down to the same simple notion: there is no truth.

Claiming there is no truth is a kind of "end around" the whole who-is-right-about-religion debate. If there is no truth to begin with, then feuds about which religion is true are pointless. There's no sense fighting about who has the right answer when there are no right answers to be had.

This tack is appealing in part because it's meant to engender a kind of tolerant peace and harmony between people. That is the point of the clever "Coexist" bumper sticker regarding religion. It's crafty, but ultimately contradictory. Everyone is "right" in a certain sense ("true for you"). In another sense, though, lots of religious people are wrong if they think their own view is true in any deep way—true to reality.

Here's another twist. When people say there is no truth, I often wonder how they want me to respond to their own statement. I think they want me to believe them, but the minute I consider the possibility that they might be onto something—the minute I start agreeing with them, in other words—I run into a problem. I cannot give the nod to their assertion, since that would be the same thing as saying their view is true, which is the one thing they will not allow me to say.

You see the problem. You can also see how the idea that there is no truth cuts the legs right out from under the Great Commission.

Notice the pattern. Something of spiritual significance is going on in the visible realm that is obviously false, yet the rank and file don't see it, so their response is completely wrongheaded.

Out of the Shadows

You can immediately see the impact of both of these lies from the perspective of spiritual combat. Islam is a threat to religious liberty the world over and a special menace to the "people of the book"—Jews and Christians. The denial of truth undermines all attempts to separate fact from fancy, giving free rein to the Father of Lies.

Each is a scheme to blind and deceive regarding something biblically significant. Each is a ploy, a ruse, a deception in the unseen world trading on the demonically imposed blindness of the masses, and the consequences are disastrous.

Remember, the key to seeing the unseen is to look for something spiritually dramatic going on in the visible realm that is so obvious everyone else should see it, but they don't. That is the tip-off. That is the "tell." That is the giveaway letting you know you're dealing with an area where the enemy has doubled down.

Others are blind to the ruse since it's driven by spiritual forces of darkness in a realm they cannot perceive but we can. We can see the scheme. We can marshal our forces of truth at that point and do everything within our means—by wisdom and truth and the grace of God—to stand firm.

Our proper response to others' blindness, though, is a soft heart—compassion, not quarrelsome conflict. The devil is our true adversary, not the non-Christian. Nonbelievers have been deceived.

Paul tells Timothy to be patient and gentle when correcting them in the hope that God will grant them spiritual sight leading to their salvation (2 Tim. 2:24–26).

Soft heart, not soft mind. And no compromise. Note this excellent word of advice—and caution—for anyone navigating the street. It comes from former slave trader turned hymnist and pastor John Newton, taken from his first public service at St. Mary Woolnoth, London, December 19, 1779. His text was about "speaking the truth in love" from Ephesians 4:15: "The Bible is the grand repository of the truths that will be the business and the pleasure of my life to set before you. It is the complete system of divine truth to which nothing can be added and from which nothing can be taken with impunity. *Every attempt to disguise or soften any branch of this truth in order to accommodate it to the prevailing taste around us either to avoid the displeasure or court the favor of our fellow mortals must be an affront to the majesty of God and an act of treachery to men.* My conscience bears me witness that I mean to speak the truth among you."[3]

There is one lie at the center of Satan's schemes that informs virtually everything you will face on the street. It is not a new deception, though. In fact, it is the very first lie, a falsehood nearly as old as time itself. We turn to that next.

CHAPTER 6

RELATIVISM: THE PRIMAL HERESY

History is testimony to a basic fact. Human lives will be ruled by one of two fundamental forces: either truth or power. Humanity will be governed either by the physical facts of God's world and the moral facts of his character, or by the forces that oppose those moral and physical facts.

I learned this painful lesson firsthand in my own travels in 1976 behind what was then called the "Iron Curtain." I was encouraging Christians in five communist countries who were being crushed under the hammer of Soviet-style Marxism.[1]

The official newspaper of the Communist Party in the Soviet Union at that time was called *Pravda*. The word means "truth." Truth, though, was not a valued commodity under Soviet totalitarianism. Truth was just a wax-nosed propaganda tool used to serve a different end. Power, not truth, was the ultimate instrument of Soviet influence.

Without truth, brute force will always be the master, and freedom to choose to live by truth will be the casualty. Humans will then be compelled to live by lies, and today lies abound.

To understand what you face on the street, then, you must

understand how the death of truth—relativism—has thoroughly captivated the culture. It is one thing for individuals to be confused about truth. It is quite another when an entire civilization is confused, a social malady abetted by government policy that frequently supports the death-of-truth madness and tilts the balance toward power—a creeping totalitarianism.

As many have said before, ideas have consequences. False ideas, though—lies about the world—cut deep gashes. One lie has been with us from the beginning, from the genesis of humanity. It is as ancient as mankind itself and has cut the deepest gash in the human soul. It is the first lie. It is the primal heresy.

The First Lie

In the beginning, humans knew no lies, of course. Their realm was ruled by the power of goodness. The truth of God's world prevailed. Power and truth were united, one. It did not stay that way for long, though. A crafty deceiver intruded. When the goodness of the author of truth was challenged, a counterfeit truth took stage.

"Has God said?" the deceiver challenged. "He's lying. He's holding out on you. He is not good. What do *you* want? What does *your heart* tell you?"

"The fruit seems good to eat. It delights my eyes. It will make me wise. I want it."[2]

"Then take it. Be free of him. Truth is not out there. Truth is within. Make your own rules. Follow your own heart. Be true to your own self."

This exchange is an interpretive paraphrase, of course, of Genesis 3:1–6, but it reflects the crux of the matter. At the fall, an alternative "truth" prevailed: the truth within, "my truth." The revolt in the garden was a rejection of the external source of truth in exchange for an internal authority. Self-rule replaced God's rule. Mankind embraced itself.

This outside/inside distinction—God's truth vs. individual truth—may sound familiar. It is the root of relativism, the primal heresy. And it did not produce the promised freedom. Instead, it brought thorns and thistles, bondage and captivity, and it continues to do so today.

> The ancient Hebrew prophet Hosea said if you sow to the wind, you will reap the whirlwind.[3] The proverb applies here. The option that promised absolute freedom brought absolute slavery. We are not the masters of ourselves. We never were. Instead, our selves—the flesh—and the deceiver now master us.

As I said earlier, human lives are ruled by one of two fundamental forces: either truth or power. This is when that clash began.

Of course, if there is no God, there is nothing left but self and power. We are the landlords, not the tenants.[4] No external moral order rules the day. No transcendent meaning drives human ambition. That is the appeal of atheism. But that is not the truth. That is part of the lie.

Relativism is the heartbeat of our age. It is the pulse of the street. Every generation has fallen prey to it, but this generation celebrates it, idolizes it. The concept, though, is a bit hard to nail down for some. Here is a brief tutorial.

Inside or Outside?

Relativism is a take on the meaning of the word *truth*. The word *relativism* is used to communicate a particular understanding of what it means to say that a belief, statement, or point of view is true.

When I tutor students on the meaning of truth, I start with a statement, then I ask two questions. First, I make a dramatic display of placing a pen on the podium. Then I say, "The pen is on the podium." Next, I ask if the assertion is true. When the students nod, I ask the critical question: "What *makes* the statement true?"

Hands shoot up. "Because I see it there," one student says.

"But if you didn't see it," I ask, "wouldn't it still be true that the pen is on the podium? Seeing might help you know the statement is true, but it isn't what makes it true."

"Because I believe it," offers another.

"If you stopped believing," I challenge, "would the pen disappear? No. And would believing really hard make a pen materialize atop an empty podium? Probably not.

"The thing that makes the statement 'The pen is on the podium' a true statement," I tell them, "is a pen, and a podium, and the former resting on the latter. It doesn't matter if anyone sees it. It doesn't matter if anyone believes it. It doesn't matter what anyone thinks at all."

Note, the truth of the statement "The pen is on the podium" is independent of any subject's thoughts—a "subject" here being any person or any group of people. It is, in other words, mind independent.

Notice, by the way, that the students' first two responses tie the notion of truth to what is happening on the inside of each student—a personal belief or an individual sensation of seeing—and not to anything that's happening outside the students.

> This inside/outside distinction is the key to understanding any form of relativism. It is the difference between subjectivism and objectivism.

The classroom exercise is a lesson on the meaning of objective truth. If the "truth maker," the condition that makes a statement true, is something about the object itself—something outside of us, so to speak, unrelated to our own thoughts, desires, feelings, or beliefs—then the truth is an objective truth. The statement accurately fits some feature of the world "out there," regardless of anyone's opinion about it.

Aristotle described it this way. If you say that it is and it is, or you say that it isn't and it isn't, that's true. If you say that it isn't and it is, or you say that it is and it isn't, that's false.[5]

Aristotle's characterization is the commonsense, garden-variety understanding of the meaning of truth. When my philosopher friend Frank Beckwith was asked what the definition of truth was, he quipped, "Do you want the true definition or the false one?" You get the point.

By contrast, think of my daughter Eva, when she was five years old, amusing herself with a book beyond her reading ability. As she recited the book's tale, out tumbled the dramatic particulars. She turned each page at proper intervals, yet her yarn bore no resemblance to anything on the page since she wasn't actually reading. The words she spoke were purely a product of her own imagination. The story was in her head, not in the book.

Put another way, the "truth" spoken was in the subject (Eva), not in the object (a *Fancy Nancy* book, in this case). It was based on something on the inside, not on something on the outside. It was mind dependent (a five-year-old mind here), not mind independent. Therefore, it was a subjective, or relative, truth.

Here is another way of seeing it. If the truth you have in mind can change simply by changing your mind, then that "truth" is only in your mind. It's not in the world. It's on the inside, not the outside. That's relativism.[6]

> If someone's "personal truth" is not a fact, then it isn't a "truth" at all since all real truths are facts. It may be a belief, of course, but if the belief does not match reality, then it's not a truth of any kind. It's an error, or a mistake, or maybe even a deception, but it is not a truth. Talking as if it were creates confusion.

In the real world, simply believing something cannot make it true. Mere belief cannot change a single thing about the way the world actually is. If you don't believe in gravity, for example, you will not float away. That is the folly of letting beliefs on the inside define truth on the outside.

Real Bad or Feel Bad?

This inside/outside distinction applies in exactly the same way to morality. One might say it's the difference between real bad and merely feel bad.

Moral objectivism is the view that moral claims are like the statement "The pen is on the podium." Philosophers call this "moral realism" because moral qualities, though not physical, are still just as real as the pen. The truth maker is an objective fact, not a subjective belief.

So, for example, when a moral objectivist says, "Rape is wrong," he means to be describing rape itself, not merely his own feeling, opinion, point of view, or preference about rape.[7] In objectivism, something about the object (an action, in this case) makes the moral statement true. Rape, therefore, is wrong because of something about rape, not something about a person, or his culture, or his genetic conditioning.[8] Objective moral truth, like all genuine truth, is mind independent.

By contrast, moral relativism is like little Eva's story. The "facts" are only in one's mind, not in the world. No act is bad in itself. The words *evil*, *wicked*, or *wrong* (or *good*, *virtuous*, or *noble*, for that matter), never describe behavior or circumstances on the outside. Rather, they describe a judgment inside the mind of a subject who has either expressed a preference or felt an emotion.

Once again, in relativism, the subject—a person's beliefs, tastes, or preferences—is the "truth maker."[9] Moral beliefs are only "true" for the person who holds them. They might not be "true" for others who have different moral convictions. That's because in relativism, moral truth is mind dependent. In a relativistic world, then, no belief of any kind—moral or otherwise—can be false since a mere belief ("my truth") is true by definition.

Moral objectivism, then, is the view that morality is like gravity. Moral relativism is the view that morality is like Monopoly. The facts of physics are features of the world, not a matter of personal whim, individual taste, or cultural convention. Monopoly, on the other hand, is manmade. The rules are made by people (at Parker Brothers, in this case) and can be changed by people. If you don't like the rules, you can alter them (variations that are sometimes called "house rules"), play a different game, or play no game at all. It's up to you.

With any objective statement, facts make the claim true. With a subjective statement, the subject's beliefs or feelings or self-identification make the claim true. Rape is only wrong, for example, if a person simply believes it so, not because of anything questionable about rape itself. Likewise, men don't menstruate, unless, of course, the "man" is a woman who self-identifies as a man.

The Triumph of the Self

This cultural swing toward self began more than a century ago, but it shifted into high gear in the '60s. I know; I was there. We chanted slogans like "Do your own thing," "Different strokes for different folks," "Live for today," and "If it feels good, do it." These were not metaphysical statements, however—statements of ultimate meaning or deep personal identity. Rather, they were simply refusals to be governed by current ethical conventions.

For the past fifty years, remnants of the Christian worldview provided a measure of restraint to that impulse of self-directed hedonistic license. Now, though, the wound goes much deeper.

Today, a single slogan sums it up: "You do you." Two personal pronouns and a verb. Nothing else. The mantra is completely self-reflexive: me about me. That's the ruling dogma. In *The Rise and Triumph of the Modern Self*, Carl Trueman describes this "expressive individualism" as the idea that "each of us finds our meaning by giving expression to our own feelings and desires."[10]

Lest Trueman's characterization be mistaken for a noble commitment to personal authenticity, make note of his phrase "finds our meaning." Rev. Martin Luther King Jr. stood true to himself against the torrent because his convictions were rooted in something outside himself—God's truth about the dignity and value of each human being.

Now, on the street, "authenticity" is nothing more than naked desire, and desire's unrestrained expression is central to one's identity. It is what Rod Dreher, author of *Live Not by Lies*, calls "the liberation of individual desire." Listen carefully: "The essence of modernity is to deny that there are any transcendent stories, structures, habits, or beliefs to which individuals must submit and that should bind our conduct. To be modern is to be free to choose. *What* is chosen does not matter; the meaning is in the choice itself. There is no sacred order, no other world, no fixed virtues and permanent truths. There is only here and now and the eternal flame of human desire. *Volo ergo sum*—I want, therefore I am."[11]

The slogan on a Ninja Warrior T-shirt reads, "Be your own hero." Think about that. Heroes are others we look up to and emulate because of some superior virtue. Being our own hero means the self is already the high-water mark. Thus, hero worship is reduced to self-worship.

Note how deeply the primal heresy has taken hold. A pandemic of narcissism besieges us and is championed as central to individual meaning and personal identity. Self-love and unrestrained pursuit of self-interest are no longer vices; they are virtues. Indeed, they are now considered inviolable human rights.

It's not that new trends encourage immoral conduct that people a generation ago would not have countenanced. Rather, those under the spell of this metaphysical narcissism seem unable to think in objective moral categories at all. There simply is no ethical order. There is only *amour propre*—the love of self.

Consider, for a moment, how gender is now viewed. "Gender" no longer refers to anything about our bodies on the outside; it is, rather, a matter of internal preference and personal self-determination. Living whatever it is you believe about yourself is now called "being authentic."

Genuine gender dysphoria is a tragic burden to bear, of course, and for those so afflicted suicide rates skyrocket. Harm results when we encourage this delusion. The proper solution to gender confusion is to treat the outside world as the locus of truth, not the inside world. That approach, though, is anathema to the emerging culture. Such defection from the dogma of narcissism is now punished. Power replaces truth.

Mordor in Our Midst

When our first parents exchanged the external rule of God and the objective truth of his world "out there" for the internal rule of their own desires "in here"—the outside/inside exchange at the heart of all forms of relativism—they plunged humanity into darkness. Like Mordor's creeping cloud, a blanket of deception looms over this generation.

Through it all, the serpent stays in the shadows, mankind unaware of the stranglehold he has on them. The captives offer darkness as light, clothing vice in the vocabulary of virtue with words like *tolerance, diversity, equity, inclusion, broad-mindedness, dialogue, justice,* and—above all—*love.* They use the vocabulary of evil to subvert the good with words like *intolerance, bigotry, inequity, exclusion, narrow-mindedness, silence,*[12] *injustice,* and—above all—*hate.*

The language deceives them.[13] The children of light, though, see what the children of darkness cannot.

> Here is why this insight matters while navigating the street. If you do not understand how thoroughly the primal heresy permeates the current culture, you will not understand the meteoric rise of antipathy to Christianity characteristic of this new generation. To them, the objective-truth-that-applies-to-everyone Christianity is modern heresy.

The first lie, the primal heresy, informs and influences virtually everything you will face on the street—from views on religion and the existence of God to ideas about sex, marriage, gender, abortion, Scripture, divine authority in the lives of men, and so on.

Be prepared. Put on your full armor. We do not lean on the bent reed of popular opinion or public approval. Rather, we reason, we cajole, we warn, and sometimes we persuade, the belt of truth being the first weapon in our spiritual arsenal.[14] Then, having done everything, we stand.

Girding our loins with truth is the first step in the battle for the souls of men, and that is the task that the remaining chapters of *Street Smarts* will be devoted to.

PART 2

NAVIGATING THE STREET

CHAPTER 7

ATHEISM: DISTRACTIONS

The simplest way I have ever found to explain my reasons for believing in God is this: God is the best explanation for the way things are. That statement sums up in one sentence my basic approach to half a century of making a case for God and for Christianity.

Atheism, on the other hand, explains nothing. It is the ultimate non-explanation, "explaining" by denying that explanations exist.

"Why is there something rather than nothing?" No reason. "What caused everything?" Nothing. "What accounts for morality?" There is no morality to account for. "Why is there evil in the world?"[1] There is no real evil in the world since there is no real morality. "What is wrong with the world?" Nothing. It just is. "How do we fix the world?" We can't fix what's not broken. We can only make it more tolerable to our personal tastes.

I realize I've painted a rather dark picture of atheism, but the portrayal is true to the worldview.[2] Great twentieth-century British philosopher and atheist Bertrand Russell put it candidly:

That Man is the product of causes which had no prevision of the end they were achieving; that his origin, his growth, his hopes and fears, his loves and his beliefs, are but the outcome of accidental collocations of atoms; that no fire, no heroism, no intensity of thought and feeling, can preserve an individual life beyond the grave; that all the labours of the ages, all the devotion, all the inspiration, all the noonday brightness of human genius, are destined to extinction in the vast death of the solar system, and that the whole temple of Man's achievement must inevitably be buried beneath the debris of a universe in ruins—all these things, if not quite beyond dispute, are yet so nearly certain, that no philosophy which rejects them can hope to stand.[3]

Dark? Yes. Painfully honest? Indeed. Accurate? Completely. On a materialistic view of the universe, things just *are*. Nothing more. No explanation for anything important. No purpose for anything dear. Rather, universal stillness. Nothing-ism. Naught to build on other than Russell's "firm foundation of unyielding despair."[4]

All this to say that the answer to the God question dictates one of two trajectories leading in opposite directions based on who is in charge—the creature or the Creator, the Potter or the clay.

> God's existence is the most decisive issue of life because the answer you give to that one question sets an irrevocable course for everything that follows. Dealing with atheism, then, is a kind of structural starting point for worldviews.

All the big questions, then—issues of origin, meaning, morality, and destiny—and all the secondary concerns, too—issues of sex, gender, liberty, equality, bodily rights, and the like—eventually come down to one question: Are we our own, or do we belong to Someone else? If there is no God, then all is clay and nothing but clay.

Thus, the God question is the first one to answer since it is the foundation for answers to all the others. Yet most Christians are not prepared for—and are apprehensive of—encounters with atheists. There are two reasons engaging atheists can be daunting.

First, the most vulnerable part of any worldview is its foundation. Undermine that, and you undercut everything resting upon it. Destroy the footings, and the whole lot crumbles. Our story starts, "In the beginning, God. . . ." If there is no God, then there is no story, and Christianity never gets off the ground. Simple.

Second, atheists are characteristically confident and aggressive, and their complaints against theism are often rhetorically clever and sometimes philosophically complex, making them difficult for Christians to counter.

Three Moves

Of course, there is a plethora of issues atheists raise and a rack of titles offered by thoughtful Christians countering them.[5] My purpose here is not to retrace that ground.

Instead, in this chapter, I want to give insight into three general moves—three distractions, if you will (plus a short bonus issue)—that you'll face with your atheist friends. I'll then provide tactical questions to get you moving forward comfortably in thoughtful conversation on those concerns with minimal risk.

Take note, the goal here is not to close the deal. We're not in harvest mode. Instead, I want to help you do a little gardening by offering a few simple questions to get you going and to get your friend thinking.

There are three diversions you will consistently confront when talking with atheists. Often, an atheist's first step is a defensive move, a deflection. By redefining the word *atheist*, he attempts to absolve himself of any responsibility to defend his own view. His second move is another redefinition, this time of the word *faith*, distorting it to make it impossible for you to defend *your* view. Finally, there's the blanket dismissal, "Believing in God is irrational; there is no evidence."

Before I go further, though, let me give you a general maneuver. My first response when somebody tells me he's an atheist is, "That's interesting. What kind of atheist are you?" (Columbo #1).

My question trades on the simple fact that atheists do not agree on everything. Most atheists are materialists—convinced that nothing exists except physical things governed by natural law[6]—but not all are. Some believe in objective morality; some do not. Some flutter back and forth between atheism and agnosticism, depending on the definitions.

Asking this question has several advantages.

First, I want the atheist to see I'm not shocked or intimidated by his announcement but rather curious about his convictions and comfortable learning more about them.

Second, this question immediately forces the atheist to think about his own view in a more precise fashion, something I'm convinced many have rarely done.

Finally, an opening question like this buys me time to consider where I might go next with my queries.

My second general question is, "*Why* are you an atheist?" (Columbo #2). I have no idea how my friend is going to respond. He might give a reason, or he might offer a vague charge that there's no evidence for God or that theism is irrational (I'll deal with those responses in a bit).

Notice, since I'm the one initiating the queries, I'm in the driver's seat. Because I'm using questions, there's no pressure on me. I'm in student mode, not persuasion mode. It's a safe place to be.

With your initial steps in place, let's move on to the distractions I mentioned earlier. The first has to do with definitions. Atheism used to mean one thing but lately has morphed into something different.

Atheism Lite

Oddly, many atheists no longer believe there is no God. Instead, they say, they merely lack belief in God. They don't claim God doesn't exist. Rather, they simply don't believe he does exist.

These atheists are not unbelievers, then. They are simply non-believers. Since a nonbelief is not a claim, it requires no defense. Thus, atheism secures the inside lane as the default view of reasonable people. Or so atheists think. That's their strategy.

Some attempt to find safe harbor in a vague agnosticism. Since they don't know God exists ("Theoretically, it's possible he does"), they're not really atheist but agnostic—in knowledge limbo on the issue.

These moves are almost always disingenuous coming from someone who is clearly a committed atheist. True agnosticism is an intellectually respectable position, of course, but that is not the outlook of the atheist here.

> *Theist*, *atheist*, and *agnostic* are not words that describe knowledge categories but rather words that describe beliefs (ergo *believer* versus *nonbeliever*). Most of our beliefs are fallible (capable of being false). We still believe they're true, though—often with good reason—even if we don't know for sure. If agnosticism means lack of complete certainty, then each of us is agnostic on just about everything we think we know.

Here is the insight that betrays the flaw in this verbal sleight of hand: atheists may lack a belief in God, true enough, but they do not lack a belief about God. They are neither agnostics nor non-believers. Rather, they are believers of a certain kind. They believe there is no God, even if they don't know for sure. That is why they're called atheists.

The root word *theism* means the existence of God, and the prefix *a* is a negation. An atheist, then, is one who holds "not God," or "God is not." In plain language, atheism is the belief that there is no God. This is not linguistically complicated. It never has been.

If I were an atheist, I would not take this route. I'd fear people would think I was cheating with words, betraying weakness, not strength. This, as it turns out, is exactly what's happening. Yes, there is a difference between nonbelief and unbelief, but there is no refuge here for the atheist. Here's why.

If you asked me which rugby team was the best in England, I wouldn't know where to start. I have no data, so I have no opinion. I am truly a nonbeliever regarding the question. Deprived of information, I am deprived of an opinion. I am neutral.

This is not the case with atheists, though. They are not neutral on the God question. If they were, they wouldn't be writing books, doing debates, or wrangling with theists. No one pontificates on their nonbeliefs. There'd be nothing to talk about.

Richard Dawkins is currently the world's most famous atheist. He makes his case in his bestselling book *The God Delusion*. If God is really a delusion, then he does not exist. Simple. Theists say there is a God, and atheists like Dawkins contend they're wrong—even delusional. Thus, atheists argue that there is no God—hardly a nonbelief.

Here is the simple calculus. There are only three possible responses to the claim that God exists.[7] You can affirm it ("God does exist"), you can deny it ("God does not exist"), or you can withhold judgment ("I'm neutral") either for lack of information or lack of interest. However, neither apathy nor uncertainty characterize those who say they "lack belief in God."

With that insight in place, here is how I would engage someone who clearly believes God does not exist yet defines his atheism as mere lack of belief:

"The way you describe your atheism confuses me a bit. Would you mind if I ask you a few questions?"

"No. Go ahead."

"I'm going to make a statement, and I'd like to hear your response to it. Okay?"

"Sure."

"Here it is: God exists. What do you personally believe about that statement?"

"Like I told you before, I don't know for certain."

"Right. I got that. But I'm not asking you what you *know*. I'm asking you what you *believe*."

"I'm agnostic."

"Agnostics have no opinion one way or the other. From what you've said so far, though, it doesn't sound to me like you're neutral on God. Maybe I can put the question another way."

"Okay."

"Given the statement 'God exists,' it seems you have one of three choices. You could affirm the statement (that would be my view, theism), you could deny the statement (that would be atheism), or you could completely withhold judgment since you have no opinion one way or another (agnosticism). Can you think of any other options?"

"No, not really."[8]

"So, which one are you? Do you affirm the statement 'God exists,' do you deny it, or do you have no opinion one way or another?"

"Like I said, I lack a belief in God."

"I get that. But just to be clear, that wasn't one of

the possible options. **Are you saying you have no opinion one way or another on this matter? Are you sitting on the fence on the God issue?"**

"I have no belief in God."

"Right, but that's a different issue. Isn't saying you have no belief *in* God different from saying you have no belief *about* God?"

"I don't know what you mean."

"Okay, let me put it this way. I believe in God, but you've been pushing back on that. You think I'm mistaken, right?"

"Right."

"So, if you think I'm wrong about God existing, then you must believe he *doesn't* exist, which is why you have no belief *in* God. Does that make sense?"

"I see your point."

"So, in your case, having no belief in God is really the same thing as believing that God doesn't exist, which is why you think I'm mistaken for believing in God, right?" [Columbo #1]

An atheist is free to define his own view as lack of belief in God if he wants. Even so, if he lacks belief because he thinks there is no God, then he still qualifies as an atheist under the standard definition, his "lack of belief" notwithstanding.

The purpose of this line of questioning is to even the playing field a bit. Both the Christian and the atheist have a conviction—a belief—and those beliefs are at odds. Fair enough. That means both have a view to defend. If you're not clear on this issue, you'll always be playing defense, and the atheist will have a free ride in the discussion. Try not to let that happen.

Fanciful Faith

The atheist's first maneuver keeps him from having to defend his own view. His second move, frequently, is an attempt to keep you from defending yours. This misstep is a common one, a mistake even Christians have unwittingly abetted, so it's an error often made on both sides of the debate.

To illustrate this misstep, suppose I claim that atheism is false since atheists don't believe in science. After all, they don't believe in God because they can't see him, but they can't see atoms either, so the existence of atoms must be in question, too. Since atoms are central to science, atheists, then, must not believe in science, and a worldview that denies science can't be true.

You can immediately see the errors here. I have misrepresented the atheist's view, easily "defeating" the distortion. This is not only bad manners, it's also bad thinking—an informal fallacy called a "straw man." Erect a caricature of someone's view (the straw man), then easily knock the scarecrow down.

This is what atheists continue to do with "faith." Peter Boghossian is an example. "The word 'faith,'" he writes, "is a very slippery pig. . . . Malleable definitions allow faith to slip away from critique."[9]

Boghossian is right on this point, of course. Definitions should not be malleable. Twisting the definition of faith to suit his own purposes, though, is not the answer, just as twisting the definition of atheism (by Christians or by atheists) is equally illicit.

Boghossian admits he's "*redefining faith* as 'pretending,'" (emphasis mine).[10] It suits his purpose. He defines the "faith virus"[11] as either "belief without evidence" or "pretending to know things you don't know."[12]

"If one had sufficient evidence to warrant belief in a particular claim," Boghossian writes, "then one wouldn't believe the claim on the basis of faith. 'Faith' is the word one uses when one does not have enough evidence to justify holding a belief."[13] This, of course, is circular since his conclusion simply repeats his redefinition of faith. It's also self-serving.[14]

Faith is critical to Christianity, so it's an obvious target. Let me say respectfully, though, that it does not matter how atheists like Boghossian define faith or even how some misinformed and confused Christians characterize it. It only matters how Christianity itself defines faith. Otherwise, the critic will be jousting with scarecrows. For this, we must go back to the Christian's authority, the Bible.

The biblical accounts are replete with appeals to evidence that justifies their claims.[15] The summary at the end of John's gospel should be enough to make this basic point: "Therefore *many other signs* [miracles] Jesus also performed in the presence of the disciples, which are not written in this book; but these have been written so *that you may believe* that Jesus is the Christ, the Son of God; and that believing you may have life in His name" (20:30–31).

No appeal to blind faith here. The Greek word for biblical faith—*pistis*—means "active trust," and in Scripture this trust is continually enjoined based on reasons and evidence, not blind leaps. Note, for example, the emphasis added in these passages:

- "Jesus the Nazarene, a man *attested to you by God with miracles and wonders and signs* which God performed through Him in your midst, just as you yourselves know" (Acts 2:22).
- "To these [apostles] He also presented Himself alive after His suffering, *by many convincing proofs*, appearing to them over a period of forty days" (Acts 1:3).

- "Though you do not believe Me, *believe the works* [i.e., miracles], so that you may know and understand that the Father is in Me" (John 10:38).
- "And according to Paul's custom, he . . . *reasoned with them* from the Scriptures, *explaining and giving evidence* that the Christ had to suffer and rise again from the dead" (Acts 17:2–3).

John, the Beloved Disciple, brings it all together for us in 1 John. He opens his letter with the evidence of his own eye-witness encounter with Christ. Notice how many senses he appeals to: "What was from the beginning, what we have *heard*, what we have *seen* with our eyes, what we *looked at* and *touched* with our hands, concerning the Word of Life—and the life was *manifested*, and we have *seen* and testify and proclaim to you the eternal life, which was with the Father and was *manifested* to us—what we have *seen* and *heard* we proclaim to you also" (1:1–3).

He closes his letter this way: "And the testimony is this, that God has given us eternal life, and this life is in His Son. He who has the Son has the life; he who does not have the Son of God does not have the life. These things I have written to you who believe in the name of the Son of God, so that you may *know* that you have eternal life" (5:11–13).

To John, faith wasn't a blind leap. It wasn't wishing on a star. It was grounded in evidence that led to knowledge. And when the evidence is so overwhelming—as it was for the earliest follows of Jesus (and many since then)—the knowledge is certain.

Be on the lookout for this faith-is-blind distortion by atheists. Unless you clear up this confusion, you'll have little grounds for discussion—and little ability to defend your view.

Our point is based on a simple rule: if someone wants to critique a view, then he must critique the view itself and not something else. If the word "faith" continues to trouble your atheist friend, see if he'll agree to a substitute. A single line of questioning should suffice to clear the air:

> **"It's obvious we have different definitions of faith. That's okay, but since we're talking about my view right now, maybe we can use my definition."**

"What's that?"

> **"Biblical faith is trust based on reasons and evidence. It's not a leap."**

"Well, I still think faith is blind."

> "What if I gave you evidence for my beliefs. What then?"

"Then it's not faith."

> "What would you call it?"

"I don't know. I just know it's not faith if you have reasons."

> **"Okay, since I'm glad to offer reasons for my views, what word would you like me to use instead?"**

"Uh . . . convictions?"

> "That works for me. So how about I talk about my convictions and the reasons I have for them, and you can respond?"

"Okay."

"Show Me the Money"

There's a reason atheists insist that Christian faith is blind. They're convinced there is no evidence for God, so belief in him is irrational and faith in him must be a leap. But the assertion is baseless; it's simply not true.

> Of course, if they're convinced there's no evidence for theism, then the atheist thinks his view wins by default since it's the only alternative—in rational terms, either A or non-A, either God or not God. The approach is appealing to the atheist since, as with the redefinition of the word *faith*, it makes his job easier by allowing him to avoid having to give independent evidence for atheism.[16]

The easiest way to get clarity on the "irrational" and "no evidence" charges is to ask probing questions.

Here's my first one: "Precisely, what is irrational about belief in God?" (Columbo #1). Here, I'm looking for specifics. It's not enough for an atheist to respond, "It's just dumb." Exactly *what* is "dumb" about it?

An irrational belief is one that either contradicts good reason or flies in the face of solid evidence to the contrary, so ask, "How does belief in God violate reason?" (Columbo #1), or "What is the evidence against God?" or "What is the evidence for atheism and, therefore, against theism?" (Columbo #2).

The only attempt I know of to show the irrationality of theism is the appeal to the apparent contradiction posed by the problem of evil. As we'll see later, though, this attempt fails.

When an atheist says there is no evidence for God, I have a few questions for him:

"What specific arguments for God have you considered?"

"I haven't seen any."[17]

"Well, if you haven't considered the arguments for God, how do you know no such evidence exits?"

"Well, I have considered some of them."

"Good. I'm curious which ones you've thought about and what, in your opinion, is wrong with them. How, specifically, have they failed?"

You might even ask, "What would count as legitimate evidence for God, in your mind?" This query will help you determine if your friend is even open to hearing evidence.

These questions are good ones even if you're not versed in arguments for God (I'll cover some of those in the next chapter). If your friend gives any content, make note of it, thank him for it, and tell him you'll give his ideas some thought. There's no obligation to answer every challenge on the spot, especially if an issue is out of your depth. Do some research later, on your own, when the pressure is off.

> The key here is not to settle for vague generalities. Ask your atheist friend to spell out the shortcomings of belief in God that he has in mind. He needs to be clear and precise on the exact reasons he thinks belief in God is unsound.

A warning is in order here. There is a difference between having credible reasons to believe something and having reasons adequate to convince a hardened skeptic. Saying there's no evidence is not the same as saying the evidence is unconvincing. That's a different matter. A piece of evidence is an indicator, not necessarily a decisive proof.

Generally, a thoughtful theist's method is what's called abductive reasoning. All things considered, what is the best explanation for the way things are? It's a cumulative case approach. That's a matter for thoughtful discussion, not thoughtless dismissal.

When atheists say, "There's no evidence," they're either not paying attention or they're misunderstanding the role of evidence.

Our fourth "bonus" challenge, though, is the oddest distraction of all.

One Less God

In *The God Delusion*, Richard Dawkins writes, "I have found it an amusing strategy, when asked whether I am an atheist, to point out that the questioner is also an atheist when considering Zeus, Apollo, Amon Ra, Mithras, Baal, Thor, Wotan, the Golden Calf, and the Flying Spaghetti Monster. I just go one god further."[18]

This silly maneuver has bewildered many Christians. Maybe that's why Dawkins thinks it amusing. To see how meaningless his move is, consider these similar claims:

- All married men are basically bachelors since they are not wed to every other woman on the planet.
- People with jobs are basically unemployed since there are gazillions of companies who haven't hired them.
- Murderers are basically peaceful folks, considering all the people they haven't killed.

Like I said, silly. That atheists believe in one less God than theists is precisely the difference between an atheist and a theist. That little difference makes all the difference. Nothing profound here.

Being an atheist is not a degreed property, as philosophers would say. You can't be mostly atheist but a little bit theist. You either believe in God or you don't. The switch is on or off.

"You're basically an atheist like me."
"What do you mean?"
"Well, you don't believe in Zeus or Apollo or hundreds of other gods, do you?"
"No. I believe in one God, the God of the Bible."

"So, I just believe in one *less* god than you do."

"Right. I agree. Why is that significant?"

"Well, that means we're almost the same. You're basically an atheist."

"So do you think I'm basically a bachelor?"

"Of course not. You're married."

"Well, there are billions of women I'm *not* married to, and a bachelor has only one less wife than I do."

"That makes no sense."

"I agree."

Even if we concurred with Dawkins and admitted we were "atheists" regarding other gods, what of it? Nothing meaningful follows from Dawkins's point.

Maybe Dawkins thinks a Christian's belief in Yahweh and rejection of other gods is arbitrary. Believing in the God of the Bible, though, is not the same as having faith in Zeus or golden cattle or airborne pasta boogeymen. We reject finite gods because there's no reason to believe they exist. We believe in a transcendent, morally perfect, eternal, omnipotent, personal Being because a multitude of reasons convince us he's real.

There's much to discuss with atheists, but clearing the air on these critical misperceptions or distortions is key to making progress.

Use these questions as friendly probes in conversation. They're formidable tools to keep you in the driver's seat in otherwise difficult interactions with those seeking to undermine the very foundation of Christianity: God.

Both atheists and Christians make claims. It's an even playing field in that sense. Both are required to give reasons for their views.

We are ready to do that, showing that our confidence in God is grounded not in wishful thinking but in a body of evidence that needs to be addressed rather than dismissed as naught.

Providing that positive evidence for God is our next step in responding to atheism on the street.

CHAPTER 8

GOD: THE BEST EXPLANATION

I began the last chapter by suggesting a general strategy I think is the easiest way to make your case for God. I said that the reason I believe in God is that he is the best explanation for the way things are.

Much of my effort making the case for God and Jesus and the Bible—and even critical elements of Christian morality—hinges on what I take to be the commonsense fit between what Christianity claims about the world and the way the world really is. You might call this principle the superior explanatory power of Christian theism.

The same approach applies to the broader question of God's existence. The important details of the theistic worldview make good sense of what we discover the world to be like. This worldview fits the world as we find it and also resonates with our deepest intuitions about origin, meaning, morality, and destiny.

This "fit" is the classical definition of truth, by the way.[1] When a belief fits the way things actually are, we say the belief is true. On the flip side, when a belief does not match the world as it is, then the belief is false.

> Note the advantage of this "best explanation" strategy. No need to dismiss the possibility of other options. We are free to consider alternatives. We're not dogmatically insisting that ours is the only explanation, just the one we think is the best explanation, all things considered.

Our confidence is based on a powerful concept: reality is on our side. God's existence makes sense of features of the world that, without him, would be unlikely in the extreme. Other worldview stories do not fare well by this standard because obvious details simply do not fit into their narrative, putting them on a collision course with reality.[2]

So, fix this fact first in your mind from the outset: God is the best explanation for the way things are. That is your best starting point, in my opinion, when dealing with atheism.

Now, here are two applications of this principle that are amazingly simple to grasp and are, therefore, quite persuasive.

Beginning at the Beginning

I was once asked during an audience Q&A to give some compelling evidence for the existence of God. "Can I ask you a few questions to get us rolling?" I said to the challenger. He nodded. "First, do you think things exist? Is the material universe real?"

"Yes, of course," he answered.

"Good. Second question: Have the things in the universe *always* existed? Is the universe eternal?"

"No," he said. "The universe came into being at the big bang."[3]

"Okay, I'm with you.[4] Now the final question: What *caused* the big bang?"[5]

At this point, he balked. "How do I know?" he said. "I'm no scientist."

"Neither am I," I admitted, "but there are only two choices, aren't there? Either some thing or no thing.[6] What do you think? Do you think something outside the natural universe caused it to come into being, or do you think it simply popped into existence with no cause, for no reason?"

At this point, the skeptic who leans on reason finds himself in a box. Both the law of excluded middle (it can't be neither option because there's no third choice) and the law of noncontradiction (it can't be both since that's a contradiction) oblige him to choose one of the only two logical possibilities.

To admit that something outside the natural, physical, time-bound universe is the world's cause would be at odds with the skeptic's naturalistic atheism. Yet, what thoughtful person would opt for the alternative? Even if he thinks it possible the universe popped into existence, uncaused, out of nothing, it's clearly not the odds-on favorite.

Imagine a man's wife asking where the new Mercedes-Benz SL parked in their garage came from. I doubt she'd be satisfied if he told her, "Honey, it didn't come from anywhere. It just popped into existence out of nothing. No problem. That's how the universe began, you know." Even ordinary folk untutored in physics realize that's not going to wash.

> Reason dictates we opt for the most reasonable alternative, and the something-from-no-thing option is not it. Indeed, it's worse than magic. In magic, a magician pulls a rabbit out of a hat. In this case, though, there's no hat—and no magician. There's just a rabbit (the universe, in our case) appearing out of nowhere.

You might recognize this line of thinking as the Kalam cosmological argument, an ancient defense of theism recently revitalized by philosopher William Lane Craig.[7] If you haven't read his books, let me give you the short course.

You can construct a logically tight syllogism to make this case, but that's not necessary for the average person when you appeal to a commonsense notion like this. Here's the simplified version: a big bang needs a big banger. I think that pretty much covers it. Every effect requires a cause adequate to explain it. Pretty obvious.

Ironically, the night I was working out the details of this point in the lobby of a large hotel in Poland, there was a huge bang in the reception area. The gabby crowd in the lounge was immediately struck silent, everyone wondering the same thing: *What was that?*

Of course, they knew what it *was*. It was a big bang. The real question in their minds was, *What* caused *that?* Did something fall over? Did a firecracker go off? Did someone get shot?[8] I promise you one thing, though. No one in that hotel—regardless of religious or philosophic conviction—thought the bang was uncaused. It never occurred to anyone that the bang banged itself.

Skeptics know this, too. Once, at a dinner party, a young man sitting across from me announced—somewhat belligerently—that he no longer believed in God. "It's irrational," he said. "There's no evidence."

In response, I raised my point about the big bang. "If you heard a knock on the front door," I said, "would you think the knock knocked itself, or would you conclude some *one* was doing the knocking and then get up and answer the door?"

He sniffed dismissively at my question, so I let the issue go. Half an hour later, over desert, though, there was a loud knock on the front door (I'm not making this up). Startled, the atheist lifted his head in surprise. "Who's that?" he blurted out.

"No one," I said. The point was lost on him, of course. His next move, though, was telling: he got up and answered the door.

That night, this young, naive atheist had encountered reality.

He knew a simple knock could not have knocked itself, yet he seemed willing to accept as reasonable that an entire universe popped into existence without rhyme, reason, or purpose.

Once, my daughter Annabeth slammed the flat of her hand down on the table with a bang and said, "If I bang my hand down, then I am the one who banged it. So, who banged the big bang?" At eight years old, she had internalized an obvious point: atheism has no resources to explain where the world came from. Theism does. Thus, it's the best explanation for the way things are.

"Who Created God?"

The question about God's origin comes up frequently with children. It also comes up with adults trying to sidestep the native persuasiveness of the cosmological argument I just offered. *Skeptic* magazine's Michael Shermer raised it during my national radio debate with him, and Oxford's Richard Dawkins thinks theism has "utterly failed"[9] because apparently there is no answer to a question even children know to ask.

> Children ask, "Who created God?" because they're children. Grown-ups ought to know this is not an appropriate challenge. The failure is with the question, not with theism.

The challenge falters at two points.

First, it disregards the argument proper by deflecting attention elsewhere. Asking, "Who created God?" does nothing to address the main concern: If the universe is not eternal, then what caused it to "bang" into existence? The question is a fair one and needs to be answered, not ignored. Since the effect is the entire natural realm, then something outside the natural realm must be its cause. Simply brushing the point aside does nothing to weaken its force.

Second, the theist is not vulnerable to the same question about cause for a simple reason: the concern only applies to things that *begin* to exist. This point is so frequently ignored by atheists—even lettered ones like Dawkins and Shermer—that it bears repeating: the question properly applies only to things that begin to exist.

Yet no one in the discussion believes God had a beginning. No theist believes it, and no atheist thinks a self-existent Being *came* into being. The notion itself makes no sense—so it's a bit odd when educated atheists ask the question "Who created God?"[10] Atheists who persist on this issue are simply flogging a straw man.

No matter what view of reality a person takes—a religious one or a nonreligious one—they must accede to an ultimate starting point for everything lest they be locked into a hopeless regress of unlimited "Who created that?" queries.

We know that since the material universe has an age and can't create itself, the physical world can't be that ultimate starting point. There must be a self-existent something outside the natural realm that is ultimately responsible for everything else that exists. It must also be something that can *decide* to cause the world to come into existence. Since only personal agents make decisions, the cause of everything must be a some*one*, not a some*thing*. That's why it makes no sense to ask, "What caused God?"

This doesn't prove God exists, of course. It only shows that the "What caused God?" question is not a meaningful one to ask a theist, though it is an appropriate one to ask a naturalist regarding the universe.

There's one final concern about this challenge that I'll mention briefly before we go to a sample dialogue, and maybe you noticed it. The question is flawed in yet another way. It's similar to questions like "Do you still beat your wife?" It presumes something that may not be true.

These are called "complex questions,"[11] since any answer to the query implicitly affirms something else that may not be true. In this case, asking, "Who created God?" assumes God was created, which is a false move, as we've seen.[12]

That said, here's how I would approach this issue in conversation:

"Who created God?"

    "What do you mean?" [That basic first question again.]

"Well, you seem to think the universe needed a creator, so you believe in God. All I'm asking, then, is, 'Who created God?'"

    "Can you see that you're assuming something when you ask that question?"

"What do you mean?"

    "Well, if I asked you whether you've stopped beating your wife, what would I be assuming?"

"That I beat my wife."

    "Right. So, what are you assuming when you ask, 'Who created God?'"

"Well, I guess I'm assuming God was created."

    "Exactly. So why would you think that if there were a God, he would need to be created?"

"Well, you think the universe was created."

    "Right, I do. I believe that because the universe came into being—which you believe, too, right?"

"Right."

    "So, let me ask you a question. Do you think that if the kind of God I'm talking about existed, then he would have been created?"

"Maybe."

    "Why would a self-existent Being need to be created? Wouldn't that be a contradiction?"

If one of your children raises this issue, you might amend your dialogue this way: "If I asked you, 'Are you still cheating on your tests in school?' what would I be assuming?" Let them chew on it a bit until they get the right answer—about their tests and about God—maybe with a little help from you.

Next, ask them, "Okay, since your question assumes God was created, what makes you think that's what happened? Is that what the Bible teaches? [Interaction] No, the Bible teaches that God is eternal. Do you know what that means? [Interaction] It means God never had a beginning, and he will never have an end. Do you see that it doesn't really make sense, then, to ask the question about the beginning of God if he had no beginning?"

You get the idea. Pursue an interactive conversation with them where you tease out these concepts with questions. I think they'll catch on quickly.

Making Contact

There's another feature of reality that theism can account for better than atheism. Let me introduce it with a question: How would we know if there is intelligent life in other parts of the universe?

Scientists know the answer: we would know if we discovered something coming from another world that could not have been produced by natural causes. And scientists *are* looking for this—or listening, rather. The project is called SETI, the Search for Extraterrestrial Intelligence.

SETI's basic principle for recognizing the existence of intelligent life beyond Earth was showcased years back in a fascinating film called *Contact*. In the movie, agnostic SETI astronomer Ellie Arroway (Jodie Foster) scrutinizes radio signals from outer space, "waiting for E.T. to call."

One night, he does, with a series of audio pulses counting out each prime number—integers divisible only by themselves and the number one—from 2 to 101. It is a complex series of twenty-six numbers conforming perfectly to an external code—what scientists call "specified complexity"—a clear sign of intelligence. Indeed, the pulse sequences through only the first four primes—2, 3, 5, and 7—before Ellie says, "There's no way that's a natural phenomenon."

But there's more. The signal is coupled with a second transmission, the image and audio of Adolf Hitler presiding over the 1936 Olympics. It was the first TV broadcast strong enough to drift into outer space fifty-two years earlier, handily returned to sender from the star system Vega, twenty-five light-years away. Interlaced within the TV signal frames is another surprise: encrypted pages of text that, when decoded, reveal detailed plans for building a one-person galactic transport. The blueprint, they say, is "the jackpot."

Ellie—along with her previous naysayers—is now completely convinced of the existence of intelligent extraterrestrials. Incontrovertible evidence—a sophisticated code revealing a detailed blueprint providing instructions to build an unimaginably complex machine—settles the issue.

Curiously, though, Ellie is unconvinced of God's existence. Why? "As a scientist I rely on empirical evidence," she tells her love interest, Palmer Joss (Matthew McConaughey), who prefers religious experience over reason.

"In that matter," Ellie concludes, "I don't believe there is data either way." Why should she believe God created everything then left us no evidence, she argues. "I need proof," she says simply.

Joss has nothing to offer other than his you've-got-to-have-faith bromides. We can offer a better solution, though—a simple one right in front of Ellie's and Palmer's eyes, but one that hadn't occurred to the writers, apparently. Had Ellie applied the same rules to the question of God that she applied to the question of E.T.s, she would have had the evidence she asked for—in spades.

Here it is. The evidence—proof, if you will—for the existence of God is the same kind of evidence Ellie took as proof for the existence of extraterrestrials: a sophisticated code revealing a detailed blueprint providing instructions to build an unimaginably complex machine—our DNA.[13]

> Ellie Arroway finds a blueprint for a spaceship and properly infers intelligence as its source. Yet every single cell in her body carries within it a code—embedded in the DNA double helix—of a detailed blueprint vastly more complex than the one for her galactic transport.

In our computer age, we all know where code like this comes from. It comes from programmers. It is designed by intelligence.

So, here's the question: Who wrote the code? Who programmed Ellie Arroway's DNA with tens of thousands of pages of information? Who combined three billion base pair "words"[14] to write the assembly instructions for human beings? Indeed, who programmed the DNA for the five billion species estimated to have lived on planet Earth?

To reprise Arroway, there's no way that's a natural phenomenon.

Right. The human genome is no accident. Rather, it is a detailed plan carefully laid out by an intelligent mind.[15] Regarding E.T.s, Arroway has the evidence she needs: a blueprint of a spaceship. Regarding God, she also has the evidence she needs: a blueprint of a human body.

And remember, computer code is binary—zeros and ones. DNA is a four-character digital code, making it much more sophisticated and much more powerful. Noted biochemist Michael Denton says, "The capacity of DNA to store information vastly exceeds that of any other known system; it is so efficient that all the information needed to specify an organism as complex as man weighs less than a few thousand millionths of a gram. The information necessary to specify the design of all the species of organisms which have ever existed on the planet . . . could be held in a teaspoon and there would still be room left for all the information in every book ever written."[16]

Fingerprints Everywhere

And DNA is just the tip of the design iceberg. Signs of intelligence—God's fingerprints, as it were—are everywhere in the natural world, with countless examples of design chronicled in scores of works—books, DVDs, and so on—authored by believers and non-believers alike.

There's the remarkable positioning of our planet in just the right place in our solar system—what even secular scientists call the "Goldilocks zone"—with just the right size; just the right seasons dictated by just the right tilt of Earth's axis; just the right magnetic field with just the right intensity; just the right-sized moon creating just the right tides and just the right continental drift; just the right ratio of oxygen to nitrogen; just the right ratio of carbon dioxide to water vapor—and on and on and on.

There are the incredibly fine-tuned constants of physics that dictate the constitution of our physical universe—the force of gravity, the strong and weak nuclear forces, the initial entropy of the universe, the cosmological constant, the proton-neutron mass difference, the expansion rate of the universe—with a minuscule change in of any one of them resulting in a universe unfit for life anywhere. It's what some scientists now call the "rare Earth" hypothesis.[17]

There's the discovery that every living cell is chock-full of microscopic nanomachines made of molecules that are irreducibly complex—alter or remove one part, and the entire machine breaks down—meaning they could not have been constructed by a step-by-step evolutionary process.[18] It's unmistakable evidence of design that even Darwin admitted would falsify his theory: "If it could be demonstrated that any complex organ existed, which could not possibly have been formed by numerous, successive, slight modifications, my theory would absolutely break down."[19]

There's the stunning ability of reptiles (sea turtles), fish (salmon), mammals (whales), and insects (monarch butterflies) to navigate to precise locations on the globe by tuning in to Earth's magnetic field.[20] It's unthinkable in the extreme that the same incredibly sophisticated virtual GPS system would independently evolve by accident in creatures far removed from one another on the proposed evolutionary tree of life.

These remarkable features (and there are many more examples) are so stunning given naturalism, they prompted astrophysicist Sir Fred Hoyle—who originally coined the term *big bang*—to admit, "A commonsense interpretation of the facts suggests that a super-intellect has monkeyed with physics, as well as with chemistry and biology, and that there are no blind forces worth speaking about in nature. The numbers one calculates from the facts seem to me so overwhelming as to put this conclusion almost beyond question."[21]

Clearly, God's "fingerprints" are everywhere for those who are willing to look. There are many ways to make this point in conversation. Here's one example:

"There's no evidence for God."

> **"Let me ask you a question. If you saw a shoe print in the sand on the beach, what would you conclude?"**

"Someone had been walking there."

> "Right, a person wearing shoes."

"Right."

> "Would you be tempted to think it was a freak accident of nature—seashells, sand, surf all rolling around together, creating an impression that *looked* like a shoe print but wasn't?"

"That wouldn't make any sense."

"Why not."

"Because, first, chance probably can't produce a shoe print, and second, there's a better explanation: a person wearing a shoe did it."

"Exactly. Now another example. Let's say you found a blueprint of some sort. Would you be tempted to think it was a crazy accident of ink spilled on paper and whipped around by the wind?"

"Of course not, for the same reasons."

"Especially if the blueprint actually described something that was incredibly complex and worked really well, right?"

"Right."

"So, what do you make of the human body?"

"It evolved by chance."

"And the DNA blueprint for the human body inside each one of our cells?"

"It evolved by chance."

"Why would you believe a human body evolved by chance, when you can't believe a simple shoe print in the sand happened by chance?"

"Well, it's possible."

"Let's say I agreed. Even if it were possible— which strikes me as unlikely, and I bet you think it's unlikely, too—do you think it's the most reasonable option? Is it the odds-on favorite?"

"That's what scientists say happened."

"But isn't there a better explanation?"

"What?"

"Someone made the DNA blueprint inside the human body."

"Who would that be?"

"God."

Quantifiable, empirical, scientific evidence is the reason notable scientists have conceded—almost against their will—a supernatural cause to the universe.

Caltech astronomer Allan Sandage—one of the world's foremost observational cosmologists—gave a lecture at a conference in Dallas in 1985 describing the astronomical evidence for the beginning of the universe. He shocked his listeners by calling it a "creation event," adding, "I now have to go from a stance as a complete materialistic, rational scientist and say this super natural [sic] event, to me, gives at least some credence to my belief that there is some design put in the universe."[22]

Antony Flew—arguably the most influential philosophical atheist of the twentieth century—became a theist in 2004. As he puts it, he simply "followed the argument where it has led me."[23] For Flew, that included the scientific evidence for the origin of the universe (point #1) and the evidence for the design of the "intricate laws" of the universe and the DNA double helix (point #2).[24]

Astronomer Robert Jastrow, former director of NASA's Goddard Institute for Space Studies, offers this stunning summary: "For the scientist who has lived by his faith in the power of reason, the story ends like a bad dream. He has scaled the mountains of ignorance; he is about to conquer the highest peak; as he pulls himself over the final rock, he is greeted by a band of theologians who have been sitting there for centuries."[25]

I am not saying these notables are right because they are famous scientists. That would be a mistake. I'm saying that people of this stature do not change their minds and swim against the prevailing ideological current for no good scientific reason. Each was convinced by the overwhelming empirical evidence that theism, not atheism, was the best explanation for the way things are.

Multiverse: The Cosmic Lottery

Of course, naturalistic atheists have not been silent in the face of this compelling evidence for design. There is a rejoinder.

What if our universe is not the only one? Maybe, Richard Dawkins muses, "There are many universes, co-existing like bubbles of foam, in a 'multiverse.'"[26] If a multitude of worlds exist—billions and billions of them stretching to infinity—then the statistical improbability of a finely tuned Goldilocks universe like ours evaporates.

Every lock's combination yields eventually to an infinite number of attempts. "Radically unlikely" morphs into "unavoidably certain." With unlimited variations, no superintellect need monkey with physics to make our world. Rather, we got lucky; otherwise, we wouldn't be alive to muse on the mystery.[27]

Of course, as philosopher William Lane Craig notes, "If an infinite ensemble of simultaneous universes does not actually exist, [the] attempt to explain away the fine-tuning of the universe for intelligent life collapses."[28] So what is the evidence for the multiverse?

Precious little. The project remains entirely theoretical and hypothetical. Since there can never be, even in principle, any empirical, observational verification, the multiverse option is, in philosopher Douglas Groothuis's mind, "nothing more than metaphysical speculation . . . invoked without logical basis simply to avoid a Designer."[29]

Further, any universe-generating mechanism—if it did exist—would *itself* need to be finely tuned for the task of manufacturing an infinite array of worlds. The atheist's alternative, then—even if plausible and verifiable—solves nothing in the long run.

Once again, a better explanation is at the ready, one that fits all the observable evidence and is not ad hoc: intelligent design. Here's a sample dialogue:

"We don't need God to explain all the fine-tuned features of physics and the solar system and biology and so forth."

"Why not?"

"Scientists suggest there might be an infinite number of universes out there. So it's inevitable you'll get one like ours, no matter how unlikely it seems to us."

"What's the evidence for thinking there might be an infinite number of universes?" [Columbo #2]

"Well, it's theoretical."

"You mean there's no empirical evidence at the moment?"

"It's speculative. They're working on it, but it seems like a reasonable explanation for the appearance of fine-tuning."

"So, you think a multiverse can ultimately solve that problem?"

"Why not?"

"Because now, instead of having to explain what caused one universe—ours—you have to explain what caused an infinite number of universes."

"Well, scientists think there must be some physical process or maybe quantum activity that can do the job. Like I said, they're working on it."

"Well, if there's a multiverse maker, of sorts,

wouldn't that mechanism itself need to be finely tuned to crank out all those universes? It looks like your solution creates more problems than it solves. What do you think?"

"Again, they're working on it."

"Well, I'm not a scientist, but I think that when something *looks* designed, and it's radically unlikely to happen by chance, and the alternatives have little to no evidence to support them, then the best conclusion is that it *is* designed."

"Scientists reject that."

"But why posit an infinite number of undetectable worlds when a simpler solution fits all the data?"[30]

"What solution is that?"

"God."

Richard Dawkins opens his bestselling book *The Blind Watchmaker* with these words: "Biology is the study of complicated things that give the appearance of having been designed for a purpose."[31]

Maybe living things—and the rest of the universe, for that matter—"appear" to be designed for a purpose because they *are* designed for a purpose. Maybe, as Cambridge-trained biochemist Douglas Axe puts it, "That [God] has acted is plain to see, and no theory can erase what we see."[32] Maybe, all things considered, God actually *is* the best explanation for the way things are.

Which is more reasonable? The existence of the cosmos and the intricate and delicately balanced design of the universe—design in both biology and physics—are accidents, or the advent of the universe and the "appearance" of its design are the result of an intelligent Designer?

I have given two substantial reasons to believe in God: the

origin of the universe and the dazzling design at every level of our world. Both point to God and not atheism as the best explanation for the way the world is.

Our final application of our "best explanation" principle against atheism is the most surprising—and possibly the most potent—since it leverages the problem of evil as evidence in favor of theism, not atheism.

CHAPTER 9

EVIL: ATHEISM'S FATAL FLAW

In 1982, I lived in Thailand for seven months supervising a feeding program in a Cambodian refugee camp named Sa Kaeo. My charge: 18,250 Khmer refugees who had escaped the holocaust perpetrated on Kampuchea by the Khmer Rouge after the fall of Phnom Penh in 1975.

The first-person accounts of the slaughter that took place were mind numbing. Even children relayed stories of unthinkable brutality. By 1979, an estimated two million Cambodians—about one quarter of the population—had perished at the hands of Pol Pot's Khmer Rouge. It was the greatest act of genocide ever inflicted in history by a people on its own population.

No thoughtful person can countenance such barbarism—such innocent suffering, such inhumanity—without recoiling from the wickedness, the depravity, the unmitigated decadence that took place there.

Surprisingly, though, the evil of atrocities like the Cambodian carnage provides an unusual opportunity for the theist and a striking liability for the atheist.

The Brighter Side of Evil

The problem of evil is the most enduring—and for many, the most persuasive—objection to the existence of a completely good and supremely powerful divine Being.

It's easy to see why. A good God would want to get rid of evil, it seems, and a powerful God would be able to get rid of evil. Yet evil remains. To paraphrase Epicurus: If God, then whence evil?

This challenge—called the deductive problem of evil—fails for reasons I have addressed in more detail elsewhere, as have others.[1] In a word, the charge does not stand up since it's certainly conceivable that a good, powerful God might allow evil if he had good reason to do so. This mere possibility is enough to nullify the contradiction, which is why it's rare for philosophically astute atheists to raise this challenge anymore.[2]

> Thoughtful attempts at explaining why God allowed evil in the first place are called theodicies. Most have merit, but they are speculative since God has not revealed his mind on this issue.

Our approach will trade on a different concern—what might be called the "brighter side" of the problem of evil: the problem itself defeats the objection.

Here is the key strategic move: Do not focus on trying to answer why God allowed evil—a daunting task. Rather, parry the apparent defeater by showing that genuine evil is evidence for God and against atheism, not the other way around.

Our strategy trades on two facts embedded in the objection.

First, every thoughtful person, no matter where or when he lives, knows that something is terribly wrong—morally wrong—with the world. The thought, *That ain't right*—the basis for the complaint about evil and God—crosses our minds repeatedly. Things are not just broken; they're bad. They are not the way they are supposed to be.

Second, when we point the finger at the bad stuff, we aren't simply saying we don't like what's happening or that we'd personally prefer things to be different. No. We're convinced certain things are wrong—profoundly morally perverse in themselves—regardless of whether anyone else thinks differently.

This second fact is the difference between moral relativism ("That's not right for me") and moral objectivism ("That's not right, regardless"), a distinction we discussed in chapter 6. If the actions themselves are evil—as people imply—if the wrongness is somehow in the behaviors regardless of what others think or feel (remember, the Khmer Rouge had no moral misgivings about genocide), then the evil is objective.

Here's the takeaway: the problem of evil is only a problem if morality is objective, not subjective. Since everyone knows evil is a problem, then everyone—even the atheist—implicitly affirms objective morality.

For all their don't-push-your-morality-on-me protests, most people know better. Deep down, they are certain that some things are bad in themselves. Count on that. This fact about the problem of evil leads to an insight lethal to atheism.

> Yes, the existence of evil is psychologically daunting for theists, but it's not the rational problem most people think it is. Indeed, for Christians, evil is an ally if they know how to leverage the problem in their favor.

In *The Brothers Karamazov*, Fyodor Dostoyevsky famously notes that if God does not exist, then all is permitted. If there is no Lawmaker—God—there can be no law: nothing properly forbidden and nothing required. If no law, then no lawbreaking—thus no evil—and no law keeping, either—thus no good. Behaviors just *are*, and nothing more can be said about them.

If no God, then no transcendent plan or ultimate purpose, either, as atheist Richard Dawkins bluntly admits: "If the universe were just electrons and selfish genes . . . blind physical forces and genetic replication, some people are going to get hurt, other people are going to get lucky, and you won't find any rhyme or reason in it, nor any justice. The universe we observe has precisely the properties we should expect if there is, at bottom, no design, no purpose, no evil and no good, nothing but blind, pitiless indifference."[3]

Grim tidings for mankind, if so.

For many, though, this is not sad news but a happy discovery signaling limitless liberties. No God means no boundaries and no restrictions—"All is permitted"—and that's the way many want things to be, at least when it comes to their own personal indulgences.[4]

The startling flipside to these limitless liberties, though, is a moral calculus that both Dawkins and Dostoyevsky see with crystal clarity: if there is no God, the liberties are limitless because there is no law. And if no law, then no broken laws, and if no broken laws, then no evil.

The atheist's complaint against evil, then, ironically places the theist on solid footing while leaving the atheist's feet firmly planted in midair. Dostoyevsky's—and Dawkins's—insight is key to understanding the problem (for atheists) with the problem of evil: if no transcendent God, then no transcendent moral laws that, when broken, result in genuine evil in the world. To counter Epicurus: if atheism, then whence evil?[5]

In a moment I want to show you how to tactically leverage that liability in your own favor using questions. First, though, a strategic concern.

Atheism: No Exit

After decades of addressing the problem of evil with audiences, I have stumbled on an insight that has simplified my task immensely.

I do not begin my talk with tactical concerns (maneuvering on the specifics) but rather begin with a strategic point (sketching out the big picture) that I have already hinted at. I want to show that the atheist himself is just as vulnerable to the problem of evil as he thinks the theist is. Indeed, more so.

To set the stage, I begin by clarifying the challenge in vivid terms, spelling out the logic of the complaint, then offering an anecdote, an illustration, or a graphic piece of news (there's always some horror in the headlines) accentuating the gravity of the atheist's protest—the Cambodian holocaust, for example. In short, I try to increase the emotional force of the objection.

Next, I tell the audience that I do not grapple with this problem first as a theologian, or as a philosopher, or even as a Christian, but as a human being trying to make sense of my world. Evidence of egregious evil abounds. How do I account for such depravity?

I'm quick to add, though—and here is the strategic move—I am not alone. Theists are not the only ones saddled with this challenge. Evil is a problem for everyone. Since evil is an objective feature of the world (hence the universal objection), every person, regardless of religion or worldview, must face its challenge. Even the atheist.

When assaulted by personal tragedy, or distressed by sordid events in the news, or personally victimized by corruption or abused by religion, some understandably reject God. ("That's when I became an atheist.")

Notice, though, that opting for atheism does nothing to resolve the original complaint. Each of those evils remains. The atheist must now take his turn offering his own explanation for evil since eliminating God doesn't eliminate the problem.

The atheist faces a complication the theist does not encounter, though. How can anything be ultimately evil or good in a materialistic universe bereft of a transcendent standard that makes sense of his moral complaints in the first place?

Atheists still must answer the question, How do I, as an atheist, account for evil in the world? How do I, from inside a materialist worldview, answer the problem of evil? As I have written elsewhere, "Removing God from the equation, though understandable, does nothing to eliminate the problem that caused someone to doubt God's existence in the first place. God is gone, but the original problem remains. The world is still broken. Atheism settles nothing on this matter. . . . Things still are not the way they're supposed to be, so the atheist continues to be plagued with the same problem he started with."[6]

So how do atheists answer their own challenge—the charge against the theist of an incurable worldview contradiction—when it's turned back on them? They can't. What could it possibly mean for an atheist to say that the world is not the way it's supposed to be when in the atheist's universe there is no "rhyme or reason" to be found—no "supposed to" about anything? Their materialist worldview provides no resources to account for—and no grounds to complain about—genuine evil.

In the final analysis, in a world without God, deep morality—objective morality—turns out to be an illusion. Whatever is, is "right." Nothing more can be said. The atheist's own answer, then, to the problem of evil—that is, the only answer left to him—is that there is no problem of evil.

Here is the irony. The existence of evil initially fueled the atheist's fury toward God, yet his own worldview turns the wickedness he was so intense about into complete illusion.

This is a solution? This is the best explanation for the way things are? This is the worldview that has the best resources to make sense of the challenge we all face with evil?

Evil, Our Ally

Here is how to show, tactically, that the really bad stuff that happens in the world is really good evidence for God.

In your conversation with a skeptical friend, first ask for his assessment of something clearly morally grotesque. Mention Auschwitz, or a recent massacre reported in the news, or any striking instance of cruelty, wickedness, or man's inhumanity to man. If the standard examples don't move him, suggest homophobia, bigotry, intolerance, racism, climate change—whatever pushes his personal moral hot button. Chances are, he's already provided examples for you.

Second—and this is the important question—ask, "When you say these things are evil [or bad, or wrong, or wicked, or 'ain't right'—whatever], are you talking about the actions themselves, or are you only talking about your feelings or personal preferences about the actions? Are they merely wrong for you, or are they wrong for anyone, regardless?"

Again, you're zeroing in here on the difference between moral objectivism and moral relativism.

In virtually every case—if he doesn't have his philosophical guard up defending his relativistic turf—he's going to tell you the truth: he is convinced the actions are evil, regardless of personal opinion or cultural consensus. He thinks the evil is objective, even if he doesn't use that word.

Now here is your closing question: Where does the standard come from that your friend is using to label some things wicked or wrong or morally vile, regardless of personal opinion, regardless of cultural conventions? What transcendent standard allows him to make a legitimate judgment that some things are really, truly wicked?

I think you see the point. Put in a playful way, it makes no sense to say things are not the way they're s'posed to be unless there *is* a way they're s'posed to be, and there can't be a way they're s'posed to be without a "S'poser." Translation: it's going to be difficult to make sense of transcendent moral law without a transcendent moral lawgiver—God.

This, of course, is the moral argument for God. Put formally: if there is no God, there is no objective morality. But there is objective morality (evidenced by evil in the world). Therefore, there is a God.[7]

As I pointed out earlier, your friend has one of two choices at this point. He can cling to his relativism and drop his objection about evil in the world. Surrendering that complaint, though, is going to be hard because he knows too much—real evil is self-evident to him or he wouldn't have raised the complaint to begin with. Or he can salvage his commonsense complaint about evil at the expense of his atheism since no materialistic scheme of things can account for immaterial moral obligations. What he can't do is have it both ways.[8]

> Don't let your friend miss the point. The reality of evil in the world does not help the atheist. It hurts him. Rather than being good evidence *against* God, evil in the world is one of the best evidences *for* God.[9]

You have probably noticed that I've been making the same point in a number of different ways. For clarity's sake, then, let me revisit my main point in sum. Here it is in a nutshell.

The problem of evil is only a problem if evil is real—obviously. To say something is evil, though, is to make a moral judgment—also obvious. Moral judgments require a moral standard—a moral law—and a moral law requires an author. If the standard is transcendent, then the lawgiver must be transcendent, too.[10]

If there is a problem of evil (and there is), then God exists. He is the best explanation for the way things are—even for the problem of evil. That is why evil is atheism's fatal flaw.

Evil in the Street

Now that we've identified some of the difficulties that arise from using evil to repudiate God, we can map out tactical responses to help us when a friend or coworker raises the issue in conversation.

I find it's best if I'm prepared with a move to get me going right out of the gate. Here is my standard opening question regarding the challenge of evil: **"What, exactly, is the problem, as you see it?"** [Columbo #1] The query may sound like an empty one—the problem seems obvious—but it accomplishes two tactically significant objectives.

First, this question immediately buys me time—if only a moment or two—so I can collect my thoughts and strategize my next moves. Second, it's always to my advantage to have a challenger spell out his concern in precise terms since it removes ambiguities for both of us.

The devil is in the details with challenges like this, and getting those specifics on the table will often expose problems that are not initially obvious. As I mentioned briefly, the charge of contradiction trades on the claim that a good God would eliminate evil if he could. The assumption, though, is false since it's conceivable God might have a good reason to allow evil. This insight, as I said, is all that's necessary to invalidate the contradiction. If he doesn't clarify the details of the contradiction he's charging you with, though, it's going to be difficult to point out his misstep.

Here is my second move: **"So, you believe in evil, then?"** [Columbo #1][11] Again, this seems like I'm restating the obvious, but it confirms an important detail in the conversation, plus it provides a smooth bridge to any of the dialogue strategies that follow.

As you'll see, the conversations that follow overlap in content. They all trade on the liabilities we've been exploring, but they approach those problems from different angles.

The first two challenge the atheist to make sense of his

complaint about evil given his atheism. The second two challenge the relativist to make sense of his complaint about evil given his relativism. The last set of exchanges focus on the grounding problem: What do objective moral obligations ultimately rest upon?

Your goal is not to memorize the details of each dialogue, of course, but to make note of the key questions you might ask (in bold) and then observe how I employ the basic concepts so you can do the same in your interactions with others.

"So, you believe in evil, then?"
"Right. That's why I don't believe in God."

"Let's just say you're right, and God doesn't exist. All those things you described as bad and evil, those things still happen, right?

"Of course."

"And those things are still evil, right?"

"Of course."

"That's a bit confusing, isn't it?"

"Why?"

"Well, how do you, as an atheist, explain those evils in the world?"

"I don't follow."

"You asked me how a good, powerful God could exist when there's so much evil in the world."

"Right."

"Now I'm asking, if atheism is true, how can there be so much evil in the world?"

"I still don't get it."

"Okay, let me put it this way. When you say things happen that are evil, **where are you getting your standard to judge things as evil in themselves?**"

"It's just common sense."

"Right, but now you're saying how you *know* evil. I'm asking a different question. For example, you may know what the speed limit is by looking at the signs. But where do speed limits come from to begin with?"

"The government, of course."

"Exactly. So, **what governing authority sets the limits that get broken, causing evil in the world?** That's my question."

This next discussion is another angle on the difficulty atheism has as a worldview to account for evil. Remember, the problem of evil is a *human* problem. Every person—and every worldview—must grapple with it. It's not just a problem for theists.

"So, you believe in evil, then?"

"Yes, of course I do. That's my objection."

"In other words, you believe some kind of standard of good has been violated, resulting in evil."

"That's it."

"So as an atheist, how does your worldview account for evil? How would you answer your own question in light of atheism?" [Columbo #3]

"What do you mean?"

"Well, there's evil in the world, right?"

"Of course."

"As a Christian, I think evil happens when people violate God's good purposes. It's why we say the world isn't the way it's supposed to be. Evil, then, fits right into my worldview. **But how does evil fit into your atheistic worldview?**" [Columbo #3]

"I don't get what you mean."

"Well, the rules must be real before they can be

violated, causing evil, right? **In atheism, though, there's no God making the rules. So where do those rules come from?** How do you solve that problem?

This next section has two exchanges that leverage our basic approach to show that relativists cannot simply help themselves to the problem of evil since their complaint about evil conflicts with their relativism.

"So, you believe in evil, then?"
"Yes, of course. That's my objection."
  "What do you mean by 'evil'? How would you define it?" [Columbo #1]
"Well, I think it's a matter of opinion."
  "So, there are no universal rules governing all people at all times in all places?"
"Of course not. It's all relative."
  "Now I'm confused. **It sounds like you're asking how God could allow so much evil in the world while also saying there is no objective standard for good and evil.** But how could there be any evil without a standard? [Columbo #3]
"But I do believe in evil."
  "But you just told me everything's relative, that there's no absolute standard. So then for you, evil would just be a violation of your personal opinions?"
"Right. It's what I *personally* believe is wrong."
  "So, you're asking me how can there be a God who allows things to happen that you don't like? Why is that a good objection against God? What am I missing here?" [Columbo #3]

"When you object to evil, are you saying that certain things bother you emotionally, or are you saying that certain actions are wrong in themselves regardless of how you feel, and that's what makes God's existence unlikely?"

"I'm not sure what you're getting at."

"Let me put it another way. Is racism wrong?" [Columbo #3]

"Of course it is."

"Now, do you mean racism is wrong regardless of what any person or any society thinks, or is it only wrong from your perspective?"

"It's wrong for me." [Relativism]

"Then I don't understand your complaint. **You don't think God exists because some things happen that are wrong for *you* but may be okay for others? How is that a problem for God's existence?**"

The next three exchanges focus on what's called "the grounding problem." How do we account for—ground—the existence of the kind of objective moral standards necessary for evil to be real if there is no God?

"So, you believe in evil, then?"

"Yes, of course."

"You're an atheist, though, so I don't understand your concern."

"What do you mean?"

"If there is no God, how can there be the kind of real evil in the world that you're concerned about?" [Columbo #3]

"I don't get your point." [Be prepared

for people to be confused about the
grounding concern.]

"Well, when you talk about evil, you're basically
saying some kind of moral rule has been broken,
that the person doing evil has broken that rule.
Right?

"I guess so."

"Then who made those rules?" [Columbo #3]

"What, exactly, is the problem?"
"It's obvious. Bad things happen. If there
really was a good God, like you say, then
he wouldn't allow all that bad stuff."

"I'm not sure I understand what you mean by 'bad.'
Can you help me out?" [Columbo #1]
"You know, rape, torture, murder—those
sorts of things."

"You just gave me examples of evil. But why would
you label *those* things evil and not call, say, kindness
or heroism evil? You must have some standard in
mind. **Where do you get the standard that
distinguishes good from evil?"** [Columbo #3]

"Is there a speed limit on the street by your house?"
[This question is meant to set up the Columbo #3
that follows.]
"Of course."

"If you exceeded the speed limit, would you be
breaking the law?"
"Sure."

"Where did that law come from?" [Columbo #3]
"The sign is right there. It's obvious.
Anyone can read it." [Here he's confused

how he knows the law with the source of
the law itself—a common mistake. Your
question is about the second, not the first.]

> "Sorry. I'm not asking if you can see the sign. I'm
> asking you where the sign came from. What if I made
> the sign? [Relativism] Would you have to obey it?"

"Of course not. Individual people don't set
the speed limits. The government does."

> "I agree completely. **So, what governing
> authority makes the laws of the universe
> that are broken when people do evil things?"**
> [Columbo #3]

"I'm not following you." [This confusion is
common.]

> "Well, you're saying that people are breaking the
> speed limit of the universe, in a sense—the problem
> of evil. **If there are no real speed limits, then
> there is no real evil. I'm just asking where
> those speed limits come from. Any idea?"**
> [Columbo #3]

Why believe in God? *Because* of the problem of evil, not in
spite of it.

There is no other way to make sense of a world thick with
the moral obligations necessary for there to be evil. If there is no
God, then there is no evil—nor any good—and we're back to
Dostoyevsky and Dawkins again: nothing required, all permitted;
no evil, no good; all blind, all pitiless, all indifferent.

Without the Potter, everything is clay and nothing but clay.
Deep inside, though, each of us knows better. The existence of God
is the best explanation for our deeply embedded understanding that
the world is not the way it's supposed to be.

The Theist's Bonus

You may have noticed that we've also answered another question without even trying.

If you have followed my thinking so far, my point has been that any sort of morality capable of making sense of real evil requires a standard set by someone in charge. Only a person can make commands and can reward virtue or punish vice. It must be the right kind of someone, of course, one who has the proper "say so" about what is right and what is wrong.

Now, this someone must get his guidelines for good from somewhere. But where? If they come from outside of him, then he is just as beholden to the guidelines as we are. We also then face the question of what makes *those* standards good, and we tumble into a pit without bottom, echoing the same question *ad infinitum.* Genuine goodness vanishes for lack of foundation. If, on the other hand, "good" simply means that this governing someone merely declared it so, then goodness is reduced to power, and genuine goodness vanishes again.[12]

This dilemma, though, is a false one because there is a third option—the theist's option.

If the someone who grounds goodness is himself perfectly and immutably good by nature, the conundrum is resolved. He is beholden to none other, yet his rules are not whims but flow naturally from his own native virtue.

The theist's alternative, then, makes perfect sense. If the moral law is good—which it must be since its violation is clearly evil— then the one from whom those laws emerge is probably good as well. Bitter springs do not produce sweet water.

This is the theist's bonus. The problem of evil does not just give us objective morality *grounded* in God. It also gives us a *good* God. No bottomless pit of infinite standards. No raw exercise of power masquerading as good. There is perfect goodness because someone is perfectly good.

It is the one alternative that makes sense of everything we've discovered so far about evil and good. And if not—if there is no perfectly good God who grounds morality—then there is no goodness at all. It is that or nothing.

> A good God made the world a certain way, the way it's supposed to be. Our fallen desires drive us toward a different end. God wants the good for us, and we do not. The problem is with us, not with God.

Whatever a good God commands will not just be good in the abstract; it will also be good *for* us. We cannot see into the future to know the consequences of our actions. God can. We do not know how things were meant to work, at least not completely. God does.

With every command, he directs us toward wholeness, helping us be the way we're supposed to be. We are the clay, and he is the Potter. Only under his hand and under the protection of his precepts can we be formed into something beautiful. As one writer has put it:

> The law of the Lord is perfect, restoring the soul;
> The testimony of the Lord is sure, making wise the
>   simple.
> The precepts of the Lord are right, rejoicing the
>   heart;
> The commandment of the Lord is pure,
>   enlightening the eyes.
> The fear of the Lord is clean, enduring forever;
> The judgments of the Lord are true; they are
>   righteous altogether.

They are more desirable than gold, yes, than much
    fine gold;
Sweeter also than honey and the drippings of the
    honeycomb.
Moreover, by them Your servant is warned;
In keeping them there is great reward.[13]

For the person who rejects the existence of a perfectly good God, yet still seeks to vindicate his own commitment to good and evil, one option remains. He must offer an alternative he thinks is able to make sense of goodness in a God-less universe.

The main goodness-without-God contender is Darwinism, though atheists have other comebacks, too. We'll consider each of those challenges in the next chapter.

CHAPTER 10

GOOD WITHOUT GOD?

The billboards read, "No God? No problem. Be good for goodness' sake," and, "Are you good without God? Millions are." The point was clear: morality in no way depends on belief in God. And why should it?

Atheists can be good, too. Christopher Hitchens regularly challenged his religious opponents to name a single act of goodness they could perform that a nonbeliever could not accomplish with equal success.[1]

The billboard campaign was intended as a broadside against a central evidence for God, the moral argument, classically one of four cornerstones of the case for God's existence.[2] Put simply, if there is no God, there is no morality. However, morality exists. Therefore, God exists.

Remember—as we discussed—that *objective* morality is the issue here. Clearly, no God is necessary for the make-me-up morality of relativism. Universal moral obligations, however, require a transcendent basis or grounding. That's the argument.

An About-Face

Atheists, at least until recently, have characteristically agreed with the first premise: no God, no morality. Fine. They understood the calculus and were willing to live with the consequences—or benefits, as some took it. Indeed, activist Jeremy Rifkin was one of many who saw the silver lining of atheism's moral nihilism and rejoiced: "We no longer feel ourselves to be guests in someone else's home and therefore obliged to make our behavior conform with a set of pre-existing cosmic rules. It is our creation now. We make the rules. We establish the parameters of reality. . . . We are responsible to nothing outside ourselves. For we are the kingdom, the power, and the glory for ever and ever."[3]

Times have changed.

While twentieth-century British atheist A. J. Ayer dismissed moral judgments as meaningless grunts of emotion ("emotivism,"[4] he called it), many atheists now want to occupy the moral high ground. While much of the culture embraces relativism ("Who are you to judge?"), many atheists are moving in the opposite direction.

The first premise—without God there is no morality—is false, they say. Millions are moral with no belief in God at all, and many are doing a better job at it than religious folk. God is not necessary for goodness. Darwinism can accomplish the task all on its own. Dawkins's "blind watchmaker" is also the "blind moral maker."

Can evolution explain ethics? Can "goodness" and "badness" be deduced from biology? Can Mother Nature—mixing genetic mutation with natural selection—supplant Father God as morality's maker? Right and wrong are obvious to most people, even "godless" ones. Mere belief in the Divine doesn't seem to add anything. Morality helps us, as a species, get our genes into the next generation. Nature selects the survivors. Moral genes win. Simple.

Five debilitating obstacles, however, prevent Darwinism from replacing God as an adequate source of morality.

Readers and Writers

Before I respond to the Darwinian option directly, though, some clarifications are in order.

First, an atheist can mimic many things Christians count as good—he can feed the poor, love his neighbor, even sacrifice his life for others—but he can never do the *summum bonum*, the highest good. He can never love God with his whole heart, mind, soul, and strength. He cannot worship the one from whom all goodness comes, and who therefore is worthy of our deepest devotion and unerring fidelity.

Of course, atheists would likely sniff at this point, but they mustn't miss the deeper implication. At bare minimum, the response demonstrates that regardless of who is right on the God question, the entire moral project is altered significantly when he is added to the equation. Simply put, the atheist and the theist do not share the same morality.

Second, careful theists do not claim that *belief* in God is necessary to *do* good, but rather that *God* is necessary for any act *to be* good in the first place, that without him, true morality has no foundation at all. The question is not whether believers and nonbelievers can perform the same behaviors—of course they can—but whether any behavior can be good in a materialistic world bereft of God.

Hitchens's challenge completely misses this distinction.

Imagine I handed you a copy of *Vanity Fair* (a periodical Hitchens frequently published in) and asked you to read it. Could you? Sure. So could I. Reading requires only that we possess a certain set of skills allowing us to comprehend the meanings of the words on the page.

Notice that, strictly speaking, for this simple act of reading, no additional beliefs about authors or publications or editors or typesetters or newsstands or delivery boys are necessary. You don't need to believe in writers in order to read, but you would never have a text to read unless there were writers in the first place. That's because the existence of authors is logically prior to the act of reading.

> What's required for someone to read is different from what's required for things like magazine articles to exist in the first place. Being able to read and having something to read are completely different things.

If you didn't believe in authors, you could still read books. If, however, your belief was true and authors did not exist, then books would not exist. Books, then, turn out to be evidence for authors.

That's why readers who denied authors would sound silly. ("I read in the newspaper that writers don't exist. Sounds good to me.") Sure, they wouldn't need to believe in authors to be good readers. They could challenge you to show them one article you could read as a believer (in writers) that they couldn't read as unbelievers, and you'd be hard pressed. Yet neither retort would rescue them from their foolishness. Articles are, by nature, the kind of thing that require authors.

Objective morality is just the same. The issue isn't whether we can act according to a moral code but rather whether we can account for the code to begin with. Denying God because you think you can be a good person without him is like dispensing with authors because you fancy yourself a first-rate reader. Morality is evidence for God in the same way that books and articles are evidence for authors.

Consequently, when atheists ask me, "If there were no God, would you still be good?" it's like asking if I'd still be faithful to my wife if I weren't married. Clearly, the question is meaningless.[5] When atheists say, "We can be moral without God," they're saying they can be law-abiding citizens in a land without laws.

This next dialogue trades on those points:

"I don't need God to be moral. Show me one good thing you can do as a believer that I can't do as an atheist."

> **"Are you familiar with what Jesus said was the greatest commandment?"**

"I think he said to love God with all your heart."

> "Right. **In Christianity, the greatest of all goods is loving God. Can you do that?"**

"Of course not, but that doesn't count since I don't believe in God."

> "I get your point, but at least it shows that what counts as 'good' changes a lot if God exists."

"Not in most things."

> "I think your challenge misses something else really important."

"What's that?"

> **"I'll use an illustration. What's the speed limit on the street in front of your house?"**

"It's thirty-five miles per hour."

> "And who set that speed limit?"

"The government, of course."

> "And if you honored the limit, would you be a good, law-abiding citizen in that case?"

"Sure."

> "You're a good citizen because there's a law to obey and you're obeying it, right?"

"Right."

"What if—for some reason—there were no government? Would there still be a speed limit on the street in front of your house?"

"Of course not."

"Right. Could you still drive thirty-five miles per hour in that case, though?"

"Sure."

"Would driving thirty-five miles per hour make you a good, law-abiding citizen?"

"Obviously not, since there is no law."

"Exactly. That's my point. Without the law, you could still do the behavior. So could I. But neither of us would be *good*, law-abiding citizens because of those actions."

Next, I want you to see the significant difficulties with appealing to Darwinian evolution to make sense of morality.

Darwinism: Troubled Waters

First, it's tempting for evolutionists to think that any trait conferring reproductive advantage must have evolved. They tell a mutation/natural-selection story, wave their Darwinian wand, and the conversation is over. Simply telling a tale about, say, the survival benefits of altruism is not enough, though.

Exactly how does Darwinism work to create morality?

Darwinism is a strictly materialistic process by definition—as one philosopher puts it, "clumps of matter following the laws of physics."[6] Behaviors are physical, but whether any behavior is morally good or bad is not in its chemistry or its physics. In what sense, then, is goodness or badness a physical quality? Right and wrong, virtue and vice, values and obligations are not made of material stuff.

> How can the mere reshuffling of molecules cause an immaterial moral principle to spontaneously spring into existence and somehow attach itself to human behaviors? It can't.

Second, the materialist account assumes that the truth of evolution—in the technical, neo-Darwinian synthesis sense—is unassailable.[7] However, lately, even nonreligious thinkers have raised serious doubts about the program's capabilities. A host of secularists are having significant misgivings about Darwinism proper. Two quick examples come to mind, but there are more.

In 2008, a group of influential evolutionary biologists met for a private conference at the Konrad Lorenz Institute in Altenberg, Austria. Now known as the "Altenberg 16," they were "united by the conviction that the neo-Darwinian synthesis had run its course and that new evolutionary mechanisms were needed to explain the origin of biological form."[8]

Noted New York University philosopher Thomas Nagel—himself a committed atheist—stunned the academic world with his book *Mind and Cosmos: Why the Materialist Neo-Darwinian Conception of Nature Is Almost Certainly False.* His subtitle speaks volumes.

> Since Darwinism itself is in doubt with many secular scientists, Darwinists may be leaning on a bent reed when counting on mutations and natural selection to solve the morality problem for them.

Let's set those concerns aside for now, though. I want to look at a third obstacle: even if Darwinism were true—even if "good" and "bad" somehow identified genetically transferable, physical traits—evolution still could not account for objective morality ("good for goodness' sake"), not even in principle.

A Firm Foundation

I referred to the grounding problem briefly in the last chapter, but I want to provide more clarity on it here. I want you to see exactly why Darwinism completely fails to account for objective morality—our key evidence here for God.

Recall our case. If there is a problem of evil (and there is), then morality must be objective. If Darwinism cannot explain objective morality and nothing else but God can, then our moral case for theism stands.

Long before scientists nailed down the details of gravity, ordinary folk could still predict how objects moved under its influence. They knew that something caused fruit to fall (for example), and they could calculate how it worked, to some degree. But they didn't know why things behaved that way in the world.

The "why it works" issue is called the "grounding" question. What is it that accounts for things being the particular—and sometimes the peculiar—way they are? The grounding question applies in science. It also applies in morality.

Moral facts are odd kinds of facts. They are not merely descriptions—how things happen to be. They entail prescriptions, imperatives—how things ought to be. They have incumbency, a certain obligation to them. What explains these unusual features?

Yes, reasonable people can know the difference between right and wrong, but why there is a right and wrong to begin with is a different question. What is its foundation? What "ground" does it rest upon? What—or who—obliges us, and why should we obey?[9]

> Atheists may know the right thing to do—and even do it consistently. That alone, though, brings them no closer to answering the grounding question: Where do moral obligations come from? What do they stand upon?

I'll dispense with a dialogue here since sample conversations in the last chapter traded on this point. What I want you to see next is how the grounding concern creates serious problems for an evolutionary account of morality.

The key question is this: According to the Darwinian approach to morality, what grounds "good" and "evil"? Is it something inside human beings or something outside them? Let's see.

The Blind Moral Maker

Most of us know the basic Darwinian story. Simply put, natural selection chooses among genetic variations (mutations), selecting those traits best suited for survival and reproduction. This process mimics design so well that Richard Dawkins famously dubbed it "the blind watchmaker."

In *Descent of Man*, Darwin argues that every human faculty—including the moral one—is the result of the same mindless process that governs all the rest—the blind moral maker, if you will. Note atheistic philosopher and committed Darwinist Michael Ruse says, "We are genetically determined to believe that we ought to help each other."[10] Michael Shermer, founding publisher of *Skeptic* magazine, explains:

- "By a moral sense, I mean *a moral feeling or emotion* generated by actions. . . . These moral emotions probably evolved out of behaviors that were reinforced as being bad either for the individual or for the group."[11]
- "The codification of moral principles out of the *psychology of moral traits* evolved as a form of social control to ensure the survival of individuals within groups and the survival of human groups themselves."[12]
- "*Moral sentiments* . . . evolved primarily through the force of natural selection operating on individuals and

secondarily through the force of *group selection* operating on populations."[13]

Shermer identifies two factors—a combination of nature and nurture—that he thinks form the "moral sentiments" or "moral feelings" in humans: (1) psychological moral traits determined genetically by evolution, and (2) codes enforced culturally for the good of the group.[14] This is a standard evolutionary characterization of the naturalistic origins of morality.[15]

I want you to think very carefully about this Darwinian account since it has implications for our question about goodness and God.

Atheists want to undermine the force of the moral argument for theism by accounting for morality in purely naturalistic terms. No God needed. The morality evolutionists must explain to successfully parry the moral argument, though, is objective morality, since that's the only kind of morality relevant to the argument. As I demonstrated earlier, relativism won't do.

Recall from chapter 6 that objective morality (moral realism) is mind independent, based on facts outside the subject, the object being the truth maker. Relativistic, subjective morality (moral non-realism), on the other hand, is mind dependent, based on feelings or beliefs inside a subject (an individual or cultural group), the subject being the truth maker.

So here is my question: What kind of morality did Michael Shermer describe in his Darwinian account, objective or subjective? Note the phrases "moral sentiments," "moral feeling or emotion," "the psychology of moral traits," and ethics that "group selection"—culture—honed and codified.

In each case, Shermer describes a morality that is mind dependent, grounded on feelings in the subject, with the subject—either an individual or a group—being the truth maker. Relativism, in other words.[16]

Atheists like Shermer and Hitchens claim to be objectivists (and seem convinced they are) yet consistently ground their morality in entirely subjectivist ways. Michael Ruse, however, is not so confused: ultimately, he says, morality is "an illusion put in place by our genes to make us social facilitators."[17] Ruse explains: "Substantive ethics, claims like 'Love your neighbor as yourself,' are simply *psychological beliefs* put in place by natural selection in order to maintain and improve our reproductive fitness. *There is nothing more to them than that.* . . . We could as easily have evolved a completely different moral system from that which we have."[18]

I'm not denying here that evolution can account for our sense of morality (though I am deeply skeptical). That is a different issue. I'm arguing that if it does, it can only produce subjective morality, not objective, and that's not good enough to explain the morality that needs explaining.

Here's a sample conversation:

> "Do you mind if I ask you a few questions to get clear on your view?"

"Go ahead."

> "I've been saying that if there really is a problem of evil, then God must exist to provide the standard for good and bad. You disagree."

"Right."

> "You believe in morality, but as an atheist, you think there's no need for God. Darwinism can explain our ideas of right and wrong." [Columbo #1]

"Correct."

> **"Can you help me understand exactly how that works?"**

"Well, mutations produce changes that cause feelings about things like altruism or kindness that nature selects to help the group. Standard stuff."

"Right. So, strictly speaking, to say something is 'good' or 'bad' is just another way of saying natural selection makes us *feel* a certain way about some behavior, so we label it 'right' or 'wrong.' Is that it?" [Columbo #1]

"Pretty much."

"So, if I understand correctly, the idea of good and evil is completely inside of the person who evolved that way. If we had evolved differently, we might have had completely different ideas of what was right or wrong."

"Yep. Just like with our physical evolution. With different mutations and environments, humans could have evolved bodies that looked very different from the ones we have now."

"Got it. **Would you say, then, that this kind of morality is centered 'inside' the subject, so to speak—inside the person or group who evolved that way?**"

"Exactly. Like you said, if we had evolved differently, we'd have different ideas of right or wrong."

"That's what confuses me. **If morality is simply certain beliefs or feelings inside a person because he evolved that way, that's just another form of relativism, right?**"

"I guess so."

"Do you see the problem that is for you?"

"Not really, no."

"Well, you raised the problem of evil in the world— objective evil—and I said that requires God. But you said no, evolution can explain that. Then you explained how evolution causes subjective, relativistic morality, not objective morality. So, how does relativistic morality help us understand why there's objective evil in the world?"

Counterfeit Convictions

Here is the fourth difficulty.

As I've noted, philosopher Michael Ruse—as a consistent Darwinist—explicitly rejects moral objectivism. He labels his view, appropriately, "moral nihilism" and himself as a "moral nonrealist."[19] In this, Ruse is being doggedly (and refreshingly) consistent. Indeed, he adds, even a person's conviction that morality is objective is part of evolution's clever deceit.[20]

This assessment raises another difficulty, one you may have already noticed. If evolution can produce false beliefs about morality, what other false beliefs has natural selection tricked us into believing? C. S. Lewis saw the problem clearly: "If minds are wholly dependent on brains, and brains on biochemistry, and biochemistry (in the long run) on the meaningless flux of the atoms, I cannot understand how the thought of those minds should have any more significance than the sound of the wind in the trees."[21]

Given Darwinism, how can our mental apparatus be trusted to know anything if at least some of the things we believe are dictated by chemistry—genetic mutation and natural selection—and not by thoughtful assessment?

Here is a sample conversation probing that concern:

> "So, you're saying that our beliefs about morality are simply a result of a Darwinian process, right?" [Columbo #1]

"Correct."

"So, we *could* have evolved a very different sense of right and wrong."

"That's correct."

"If I'm following you, that would mean that no thing is wrong in itself—wrong no matter how our evolution went—but only "wrong" because our evolution made us think it was wrong."

"Right."

"Then beliefs like mine—that some things are wrong in themselves—are actually false beliefs that my evolution caused me to think are true."

"Yes, I guess that would follow, strictly speaking."

"Well, that raises another question for me."

"What's that?"

"If evolution causes us to have false beliefs about morality, then what other false beliefs has evolution caused us to have? How can we trust any of our rational faculties if evolution tampers with our thinking like that?"

Physics Is Everything

The "good without God" option faces yet another obstacle.

I once witnessed a magnificent spectacle created by falling dominoes. Legions of little blocks standing in formation morphed into a stunning work of art when the creator of the massive puzzle gave the first domino a flick. As, one by one, each domino fell against another in succession, a marvelous panorama unfolded before my eyes.

The picture that appeared was not the result of random events. It was determined beforehand by the order of the dominoes and the constraints of the laws of physics. Repeat the exact setup, repeat the exact result.

Purely physical systems behave like that sea of toppling dominoes. Physical objects "collide" with each other throughout the universe in very precise ways based on their initial conditions and governed by uniform natural law. This precision is what allows science to operate in the first place. The deterministic nature of physical systems makes experimental repeatability possible.[22]

Generally, science acknowledges two kinds of causes. The first is the kind of cause evident in the cascade of collapsing dominoes—event causation. The second (the finger flick) is the kind of cause that initiates the cascade to begin with—agent causation (a human agent, in this case).

Here is the problem for atheists who are materialists—which would be most of them. Agent causation simply cannot exist for the atheist. It's an illusion. In a strictly physical universe, there are cascading dominoes "all the way down."

Mathematician Stephen Hawking and physicist Leonard Mlodinow call it "scientific determinism": "Given the state of the universe at one time, a complete set of laws fully determines both the future and the past. This would exclude the possibility of miracles or an active role for God."[23]

Quite right. These two sentences sit side by side for a reason. By stipulating that natural law "fully determines" every event in history, the authors aim to squeeze God permanently out of the equation. Simply put, physics is everything. Theology is unnecessary.

However, something else important is squeezed out as well: morality—yet another reason a purely materialistic process like Darwinian evolution is not capable of explaining the kind of morality that persistently points to the existence of God.

Do not miss this point: in a physicalist, atheistic universe, event causation governs everything—even human choices. There are no exceptions. The determinism is absolute. Everything, including human nature, must submit to the sovereignty of physics:

- "Since people live in the universe and interact with other objects in it, scientific determinism *must* hold for people as well."[24]
- "Do people have free will? . . . Though we *feel* that we can choose . . . biological processes are governed by the laws of physics and chemistry and therefore are *as determined as the orbits of the planets.*"[25]
- "Our physical brain, following the known laws of science . . . determines our actions, and *not some agency that exists outside those laws.*"[26]
- "So it seems that we are no more than biological machines and that *free will is just an illusion.*"[27]

It's hard to believe brilliant men like Hawking and Mlodinow do not see how destructive this move is to their own case, but I think you will see it readily.

Let me put the question this way: Did the laws of physics determine the order of the words on the pages of *The Grand Design*? Or did Professors Hawking and Mlodinow make that call? Did they *ponder* the evidence for their theories, *consider* the implications of the facts, *posit* conclusions, then *choose* the right words and *select* the order that would best *communicate* their views and *persuade* readers of the *rationality* of their own ideas?

Note that each of the emphasized words denotes free acts of will made by conscious agents. Without genuine freedom, the pondering, considering, positing, choosing, selecting, communicating, persuading, and reasoning would all be impossible.

By squeezing out free will in his attempt to squeeze out God, Stephen Hawking squeezes himself out of the picture as well. He disqualifies himself as author, scientist, man of reason—and also humanitarian, kind coworker, loving husband, and so forth, since moral virtues also require human freedom. Scientific determinism makes morality unintelligible.

The only way out is to acknowledge the obvious—agents (like Hawking) are not subject to the dictates of natural law. Rather, they can intervene to change the course of natural events. They can start the dominoes, stop the dominoes, or redirect the dominoes at will.

When moral issues are at stake, this is called moral freedom. Without it, there is no evil or good, just molecules in motion. Consequently, any physicalistic system—like Darwinian evolution—trying to make sense of objective morality falls flat like a house of cards.

A sample conversation might look like this:

"What kind of atheist are you?"
"I'm a materialist."

"So, on your view, everything that exists is made up of physical stuff governed by the laws of physics and chemistry, is that right?" [Columbo #1]

"That's right. We live in a completely physical universe governed by natural law. There's no God, no souls, no miracles—nothing like that. Science is all we need in order to know everything there is to know about the world. Eventually, we'll figure it all out given enough time."

"Okay, I think I understand you, but that raises a question for me."

"What's that?"

"According to your view, all your thoughts, emotions, reasoning, decisions, etc., are

governed completely by the laws of physics
and chemistry."

"You got it."

"Right, but if all your choices are determined
the way you say, and there is no genuine
freedom, how can there be any morality,
since morality requires freedom to choose the
good from the bad?"

Darwin, No Exit

The Darwinian dismissal of God as a necessary grounding for genuine morality faces serious obstacles:

- How does a strictly materialistic process governed by the laws of physics and chemistry—like Darwinian evolution—create nonphysical moral obligations that apply to humans?
- If Darwinism's adequacy to explain biological novelty is being reexamined by secular scientists, why trust it to explain morality, too?
- If the best evolution can do is account for subjective, relativistic beliefs about morality, how can it undermine the moral argument for God, which explains the existence of real, objective evil in the world?
- If evolution produces false beliefs about morality, what other false beliefs has natural selection tricked us into believing?
- How can a deterministic Darwinian world account for the genuine freedom that morality requires?

At best, Darwinism might account for beliefs about actions that humans falsely label "moral" because nature's deception accomplishes some evolutionary purpose. But it is deception, nonetheless.

Evolution might be able to explain subjective moral feelings. It can never explain objective moral obligations. Biology can't make anything bad in itself.

These are all intractable problems for atheists. The difficulties are so deep, it's impossible for evolution to rescue the atheist's moral project. In atheism, there is no such thing as "goodness for its own sake"—goodness for the inherent good of goodness—because goodness of that sort cannot exist without God.

No, Darwin will not help the atheist here. The moral argument for God stands. Evolution can't touch it.

CHAPTER 11

JESUS, THE SON

When I was a young Christian in the early '70s sporting OshKosh bib overalls and hair down to my shoulders, I wore a hip necklace identifying me as a Christian. It was called an *ichthus*, the Greek word for "fish."

The pendant consisted of two intersecting arcs with lines extending past the junction point on one side, forming the silhouette of a fish. You can still see it on bumper stickers or in ads for businesses run by believers.

The Greek word itself (ΙΧΘΥΣ) nestled inside the body, completes the icon—a simple symbol summarizing ancient Christians' core theology regarding the one they followed as Lord.

The *ichthus* formed an acrostic, with each letter representing Greek words identifying four vital pieces of the Christian message about the first-century Jewish carpenter: *Iesous* ("Jesus"), *Christos* ("Christ"), *Theou* ("God's"), *uios* ("Son"), and *soter* ("Savior").

The adornment was *de rigueur*—the current fashion—for hippies who got religion during the Jesus movement. It was also a convenient novelty piece, sparking conversations with inquisitive strangers.

The fish acronym sums up the Christian message: the man Jesus was the Messiah ("Christ"), God's only Son, the Savior.

The acrostic also serves as a handy summary of the basic theology essential to the Christian understanding of Jesus of Nazareth. *Jesus* was a true human being who came to Earth as God's promised "Anointed One," the *Christ*. He was no mere mortal, though. He was *God's* own *Son* (God in human flesh, that is), God come down, "Immanuel"—God *with* us—the chosen *Savior* of the world.

Every detail of this ancient creed is under siege today. Is Jesus a true man of history? Is he merely the son of God but not God himself? Is he the Christ, the world's one and only Savior?

In this chapter, I'll tackle the first two questions. In the next chapter, I'll cover the last one.

The Problem of Jesus, the Man

In 1890, Sir James Frazer published a work titled *The Golden Bough*. In it, he argues that ancient mythical deities like Osiris of Egypt, Adonis of Syria, Attis of Asia Minor, and Tammuz of Mesopotamia were all dying and rising fertility gods. Frazer then suggests that the story of Jesus is just a recycled version of these pagan religions.

Now, in the age of Google, Jesus "mythicism"—the notion that the Gospels are sophisticated plagiarisms, pilfering details from ancient myths and cobbling them together to fabricate the story of the dying and rising god/man from Nazareth—has gone viral. While fielding questions from a capacity crowd of twelve hundred students at Purdue University, I responded three times to some version of this challenge.

My opening aside to the first challenger was that he had been spending too much time on the internet. I did not mean it as a joke, but apparently the audience took it that way given the explosive laughter that followed. I said it because stories like this go round and round in the digital ether like a dog chasing his tail, taking us nowhere since the charge has no basis in fact.

Are the online details of these ancient myths themselves

accurate to the original accounts? Not completely. Are there genuine, precise parallels between the dying and rising gods of legend and the life of Jesus of Nazareth? Almost none. Do the records of these ancient myths predate the time of Christ? Some do not. Do details in myths before Christ prove that the same details presented in the Gospels are fictions? Not at all. Is Jesus just a mythical copycat messiah? Not a chance.

Books like Ronald Nash's scholarly *The Gospel and the Greeks*[1] or Lee Strobel's popular work *The Case for the Real Jesus*[2] spend time putting to rest the particulars.[3] In the interest of space, I'll offer three decisive academic assessments.

First, the scholar who has most exhaustively analyzed this question, historian Tryggve Mettinger, summarizes the issue by saying there simply is "no *prima facie* evidence that the death and resurrection of Jesus is a mythological construct, drawing on the myths and rites of the dying and rising gods of the surrounding world."[4]

At least seventeen ancient secular sources,[5] along with significant archaeological evidence from that period,[6] give testimony to Jesus as a man of history. Here is a summary of what we learn from just four primary sources from that era. They are respected authorities from antiquity who recorded details about Jesus with no hint he was a legendary, mythical, fictional figure: a Roman historian, Cornelius Tacitus (*Annals*); a Roman government official, Pliny the Younger (letter to Emperor Trajan); a Greek writer, Lucian (*The Death of Peregrinus*); and a Jewish historian, Flavius Josephus (*Antiquities of the Jews*).

- There was a virtuous man named Jesus.
- He had a brother named James.
- He lived during the reign of Tiberius.
- He was crucified under Pontius Pilate.
- He was reported to be alive three days later.

- The multitude who followed this Christ were called Christians.
- And they worshipped Jesus as a god.

Second, the historical evidence for the Jesus of the Gospels is so compelling, it prompted Pulitzer Prize–winning historian Will Durant to write, "No one reading these scenes can doubt the reality of the figure behind them. . . . After two centuries of Higher Criticism, the outlines of the life, character, and teaching of Christ remain reasonably clear and constitute the most fascinating feature in the history of Western man."[7]

Third, the most stunning broadside against Jesus mythicism comes from a former Christian, now an agnostic and critic of the Gospels—*New York Times* bestselling author Bart Ehrman.

During a public lecture, Ehrman fielded a challenge to the historicity of Jesus. I quote Ehrman's response at length for its power and refreshing candor. The questioner said, "I do not see evidence in archaeology or history for a historical Jesus." Ehrman reacted immediately: "Well, I do. I mean . . . I have a *whole book on it.*[8] There is a *lot* of evidence. There's so much evidence that . . . [frustrated pause]. I know, in the crowds you all run around with, it's commonly thought that Jesus did not exist. Let me tell you . . . this is not even an issue for scholars of antiquity. *It is not an issue.* . . . There is no scholar in any college or university in the Western world who teaches classics, ancient history, New Testament, early Christianity—any related field—who doubts that Jesus existed."[9]

Of course, Ehrman pointed out, one can't simply count academic heads. But the experts speak with a single voice for a reason. He gave it: "The reason for thinking Jesus existed is because he is abundantly attested in early sources. . . . Early and independent sources indicate *certainly* that Jesus existed. One author that we know about *knew Jesus' brother* and *knew Jesus' closest disciple, Peter.* He is an eyewitness to both."[10]

Ehrman then closed his response by chastising skeptics who think the accounts in the Gospels are merely myths: "I'm sorry. Again, I respect your disbelief, but . . . I think that atheists have done themselves a disservice by jumping on the bandwagon of mythicism because, frankly, it makes you look foolish to the outside world. . . . You are much better off going with historical evidence . . . rather than coming up with the theory that Jesus didn't exist."[11]

Jesus never existed? According to this noteworthy academic—and one of the most hostile critics of Christianity—there is no lettered person in the field who affirms that notion. Instead, Jesus mythicism is the myth.

> That the Jesus of the Gospels is a hodgepodge compilation of ancient deities and not, rather, a notable figure in history is a complete fiction thoroughly discredited by experts in the field. The only place this notion survives is on the internet, not in the academy proper.

Curiously, when the apostle Paul addressed Greek pagans on Mars Hill,[12] they listened patiently until he mentioned Jesus' resurrection from the dead. Then they scoffed, ridiculed, derided, and dismissed him—hardly a group committed to myths of dying and rising gods.

Of course, none of these citations proves Jesus was the Messiah. They do clearly establish from secular sources, though, that a man named Jesus—matching important details of the Jesus of the Gospels—existed.[13]

Here is a sample dialogue of how you might employ these insights in conversation:

"There's no evidence Jesus ever existed."

"I'm not completely sure what you're getting at."

[Columbo #1]

"There's just no evidence. Jesus was a myth cobbled together from a bunch of other ancient myths."

"How did you find this out?" [Columbo #2]

"It's all over the internet."

"Can I ask you a few questions about that?"

"Sure."

"What year is it now?"

"Twenty twenty-three."

"Two thousand twenty-three years . . . from when?"

"Well, the time of Christ, allegedly."

"Does it strike you as strange that the entire world operates on a calendar based on the birth of a man who never existed? Doesn't that seem unlikely?"

"It's possible."

"Did you check out any of those ancient myths yourself to see whether they paralleled the life of Jesus?"

"No, not really."

"Did you check out any scholars who specialize in the history of the ancient Near East to see what they think?"

"I haven't read any."

"What makes you confident, then, that there's no evidence for Jesus if you haven't looked at the people who specialize in that history?"

"Well, I've never seen any evidence."

"Would it surprise you to know that virtually no academic in the world specializing in the history of the time of Christ—even critics of Christianity—thinks Jesus is a myth?"

"Well, that's not what I read on the internet. Why do they think Jesus was real?"

"Because there are over a dozen ancient references outside of the Bible that mention Jesus. Plus, there's archaeological evidence, too."

Notice that one of the particulars the ancient historians recorded about Christ was the early church's conviction that Jesus was God.

The Problem of Jesus, the God

The idea that Jesus is God can seem a bit odd to readers of the Bible. According to Scripture, the Father is God, and he is in heaven, and Jesus was on earth, so they cannot be exactly the same. Yet, according to the same Bible, it appears Jesus is God as well. Yet there are not two Gods, but one.

It turns out, those who find this odd are right. It *is* odd. And, no, Jesus and the Father cannot be exactly the same. Both are God, but they are not both each other, strictly speaking. Jesus is a true man who is different in a fundamental way from the Father, yet also fully God, who is like the Father in a fundamental way. And, yes, there are not two Gods, only one.[14]

This conundrum has only one solution if we take the biblical record seriously. In fact, the way Christian thinkers have resolved this apparent conflict—which, later, when fleshed out to include the Holy Spirit, came to be called the "Trinity"—is not a problem but rather a solution to a problem because it makes the most sense of all the biblical data.[15]

First-century Jews were fiercely monotheistic, their theology characterized by two features, "that the one God is sole Creator of all things and that the one God is sole Ruler of all things."[16] God was the Lord and the Lord was God. This calculus was fundamental.

The first Christians were all Jews like that—faithful Jews,

monotheistic Jews—yet they faced a circumstance they couldn't entirely explain (at least initially), but neither could they easily dismiss it. As C. S. Lewis puts it, "People already knew about God in a vague way. Then came a man who claimed to be God; and yet He was not the sort of man you could dismiss as a lunatic. He made them believe Him. They met Him again after they had seen Him killed."[17]

Because they were convinced this Jewish Rabbi rose from the dead, as he predicted,[18] these Christians' earliest testimony of him was that Jesus was indeed Lord. Not a noble person of distinction. Not a mere governor, nor military liege, nor earthly monarch ruling a portion of creation. Rather, the Lord who made creation. The Lord who held creation together.[19] Thus, the Lord of all creation. *The* Lord.

> The New Testament record shows clearly that early Christians were convinced Jesus was both creator of all and, therefore, ruler of all—the Lord God, in short.

These ancient Christians were not trying to be theologically clever. Rather, their confession was the inevitable result of an encounter with the God who "showed up." It's what they concluded when they, as Jews, met their Messiah face to face. Clearly, the Christians counted Jesus as divine from the earliest days of the church, yet this created a conundrum.

Here is the problem they faced. First, there is only one God (Isa. 43:10; 45:5). Second, Jesus is a distinct person from the Father. We know this because Jesus interacts with the Father in personally distinct ways—he prays to the Father (John 17), he submits to the Father (Matt. 26:39), and the Father speaks when Jesus is present listening (Luke 3:21–22). Finally, Jesus is fully God. We know this because Jesus is called God (John 1:1; Rom. 9:5), he possesses divine attributes (e.g., Creator, John 1:3), and he exercises divine privileges (e.g., receives worship, Matt. 2:2, 11; 28:9).[20]

These awkward facts are what led the early church to conclude, eventually, that although God is one in essence (strict monotheism), he is more than one in person. It was the only way to resolve what at first seemed to be an irrepressible contradiction.[21]

Thus, the deity of Christ turns out to be a solution to a problem, and not really a problem itself. It's the only understanding of the revelation that harmonizes all the parts. Here's what a dialogue with a unitarian[22] (such as a Jehovah's Witness) might look like:

"I know you object to the Trinity because you think it's not scriptural, but could you please tell me exactly why?"

"Because the Bible teaches there's only one God."

"I agree."

"No, you don't. You're Trinitarian."

"Right. But believing in one God is part of the definition of the Trinity. No problem for me."

"But you think the Father, Son, and Spirit are all God. That's three gods, not one."

"Actually, our view is a little different from that. Our view is that the one God has three separate centers of consciousness, but each equally shares the one divine nature, so each is equally God—one 'what' and three 'whos,' so to speak."

"But that doesn't make sense. Who did Jesus pray to if he's God? Nobody prays to himself."[23]

"You're right. Jesus didn't pray to himself. He prayed to the Father."

"So you admit that Jesus is different from the Father."

"Of course I do. That's part of the definition of the Trinity."

"Don't you see how confused that is?"

"Confused? Didn't you just tell me you agreed with me so far?"

"How?"

"Well, you said you believe the Bible teaches there is only one God, right?"

"Right."

"So do I. You also agree that Jesus is so different from the Father they can both talk with each other, right?"

"Right."

"Then, so far we are in complete agreement on what the Bible teaches. Are you with me?"[24]

"Sure. But you also believe Jesus *is* God."

"Right, but what if I could show you this is *also* something the Bible teaches?"

"But it doesn't."

"Can I give you one example? **Who is the creator of everything that's ever been created?**"

"Jehovah. Isaiah 44:24: 'I, the LORD, am the maker of all things, stretching out the heavens by Myself and spreading out the earth all alone.'"

"Right. I agree. Good verse: 'I, *the* LORD . . . by *myself* . . . all *alone.*' By the way, when John talks about the Word in the beginning of John 1, who is he talking about?"

"He means the one who was born as Jesus: 'The Word became flesh, and dwelt among us'" [v. 14].

"Exactly. But John also says in that same passage—in verse three—that the Word created all things that were ever created: 'All things came into being through Him, and apart from Him nothing came into being that has come into being.' Have you read that before?"

"Sounds familiar."

"So, if the Bible teaches that *Jehovah* is the Creator, and it also teaches that a different person, *the Word*, is Creator, then *you* have a contradiction. So how do you solve that problem?"

"I'm not sure."

"This is why the early church used the word *Trinity*: three distinct persons all sharing the same single divine nature. It solves the problem."

Cosmic Confusion

The solution the early church settled on continues to raise concerns, though, especially the concern that the three-in-one formula is contradictory. As one challenger puts it, "According to the celestial multiplication table, once one is three, and three times one is one, and according to heavenly subtraction if we take two from three, three are left."[25]

We might sympathize with this agnostic's frustration, but there's no need for alarm. The "divine multiplication table" is not contradictory when properly understood.

The stumbling block for many is the three-in-one notion. However, not all three-in-ones are contradictions. There are three angles in one triangle (a "tri-angle"), yet no one balks at this concept. One family can have three members: Dad, Mom, and little Johnny. No problem there, either.

These are not illustrations of the Trinity, mind you. It's just a way of parrying this objection by giving examples of three-in-ones that are not contradictions. As long as the way a thing is three is different from the way it is one, there is no conflict, no inconsistency, and no incongruity.

Here is how I would manage the discussion:

"The Trinity doesn't make sense."

"Really? Why not?"

"It's an absurd contradiction."

"Can you tell me specifically what the contradiction is?" [Note my initial requests for clarification.]

"Because you can't have three in one. It's a contradiction. You have three gods and one God at the same time. That's nonsense."

"You're right. That would be nonsense if that's what we meant by the Trinity.[26] I think I see the confusion. Let me ask you a question. **How many people are in your family?**"

"Four. My wife, me, and our two kids. Why?"

"So you have four people in your family? You have four in one? Impossible. That's a contradiction. If you can't have three in one, how can you have four in one?"

"That's different."

"How?

"Because a family is one thing and the people who make up that family are another thing. They're not the same, so there's no contradiction."

"Exactly. That's my point. **As long as the one (one family) is different from the four (four people), you're in the clear, right?**"

"That's right."

"The same with the Trinity. **When Christians talk about the Trinity, they mean the one (one God) is different from the three (three persons).** Do you see how that's not a contradiction?"

"Well, you've got a point, but that doesn't make it true."

"You're right. It doesn't. But it does show it's not contradictory, right?"

"I Am God. Worship Me."

As for Jesus never uttering the words "I am God. Worship me," as Muslims often observe, there is a point here. As far as the record reveals, he never uttered those exact words—or anything that, to our ears, would be equivalent. But is that significant?

If I said, "Here are my daughters, Annabeth and Eva," but never said the exact words "I am a parent," would it make sense to claim I never said I was a dad? Hardly. I can affirm I'm a parent in a host of unmistakable ways.

In Jesus' case, he said many things that made his divine claim clear. Remember, Jesus wasn't speaking to moderns. He was speaking to first-century Jews. His claims, in Jewish parlance, were unmistakable.

By calling God his Father and saying he was the Son of God, Jesus was asserting equality with God, a clear claim to deity. The Jews, to their ears, understood it perfectly: "You, being a man, make Yourself out to be God" (John 10:33).[27]

That kind of claim was blasphemy, a capital crime[28] (the same as it would be in Islam, by the way), which is why the Jews sought to kill Jesus several times, yet he eluded them. They eventually succeeded, though, and blasphemy was the precise reason the Jewish court had him executed: "'Are You the Christ, the Son of the Blessed One?' And Jesus said, 'I am. . . .' Tearing his clothes, the high priest said, 'What further need do we have of witnesses? You have heard the blasphemy. . . .' And they all condemned Him to be deserving of death" (Mark 14:61–64).

Note, Jesus was not condemned for claiming to be Messiah. The Jews expected a deliverer, so it could hardly be a crime to claim to be the Promised One. Jesus blasphemed by claiming he was the Son of the Blessed One—God himself.

Again, this doesn't prove Jesus was God, but it's clear he made the claim—in multiple ways, on multiple occasions. To unpack that point, here's how a conversation might look:

"Where did Jesus ever say, 'I am God. Worship me'? He never did."

> "Well, I think you're right about Jesus not using those exact words. But let me ask you a question. **Is that the only way someone could claim to be God? Could Jesus claim to be God using other words?**"

"How could he do that?"

> "As a Muslim, what other words would indicate to you that someone was claiming divinity? What if someone used the sacred Jewish name for the eternal God and applied it to himself?"

"Did Jesus do that?"

> "Yes. He said, 'Before Abraham was born, *I am*.'[29] That's God's name for himself right out of the burning bush in Exodus 3:14. **What if one of his closest followers claimed Jesus created everything that was ever created?**"

"Where is that?"

> "That's in John 1:3. **What if Jesus never said,**

'Worship me,' but he readily *received* worship from others?"

"That would be pretty bad."

"Well, you can find that in Matthew 14:33. There are half a dozen verses like this in the Gospels.[30] One last thing."

"What's that?"

"Do you know *why* Jesus was executed?"

"Well, he made the Jews mad."

"He sure did. You can read in the historical account of his trial about why they were mad. **Jesus was sentenced to death for blasphemy, for claiming to be the Son of God—which the Jews clearly understood as a claim to deity."**

"I didn't know that."

"So, one, he was identified as the omnipotent Creator of everything that ever was created; two, he applied to himself the unique, holy name for God; three, he received worship from men; and four, he was executed for blasphemy for claiming to be the Son of God. Is it fair to say that's pretty close to saying, 'I am God'?"

The Problem of God, the Son

At this point, you may be thinking I have misspoken, that Jesus claimed only to be the Son of God and not God himself, and that would be understandable since "Son of God" is the language Scripture often employs. However, you also may have assumed something else based on that language that is not quite right.

Nowadays, many think that all people are children of God, after a fashion. In their minds, being a son (or a child) of God simply means "a person created by God." He made everyone, so we are all sons and daughters of God, in a manner of speaking. And on that point, they are right. We are all made by God, to be sure, and we are like him in an important way since we bear his image.[31]

Early Christians, however, did not mean what we mean today when we apply the "son of God" or "child of God" language to ourselves twenty centuries later. We misunderstand their meaning because we are trying to translate a first-century Jewish expression by importing modern ideas into ancient vocabulary—a common mistake.

Words do not get their meanings from a dictionary. That approach has the tail wagging the dog. Instead, they get their meanings from the way they are used by people in ordinary conversation, and then those meanings find their way into a dictionary. The regular use of a word (or phrase) determines its meaning for the people who use it. Keep calling a cat a *gato* (as they do in Mexico), and people will figure out what you're referring to.

The first Christians meant something particular and precise with the phrase "God's Son," and they did not mean a generic child of God in the brotherhood of man. In their minds, when a father produces a true son, he sires a child who is of the same nature as himself. So, just as a human begets a human being, a god begets a divine being. Any "son of God," then, would be a god himself, and in a strictly monotheistic society, not *a* god, but *the* God.

This point was not lost on the Jews of Jesus' time, of course. John records, "For this reason therefore the Jews were seeking all the more to kill Him, because He . . . was calling God His own Father, making Himself equal with God" (John 5:18). In this sense, then, Christ is unique among humans, sharing the very same divine nature as the one who begot him—in Jesus' words, "I and the Father are one" (John 10:30).

Note Gabriel's statement to Mary in his annunciation: "The Holy Spirit will come upon you, and the power of the Most High will overshadow you; and for that reason the holy Child shall be called *the Son of God*" (Luke 1:35).

Thus, the virgin birth was a singular event with a singular consequence. Through the miracle of Jesus' conception, Christ bears the exact same nature as his heavenly Father, a point the Bible makes clear:

- "And He is the *radiance of His glory* and the *exact representation of His nature*, and upholds all things by the word of His power" (Heb. 1:3).
- "*He is the image of the invisible God*. . . . For in Him *all the fullness of Deity dwells* in bodily form" (Col. 1:15; 2:9).

Note something unusual about Jesus' statements. In John 5:18, Jesus indicates he is somehow distinct from the Father, but in John 10:30, he indicates he is somehow the same as the Father.

Classical Christianity describes it this way: Jesus is a distinct person from the Father but shares the same individual divine essence as the Father.

Here's a way you might clarify the "Son of God" confusion in a conversation:

> **"What if I said a person was gay. What would you think I meant?"**

"That he was a homosexual, of course."

> "But what if I then said, 'He's not a homosexual; he's *gay*. He's the most cheerful guy I know.' What would you say?"

"I'd say that's confused."

> "I agree. It's confused to our ears in the twenty-first century. A hundred years ago, though, those words would have made perfect sense because back then the word *gay* meant something completely different."

"So, what's your point?"

"The point is, when we read the words of ancient people, we need to understand those words according to *their* meaning, not our meaning now."

"Okay."

"So how do you think that relates to your claim that Jesus was not God, but the Son of God?"

"I don't follow you."

"I'm asking what Jesus' claim to be the Son of God meant to the people who heard him in his day."

"How would we know?"

"Here's how: they tried to kill him because they said he was claiming to be God."

So, according to the New Testament, Jesus is the Son of God in a way no other "child of God" can be—the Son of God is *God*, the *Son*.[32]

The Irrefutable Argument

To strengthen our case that Scripture teaches the deity of Jesus of Nazareth, I want to introduce you to an ancient argument.[33] I have called this approach "Deity of Christ, Case Closed" since, in this instance, the biblical record is so clear, the conclusion cannot be countered. Plus, it's easy to present the point using a simple interactive exercise I'll show you.

This line of thinking is useful for anyone questioning the scriptural case for Christ's divinity, but it's especially handy with door-to-door evangelists like Jehovah's Witnesses. For the sake of illustration, I'll roll out my points as if I were talking with a Jehovah's Witness, but the basic biblical rationale is the same for everyone.

Discussions with Jehovah's Witnesses on the deity of Christ

frequently focus on the apostle John's introduction to his biography of Jesus, which starts with these words: "In the beginning was the Word, and the Word was with God, *and the Word was God.*"[34]

All standard Bible translations read basically the same. However, the Jehovah's Witness's *New World Translation* (NWT) renders the verse differently: "In the beginning was the Word, and the Word was with God, and the Word was *a* god."

> The Word, then, according to the Witnesses, was unique—*a* god, of sorts—but not *the* God. Rather, the Word was the very first created being.

Discussions centered on John 1:1 are almost never productive because determining the correct translation depends on nuances of Greek grammar that are beyond most of us.

Bypass that conflict like this. Say, "Do you know Greek? No? Neither do I. But we both know English. So why don't we drop down two verses to an important passage that reads the same in both our translations?"

Verse three says, "All things came into being through Him [referring to the Word in verse one], and apart from Him nothing came into being that has come into being." The NWT is virtually identical: "All things came into existence through him, and apart from him not even one thing came into existence."

Have your visitor read the verse out loud and acknowledge that there is no difference in meaning between your translations. Explain that you want to use a simple drawing as an illustration to help him clearly see the implications of the words of this verse.

Take out a napkin or a piece of scratch paper and draw a large box. Explain that this box represents everything that exists or ever existed (label it that way). Since the box "contains" everything that is, nothing is outside the lines. Every existing thing is inside the boundaries of the box.

Next, run a line through the middle of the box dividing everything that exists into two categories. It will look something like this:

EVERYTHING THAT EXISTS

On the left side, write "All things that never came into being"
(or "All things that never came into existence," to use the words of
the NWT)—that is, all things that exist, but have never been created. Ask your friend, "What goes in that box?" If he says, "God,"
he got the right answer. God is the only thing that exists that has
never been created. God alone is eternal and uncreated. Put the
word "God" in the left-hand side of your box.

Label the right side "All things that came into being" (or
"existence")—that is, all created things. Write "All created things"
there. According to John 1:3, everything in this box was created
through the Word, who became Jesus. Ask your friend if he understands this. Now write "Created through the Word" on the right side.

Your box should now look something like this:

EVERYTHING THAT EXISTS

All things that never came into being:	All things that came into being:
GOD	ALL CREATED THINGS (created through the Word; John 1:3)

Take a moment to remind your friend how this illustration is
structured. The larger box includes everything there is, was, or ever
will be. Each existing thing falls into one of two categories: created
or not created.

Either a thing was created or it was not created—there is no third option—so the two categories are all-encompassing. A thing can't be both created and not created, so the two categories are mutually exclusive. Therefore, every existing thing must go in one box or the other. It can't go in both, and it can't go in neither. Simple.

Next, to determine which category Jesus belongs in, take a coin out of your pocket. Tell your friend the coin represents Christ, the incarnate Word. Hand him the coin and ask him to place Jesus in the category where he belongs.

The first impulse of a Jehovah's Witness, of course, will be to place Jesus in the category of "all things that came into being" because that's what his theology dictates. Jesus was the first created being, and everything else was created by Jehovah through Jesus.

But John 1:3 does not allow that option. Look at the wording carefully. John says, "All things came into being through Him, and apart from Him nothing came into being that has come into being," or in the NWT, "Apart from him *not even one thing* came into existence."

In this verse, John says the same thing in two different ways for emphasis and for clarity: everything that ever came into being owes its existence to the Word, who caused it all to exist. If Jesus caused all created things to *come* into existence, then he must have existed before all created things came into existence. Therefore, the Word could not have been created.

By contrast, if Jesus created everything that has come into being, and Jesus also came into being (as they contend), then Jesus created himself. But this is impossible. He would have to exist as Creator before he could exist as a created thing, which is absurd. Therefore, Jesus can't be placed in the square labeled "All things that came into being."

At this point, your visitor may want to place Jesus somewhere outside the larger box, but that won't work. These categories are all-encompassing and mutually exclusive; there's no "place" outside to put Jesus. Everything must be inside the box, on one side or the other.

If the Word can't be placed on the right side with created things, then he must go on the left side with uncreated things. Jesus is the uncreated Creator. Therefore, Jesus is God.

Jesus, the man of history, the carpenter from Nazareth, is God's Son, God come down—Immanuel, God with us. That is what the record teaches. But does it also teach that Jesus was the world's only Savior? That comes next.

CHAPTER 12

CHRIST, THE SAVIOR

I have argued that Jesus was a true man of history, and that this man, according to the historical record, was also the true God of creation. He is the Son of God—the man who God became.

I went into some detail for two reasons. First, we cannot make a case for the truth of Jesus unless we are reasonably precise about what that truth is. Second, false ideas about Jesus abound. A firm grasp of the truth is our first defense against those errors (Eph. 6:14).

Now I would like to show you why this man, God's Christ— the rescuer—is the only hope for the world and, thus, the only possible Savior.

The calculus here is vital. Each of those elements—Jesus, Christ, God's Son, and Savior—are woven together. They cannot be separated without the whole fabric of the Christian story unraveling. If Jesus the man of history is not God the Son, then he could not be the Christ, the world's Savior, either.

That God humbled himself, stepped down, and took on human flesh is a detail so familiar to Christendom that the luster is often lost. Yet it is no minor matter. It is not a dispensable footnote in the biblical record, a negligible twist of Christian theology. Rather, it is central to the grand story of reality the biblical text tells, and it's central to the claim that Jesus alone saves.

Sometimes singular problems require singular solutions. The world is broken. This we all know. We are broken, too. This we also know. What we do not all realize, though, is that we are the problem. It was our brokenness that fractured the world to begin with.

Thus, before the world can be the way it's supposed to be once again—before all wrongs can be righted, all evil can be vanquished, and all good can be restored—*we* need to be the way *we're* supposed to be once again. Our brokenness must be repaired before the world can be repaired, lest we ruin the world once again.

We cannot rescue ourselves, though. Help must come from outside our fallen number, from outside our world. Rescue comes from Immanuel—the man who is God, who came down to be with us.

Why the God-Man?[1]

The humanity of Jesus as a historical fact is central to the Christian story. Take any other religious leaders and remove them from history, and their religions remain since it is the teachings—not the founders—that ground their faith. If those founders are fictions, the teachings remain with full force.

Not so with Jesus. Take Jesus out of Christianity, and Christianity disappears. Some suggest that nothing is lost if Jesus never existed since the marvelous story remains. Paul disagrees. If Jesus' resurrection is a myth, he says, and the witnesses traded in lies, then Christians are a pitiful lot.[2] And they're fools, too, I might add, since their witness cost many of them their lives.

Everything essential to our convictions about Christ relies on Jesus being a genuine man of history. It is not surprising, then, that so much ink has been spilled to deny it. These efforts fail, though, as I've shown. Nothing in the record suggests that Christians have misplaced their confidence. That is the first thing to get clear on.

Here is the second. Central to the entire redemptive enterprise is that Christ is not only a true man but also true God. The Messiah is God himself. It was the key issue of Jesus' life and is a *sine qua non*—an indispensable element—of Christianity.

In the face of conflicting public reports, Jesus asked his disciples, "Who do *you* say that I am?" It is the most important question anyone can answer, and clearly only one answer will do—Peter's answer: "You are the Christ, the Son of the living God" (Matt. 16:15–16). The Messiah, in other words, the God-come-down.

Indeed, John's entire gospel has the singular purpose of decisively answering the question of who Jesus was and tying that answer directly to salvation: "These [miracles] have been written [recorded] so that you may believe that Jesus is the *Christ*, the *Son of God*; and that believing *you may have life* [salvation] in His name" (John 20:31).[3]

Jesus' divine nature and his ability to save sinners are inseparable.

Clearly, Jesus came to save. The angel appeared to Joseph in a dream, saying, "[Mary] will bear a Son; and you shall call His name Jesus, for He will save His people from their sins" (Matt. 1:21). Yet, only God can save: "I, even I, am the LORD, and there is no savior besides Me" (Isa. 43:11). Peter combines the two in Christ when he writes about the righteousness of "our God and Savior, Jesus Christ" (2 Peter 1:1).

> On the day of Jesus' birth, the angel made clear that the "good news" for "all the people" was that the babe the shepherds would find in a manger would not only be the Savior—the Christ—but also the Lord (Luke 2:10–11).[4]

Paul makes the same point: "If you confess with your mouth Jesus *as Lord*, and believe in your heart that God raised Him from the dead, *you will be saved*" (Rom. 10:9). Jesus told the Pharisees, "Unless you believe that *I am He*, you will die in your sins" (John 8:24), and, "Before Abraham was born, *I am*" (v. 58). Jesus in both cases used the Greek *ego eimi* to identify himself with the ancient name of God given to Moses, "I Am Who I Am" (Ex. 3:14).[5] The Jews understood his point clearly and sought to execute him (John 8:59).

The Perfect Sacrifice

This strange metaphysical union of man and God solved a pressing problem.

I will introduce my point with a question: What is the most famous verse in the Bible? Easy. John 3:16: "For God so loved the world, that He gave His only begotten Son, that whoever believes in Him shall not perish, but have eternal life." This noble truth, though, raises a concern.

Are Christians claiming that God took a man who was not guilty and treated him as if he were guilty? Then he made him suffer an unspeakably brutal death as an expression of God's love in pardoning those who actually were the guilty ones? Really?

Most people see how the cross could be evidence of Jesus' love in that scenario, but how is it evidence of God's love ("For God so loved the world")? How is savaging the innocent on behalf of the guilty an act of divine benevolence? How does this kind of God escape the charge of "cosmic child abuse"?

Here's how. Humans were guilty, so a human had to pay. Yet, what kind of human could make a boundless payment adequate to cover the endless punishment due for the sins of the entire world? How could a mere man, Jesus, in the short span of three hours on a cross, pay for an eternity of even one person's sin, much less the sins of anyone and everyone who believes? How is that mathematically possible?

> Who could fulfill such a task? Only someone who was
> not a mere man. Only the God-man, Immanuel, the
> Savior.

Only Jesus, as God, could turn his sacrifice on a cross into a testament of God's love for the world, since it was God's own blood, freely shed by Christ,[6] that purchased Christ's church: "Be on guard for yourselves and for all the flock . . . to shepherd the church of God which He purchased with His own blood" (Acts 20:28). When did God bleed? When he was crucified on a Roman cross.

Only in Jesus, the Son of God, could a man suffer a finite amount of time yet cover an eternal debt for a countless multitude, since the man was himself the God of infinite grace. Only the Christ—God's rescuer—could do this.

Christ—The Rescuer

The word *Christ* is the Anglicized version of the Greek word *Christos*, meaning "anointed one" or "messiah." Messiah is a uniquely Jewish notion. Unfortunately, the word *Christ* has undergone a transformation—and corruption—in meaning over time.

Nowadays, depending on which source you cite, *Christ* could mean a cosmic spirit, or an impersonal mind principle, or a state ("Christhood") attained by various "ascended masters," or the "I AM Presence," or the mystical spiritual spark of divinity in all of humanity, and so on. The biblical record, of course, knows nothing of this nonsense.

In the biblical account, the rescuer is one born of a woman, who suffers injury while striking a fatal blow to the snake—the devil of old—undoing the destruction caused by the serpent and liberating those he's enslaved: "He [the woman's 'seed'] shall bruise you [the snake] on the head, and you shall bruise him on the heel"

(Gen. 3:15). This prophecy is a ray of hope, a veiled reference to the Messiah who was to come.

How would the Messiah rescue the world? God initiates a plan, found in the opening lines of Genesis 12, called the Abrahamic Covenant.

First, God sovereignly sets apart and commissions one man: Abram. Next, he promises to bring a nation forth from that man. Finally, God promises that this man, through the nation he will beget—the Jews—will be a blessing to the *goyim*—all the gentile nations of the world.

Everything that follows in the writings flows from this magnificent promise—the very backbone of salvation history. As their own story unfolds, Abraham's people—God's chosen race, selected by him to rescue the world—produce the only one who can accomplish that task: *Mashiach*, the Messiah.

For this Christ, Israel anxiously waited, an expectation displayed clearly in Jesus' birth narratives, with each player cited recalling the promise to Abraham.[7]

- Zacharias at the birth of his son, John the Baptist, blesses God, who "has raised up a horn of *salvation* for us . . . to remember His holy covenant, *the oath which He swore to Abraham* our father" (Luke 1:69, 72–73).
- At the annunciation, Mary in her "Magnificat," exalts the Lord, who "has given help to Israel His servant, in remembrance of His mercy, as He spoke to our fathers, *to Abraham and his descendants forever*" (Luke 1:54–55).
- At Jesus' dedication in the temple in Jerusalem soon after his birth, Simeon beholds the baby Christ and prays, "Now Lord, You are releasing Your bond-servant to depart in peace . . . for my eyes have seen Your *salvation*, which You have prepared in the presence of *all peoples*, A LIGHT OF REVELATION TO THE GENTILES" (Luke 2:29–32).

As predicted, that "anointed" king is a descendant of David: "I will raise up your descendant after you, who will come forth from you, and I will establish his kingdom. . . . Your house and your kingdom shall endure before Me forever; your throne shall be established forever" (2 Sam. 7:12, 16).[8]

He is born in Bethlehem, the city of David: "But as for you, Bethlehem Ephrathah . . . from you One will go forth for Me to be ruler in Israel. . . . He will be great to the ends of the earth" (Mic. 5:2, 4).[9]

David himself, in Psalm 22, predicts Messiah's brutal death. The entire psalm reads like a detailed, first-person account of Jesus' crucifixion, hundreds of years before such executions were a form of capital punishment.[10]

The Promised One

Jesus, the Messiah, was a man of destiny. The ancient writings predicted the place of his birth, his family lineage, how he would die, and the stunning impact he would have in life and in death. It's no wonder, then, that belief in Jesus as the one and only Christ is crucial to the Christian message.

- Jesus is called Messiah 543 times in the New Testament.
- Jesus said that eternal life is knowing him as Messiah: "This is eternal life, that they may know You, the only true God, and Jesus Christ [Messiah] whom You have sent" (John 17:3).
- That Jesus was Messiah was central to his own claim at his trial: "And the high priest said to Him . . . 'Tell us whether You are the Christ, the Son of God.' Jesus said to him, 'You have said it yourself'" (Matt. 26:63–64).
- Peter's first sermon to the Jews on Pentecost was to preach that God had made Jesus "both Lord and Christ," his

resurrection bearing witness, and they were told to repent (Acts 2:36–38).

- Those who deny that Jesus is the Christ who came in the flesh are deceivers, liars, and the antichrist (1 John 2:22–23; 2 John 1:7; Jude 4).

Therefore, because of God's Son, the Savior, there is no condemnation for those who are in Christ (Rom. 8:1). There is nothing that can separate them from the love of God, which is in the Christ (Rom. 8:38–39). There is no one "able snatch them out of the Father's hand" if they are Christ's (John 10:29). There is no fear remaining for those the Father has given to Christ since he loses none but raises them up on the last day (John 6:39).

The Stumbling Stone

Probably the most offensive detail of our Christian message is that a person must put his trust in Jesus—and only Jesus—to escape eternal punishment for his sin.[11] Peter calls it "A STONE OF STUMBLING AND A ROCK OF OFFENSE" (1 Peter 2:8, quoting Isa. 8:14). It is also gospel bedrock.[12]

The public pressure to treat all religions as equally valid routes to God creates a tremendous emotional incentive to modify the Christian message. Don't do it. A more modest message might comfort others for the moment, but it will never heal since it cannot cure.

> When people want to make Christianity kinder and gentler, they often tinker with the cross. To keep seekers from stumbling, they remove the stumbling block. They back down from the message God entrusted to us both to proclaim and to guard.

To stand with Jesus on this issue invites a tsunami of scorn and abuse in our culture. It is the first claim jettisoned when Christians itch to become more "tolerant." They replace the gospel of rescue from God's wrath with a watered-down Christianity of worldly love, acceptance, and inclusion.

To side with the crowd on this, though, is spiritual treason.

The disciples did not choose the name *Christians* for themselves. Others did. Followers of Jesus described themselves simply as "the Way" (Acts 9:2). The reason was clear. That was how Jesus described himself: "I am the way, and the truth, and the life; no one comes to the Father but through me" (John 14:6). Lest anyone be tempted to read ambiguity into that statement at the end of Jesus' ministry, take counsel from this one at the very beginning: "Enter through the narrow gate; for the gate is wide and the way is broad that leads to destruction, and there are many who enter through it. For the gate is small and the way is narrow that leads to life, and there are few who find it" (Matt. 7:13–14).[13]

Controversial? Yes. Confusing? No. The claim is clear. New Testament writers repeated it constantly in a variety of ways, offering nine lines of argument to solidify their point.[14]

1. Jesus is the world's only source of salvation: "For God so loved the world, that He gave His only begotten Son, that whoever believes in Him shall not perish, but have eternal life" (John 3:16).
2. Jesus is the Father's choice: "Jesus . . . said to them, 'This is the work of God, that you believe in Him whom He has sent'" (John 6:29).
3. Thus, rejection of Jesus is rejection of the Father himself: "He who does not honor the Son does not honor the Father who sent Him" (John 5:23).
4. Rejecting Jesus brings wrath; believing in Jesus rescues

from wrath: "He who believes in the Son has eternal life; but he who does not obey the Son will not see life, but the wrath of God abides on him" (John 3:36).

5. Jesus alone provides forgiveness of sin: "Therefore I said to you that you will die in your sins; for unless you believe that I am He, you will die in your sins" (John 8:24).

6. Many impostors will claim to provide other ways of salvation: "See to it that no one misleads you. For many will come in My name, saying, 'I am the Christ,' and will mislead many" (Matt. 24:4–5).

7. But there are no alternatives: "There is salvation in no one else; for there is no other name under heaven that has been given among men by which we must be saved" (Acts 4:12).

8. Jesus will be man's final judge: "Christ Jesus . . . is to judge the living and the dead" (2 Tim. 4:1).

9. Therefore, all nations are to be given this gospel: "Repentance for forgiveness of sins would be proclaimed in His name to all the nations" (Luke 24:47).

There is only one answer to the Philippian jailer's question, "What must I do to be saved?" Paul gives it: "Believe in the Lord Jesus, and you will be saved" (Acts 16:30–31). Simple and straightforward, uncomplicated and unambiguous. Do not be confused.

That is the foundation. That is the indispensable core. The claim, though, stirs up of a host of objections.

On the Street

I have spent a bit of time on the idea that the world's Savior must be God himself—and verifying this truth from the biblical text itself—because I want the point firmly fixed in your mind. If you have any uncertainty as to *why* Jesus is necessary for someone's salvation, it will be difficult for you to insist *that* Jesus is necessary for their salvation—especially in the face of opposition.

Why is Jesus the only way? He is the only one who solved the problem. That's why. Indeed, he is the only one who could.

One day, every single one of us, the morally great and small alike, will stand before God to be judged for our own crimes, such as they are—some more, some less. Either we pay for them ourselves, or we let Jesus pay for them for us. Those who are not joined to Christ in this life will stand alone in the next to endure God's penalty. That is the calculus. Be clear on that.

Before we move on to challenges, I want to make a tactical suggestion. It's always prudent to enlist Christ himself as your ally on the "one way" point if you can. Since most people have a high regard for Jesus, shifting the burden of this challenge onto him gives you an advantage.[15] Here's an example:

"You Christians think your way is the only
right way."

    "We do, but why is that a problem?" [Columbo #1]

"It's so arrogant!"

    "Can I ask you a question?"

"Sure."

    "Where do you think that idea came from?"

"It came from arrogant, narrow-minded
Christians."

    "Well, actually, it came from Jesus himself. Do you think Jesus was arrogant and narrow-minded?"

"Of course not. He was a great man who
taught love and acceptance."

    "He also taught he was the only way to heaven, and he said it many times in many ways. **So, I'm just curious, do you think Jesus was mistaken?"**

Notice the insult built into this encounter: the Christian is arrogant. There's a reason I included that.

It's common for challengers to subtly change the subject by shifting the issue from Jesus to the Christian's character. The Christian is arrogant, or intolerant, or bigoted, or something of the sort. You've both been talking about one thing—the need for Christ's forgiveness—and the talk is shifted to something entirely different—the Christian's character. The person changes the subject. He gets carried away with a distraction and never addresses the original issue: Jesus.

The first has nothing to do with the second, of course. People with questionable integrity can be correct on lots of things, even religious things. Here, the attack is on the person and not on the point, so the effort is simply a distraction.[16]

If the Christian has been acting unseemly, shame on him. But this is not usually what's going on. It's not the Christian's behavior that's triggered the charge but rather the Christian's conviction.

When this happens, it might be helpful to point out the switch using a question. For example:

> **"I'm curious, why did you change the subject?"**
> "What do you mean?"
>> "Well, a moment ago we were talking about Jesus, and now we're talking about me—in particular, about a flaw in my character."
> "That's right. You're arrogant to claim Jesus is the only way."
>> "Well, I hope I'm not arrogant, and I apologize if I came across that way. But I have a question. **Even if my claim were arrogant, how would that make it false that Jesus is the only way**? What does the one have to do with the other? Is it possible a claim that is 'arrogant' could still be true?"
> "I guess so."

"Good. **Then why do you think Jesus' claim to be the only way isn't true?**"

Do not let this maneuver distract you. Here is a different way to expose the problem. Offer an illustration that makes the point, like this:

"You're arrogant to think your way is the only right way."

> "I don't mean to be rude, but that strikes me as an odd response."

"Why?"

> "Let me try to explain why with an illustration."

"Okay."

> "Let's say you go with a friend to a doctor because he's feeling ill. The doctor says he has a dangerous disease that needs a precise treatment or he'll die. Your friend then tells the doctor, 'You're mean. I'm going to find a nicer doctor.' What would you think of your friend if he did that?"

"I'd think it was pretty dumb."

> "Why?"

"Well, even if the doctor *was* mean—and he probably wasn't—his diagnosis still could be right."

> "Good point. What else?"

"It's also dumb because my friend might really be sick, and if he doesn't get help, he'll die."

> "Exactly. I agree. Now let me change the illustration just a bit. A Christian tells you you're dying of a spiritual disease called sin that only Jesus can cure, and you say he's mean—or more specifically, he's arrogant. How is that any different from the guy in the illustration?"

The analogy is apt because pointing out a character flaw in the Christian will never bring anyone any closer to knowing if his diagnosis is correct. It's foolish, too, since there's always the possibility the Christian is right.

> Character attack—simple name-calling—is the go-to response for virtually every controversial opinion raised in this culture, unfortunately. It happens so frequently, those who do it don't realize they're out of order—both in reasoning and in manners.

Here's the rule of thumb: whenever the challenge is about the person, not the view, the challenger is aiming at the wrong target. He can't refute a view by attacking something else—in this case, the Christian. When this happens, ask your friend why he's changed the subject. Then graciously explain what you mean, since he probably is not aware of what he did.

There's one other thing I want you to consider when you're faulted for thinking you're right about religion: *everyone* thinks his views about religion—whatever those views happen to be—are right. The Christian, apparently, is the only one faulted for it.

When you're faulted just for thinking you're right about religion, you might probe a bit with questions like these that cover this challenge. I've also included some other related issues in this next interaction:

"You Christians think you're the only ones who have the truth. That's arrogant."

> "I don't understand. **Why am I arrogant just because I've thought about an issue and come to a conclusion I think is correct?**"

"Because you think everyone else is wrong but you. That's pretty egotistical."

"Do you mind if I ask you a question about that?"

"Go ahead."

"What do *you* think is the right way to get to heaven, or to please God, or however you want to put it? Do you have an opinion?"

"Well, I think being a good, kind, loving person is the answer. I think that's what religion is all about."[17]

"Well, I agree that God cares about that, but you sound like you're convinced being good is the one thing that matters. Did I get you right, or am I missing something?"

"Yep. Being a good person is what counts."

"That's confusing."

"Why?"

"Because you were just faulting me because I thought *my* way was right, but it turns out you think *your own* view is right, instead. Aren't you doing the same thing you were telling me not to do? I'm not bothered by it, but **it does make me wonder why it's okay for you to think *you're* right on religion, but it's not okay for me to think I'm right on religion.**"

"But your view is unloving."

"Really? Why?"

"Because you're threatening people with hell."

"For the record, that's not my threat, it's what Jesus taught, but let's set that aside for the moment. I have a question about something else."

"Okay."

"If there were a truck barreling down the road at you, and I yelled at you to get out of the way, would that be loving or unloving?"

"That would be loving."

"Why?"

"Because you'd be warning me of danger."

"Exactly. Would it be fair to say that what Christians are doing is giving a warning?"

"What's the warning?"

"Hell. Now, even if Christians are mistaken, is it loving or unloving for them to warn someone about hell and offer a way to avoid it?"

"Okay, it may not be unloving, but Christians are still mistaken."

"Why?"

"Because there are many ways to get to God. Look at all the other religions. Haven't you ever heard the saying 'There are many paths to the top of the mountain'?"

"Sure, but I have a question about that, too. **How do you know all those paths lead to God?**"

"Because all religions teach basically the same thing."[18]

"What about the differences?"

"What do you mean?"

"Well, Christianity teaches that Jesus is the Son of God and the Savior. Both Judaism and Islam vigorously disagree."

"So, what's your point?"

"At least one of those three religions must be mistaken on something really important."

"But God doesn't care about that. He cares only whether you're a good person."

"But even the notion of what's good is different between those religions. For

Christians, it's good to worship Jesus, but for Jews and Muslims, it's a sacrilege."

"Then those people should do what's good from their point of view." [Notice how he just relativized the idea of goodness.]

"But I still have the same question: Why are you so convinced God doesn't care even about crucial differences? Every religion thinks certain things in its theology are vital. **The Jews and the Christians can't both be right about Jesus, can they?**"

"Well, no."

"That means some religions are mistaken on critical things—even on what it means to be a good person. How can they all lead to God?"

Good Enough

There is one other issue I'll mention that you'll encounter and need to be prepared for.

It seems common knowledge to many that good people go to heaven and bad people go to hell. Take a poll, and you'll see. You'll also find out that most think they're "basically good" already—or at least good enough.

God, according to this view, is concerned with the way people behave "on average." If the good outweighs the bad, then God winks at the occasional moral lapse.

When you ask people for a definition of *basically good*, though, you'll notice something interesting. The line dividing good folk from bad lies somewhere below them, so they always seem to make the "good person" cut. Sure, they're not perfect, but nobody is.

Justice never works like that, though, does it? Our civil law demands that "on average" each person obey every law always, not most laws usually. You may be an upstanding citizen all your life, but a single crime is still going to bring you before the court.

God's law is the same. There's a reason being "basically good" will do us no good: all law requires complete compliance. Note that James writes, "For whoever keeps the whole law and yet stumbles in one point, he has become guilty of all. For He who said, 'Do not commit adultery,' also said, 'Do not commit murder.' Now if you do not commit adultery, but do commit murder, you have become a transgressor of the law" (James 2:10–11).

James confirms a commonsense notion. Laws are meant to be kept, and any violation deserves appropriate punishment. If you keep ninety-nine laws but violate the hundredth, you are a lawbreaker, nonetheless, and retribution awaits you.

Put simply, the problem with goodness is that none of us—from the least to the greatest—is ever good enough. God's law puts us all under sin, as Paul writes, "that *every* mouth may be closed and *all the world* may become accountable to God" (Rom. 3:19).

Further—and this is critical—no amount of good behavior can pay for bad behavior. Since law requires consistent goodness, the good we're obliged to do cannot cancel out the bad we've done.

Here's a sample conversation that trades on this point:

"I think I'm good enough the way I am. I'm a good person."

    "Can I ask you a question about that?"

"Sure."

    "Let's say you get pulled over for speeding. You tell the police officer he's right, you were driving too fast, but before you got on the freeway, you made complete stops at every stop sign. Do you think that will matter to him?"

"No."

    "Why not?"

"Because I'm supposed to stop at stop signs *and* not break the speed limit."

"That's right. So why do you think God's system of justice—which is perfect—would be different? Do you keep *all* of God's laws?"

"Well, I try. I do my best."

"But that wasn't my question. **I'm simply asking if you do *everything* God wants you to do.**"

"Of course not. Nobody's perfect."

"Right. So you need forgiveness, then, don't you? That's why you need Jesus."

If you are looking for a psychological lift for the moment, a temporary bromide to relieve the distress of life—Marx's "opiate of the people"—then you are welcome to any religious fantasy you like.

If, however, you want genuine healing instead of emotional distraction, then you need a genuine healer, a rescuer. Only one can provide that: Jesus Christ, God's Son, the Savior.

CHAPTER 13

THE BIBLE: ANCIENT WORDS, EVER TRUE?

Whenever I hear the opening lines of the song "Ancient Words," I am moved: "Holy words long preserved for our walk in this world. They resound with God's own heart. Oh, let the ancient words impart."[1]

Being aware of God while gazing at the ocean is all well and good, C. S. Lewis notes, but if you want to go anywhere on that sparkling sea, you must have a map.[2] Going somewhere with God is no different. In his case, though, the map is not made of symbols, but of words—ancient words.

Navigating a sea of words has its hazards. There are reefs that can wreck you if you're not careful. In this chapter, I want to help you with two issues as you navigate the sea of the Bible's ancient words: reading the word map accurately and plotting a safe course through some of the more treacherous waters of skeptics' challenges.

Let me begin, though, with some strategic advice.

God's Inerrant Word?

Be assured, I am firmly committed to biblical inerrancy. Scripture is God's Word, without error in everything it clearly affirms. If God can't err, then his words can't err. That's the logic.

Of course, to understand the point of a text, we need to be clear on (1) the flow of thought of the passage (its context), (2) the audience it was written for (its historical/cultural setting and purpose), and (3) the normal conventions of language of the intended audience (figures of speech, idioms, genre,[3] etc.).[4]

On strategic grounds, I do not think it is profitable to wrangle with non-Christians on the issue of inerrancy. It invites trouble, and we don't need to convince a skeptic of inerrancy to communicate the gospel effectively.[5] The trouble it brings is an avalanche of alleged discrepancies and contradictions, all provoked by your claim that the Bible, God's Word, has no errors. Those charges can be answered—and whole tomes have been written doing so—but for most witnessing situations, it's an unnecessary distraction. Best to try to stay on course. If you sidestep the God's-inerrant-Word issue, you will sidestep those challenges, too—all of them.

What's more, we do not need to demonstrate inerrancy to make our case for Christianity. The early Christians had no intact New Testament to point to as the inerrant Word of God when they evangelized.[6] The gospel stands or falls not on something written in Scripture, strictly speaking, but on something that happened in history: the death and resurrection of Jesus of Nazareth.

> Under God's guidance, the Bible accurately records the historical events that make all the difference, but it's the events that secure the truth of Christianity, not the record of those events.[7]

Further, the inerrancy of a text is never necessary to communicate truth about the world. There are millions of books overflowing with truth—including spiritual truth (Christian bookstores are filled with them)—that were written by mere mortals and not penned by divinely guided hands. Even if the Bible were purely the product of men opining about God and not words breathed by God through men,[8] this would not necessarily make the message of Scripture false.

As a strategic matter, then, I don't build my case for Christ on inerrancy. Instead, I argue that the Gospels are historically reliable, on the main.[9] Christianity stands or falls not on inerrancy but on facts of history about Jesus of Nazareth. If the critical events recorded in the Gospels happened, then Christianity is on solid ground.

Here's how I might make those points tactically in a conversation:

"The Bible is full of contradictions."

> **"If that were true—which I'm not conceding here—why would that be significant?"**

"Well, that proves it's not the Word of God."

> "But that's not what I'm arguing here."

"Don't you think the Bible is God's Word?"

> **"I do, but that's not relevant to the point I'm making."**

"What's that?"

> "Let me ask you a question. **Do you have any books in your library that you think tell you things that are accurate about the world?"**

"Sure."

> "Are any of them divinely inspired?"

"Of course not."

> **"Then a book doesn't need to be divinely inspired to give you truth, does it?"**

"I guess not."

"So, all I'm asking is that you consider the historical record of Jesus' claims and the things written by those he trained to follow after him to see if they speak truth or not."

Navigating successfully with any map, though, requires that you decipher the symbols correctly and read the terrain accurately. The same is true with God's Word. Read it wrong, and you're liable to run up on a reef. Here are two key concepts that work together to keep you safe—one you should never do, and one you should always do.

Never Do This

I was once asked what the single most important, practical piece of wisdom was that I could pass on to a fellow Christian. Here it is: never read a Bible verse. As odd as that may sound at first, it reflects a commonsense principle that you follow every time you read anything—including this book—but one that often gets ignored when people read Scripture.

Take this line, for example: "It's not bouncing off tough turf." What could that possibly mean? You read it once before, though— it's from chapter two of this book—and I'm sure there was no confusion when you read it then. There's a reason.

The first time you encountered that sentence, you weren't confronted with an isolated line that needed deciphering. You'd been reading a series of sentences that, taken together, provided the flow of thought that gave clarity to the meaning of each individual sentence. In that case, I was discussing Jesus' parable of the sower in Matthew 13, the "tough turf" being the road the first seeds were sown on.

That's the way I want you to read your Bible. Follow this rule: never read a Bible verse.[10] If you want to know what an individual verse means, you can't simply read the verse. You must read the larger context to capture the flow of thought that gives clarity to the writer's meaning.[11]

Here is why this skill is critical for you as an ambassador for Christ. You will have friends or coworkers challenge you on passages of Scripture because they've ignored the context and, therefore, misunderstood the point the author was making.

For example, Jesus said that some of his disciples would not taste death until they saw the Son of Man coming in his kingdom (Matt. 16:28). Skeptics are quick to point out the apparent error: the disciples are dead, and Jesus hasn't returned.

Jesus was not talking about his second coming, though, as the very next verse makes clear. Six days later, Jesus took Peter, James, and John up on a high mountain and was gloriously transfigured before them, his face shining as the sun and his garments white as light (Matt. 17:1–2). The chapter break unfortunately separates these two lines for modern readers (there were no verse numbers or chapter breaks in the original). Reading the full context, though, makes Jesus' intention clear. Context is king, as the saying goes.

So that's the first key concept: never read a Bible verse. Here's the second.

Always Do This

I never liked the question, "Do you take the Bible literally?" It comes up frequently and deserves a response, but I think the question is ambiguous—and, therefore, confusing—making it awkward to answer.[12]

For faithful Christians wary of watering down the message, their first impulse is to answer, "Yes." But now they face a challenge. Is everything in Scripture literally true? Clearly, even those with a high view of the text don't take every verse literally. Jesus is the "door," but he's not made of wood. We are the "branches," but we're not sprouting leaves.

On the other hand, we do take seriously accounts others find fanciful and far-fetched: a man made from mud (Adam), loaves and fishes miraculously multiplied, vivified corpses rising from graves, and so on. A short yes-or-no response to the "Do you take the Bible literally?" question, then, would not be helpful. Neither answer gives the full picture. In fact, I think it's the wrong question since frequently something else is driving the query.

Even non-Christians read the Bible the ordinary way most of the time—when the issues are not controversial. They readily take statements like "Love your neighbor as yourself" or "Remember the poor" at face value. When citing Jesus' directive "Do not judge," they're not deterred by the challenge "You don't take the Bible literally, do you?"

> When critics agree with a passage, they take the words
> in their ordinary and customary sense. They naturally
> understand that language works a certain way in
> everyday communication, and it never occurs to them to
> think otherwise. Unless, of course, the details of the text
> trouble them for some reason.

A critic will often abandon the "literal" approach when he reads a verse that bothers him. Jesus as the only way of salvation? No way. Homosexuality a sin? Please. A "loving" God sending anyone to the eternal torture of hell? Not a chance. This subtle double standard is often at the heart of the taking-the-Bible-literally challenge.

Note, the objection with these teachings is not based on some ambiguity that makes alternate interpretations plausible. The Scripture affirms these truths with the same clarity as "Love your neighbor." No, these verses simply offend. Suddenly, the critic becomes a skeptic and says, "You don't take the Bible *literally*, do you?"

Here is how I would answer. **I'd say I take the Bible in its**

ordinary sense—that is, I try to take the words with the precision I think the writer intended.

I realize this reply might also be a bit ambiguous, but here, I think, that's a strength. Hopefully, my comment will prompt a request for clarification. This is exactly what I want. I'd clarify by countering with a question: **"Do you read the sports page literally?"**

If I asked you this question, I think you'd pause because there is a sense in which everyone reads the sports page in a straightforward way. Certain facts are part of every story in that section. However, you wouldn't take everything written in a woodenly literal way that ignores the conventions of the craft.

"Literally?" you might respond. **"That depends.** If the writer seems to be stating a fact—like a score, a location, a player's name, a description of the plays leading to a touchdown—then I'd take that literally. If he seems to be using a figure of speech, I'd read that figuratively, not literally."

Exactly. Sportswriters choose specific—and sometimes colorful—wording to convey a solid sense of the particulars in an entertaining way. We recognize words like *annihilated*, *crushed*, *mangled*, *mutilated*, *stomped*, and *pounded* as figures of speech used to communicate events that actually ("literally") took place. We never give those details a second thought because we understand how language works.

When a writer seems to be communicating facts in a straightforward fashion, we read them as such. When we encounter obvious figures of speech, we take them that way, too.

That's the normal way to read the sports page. It's also the normal—and responsible—way to read any work, including the Bible. Ask, "What is this writer trying to communicate?" This is exactly what I'm after when I say, **"I take the Bible in its ordinary sense."**

Of course, someone may disagree with the point the Scripture makes. Fair enough. There's nothing dishonest about disagreement. Or they might think some Christian is mistaken on its meaning. Misinterpreting a passage is always possible. Conjuring up some meaning that has little to do with the words the writer used, though, is not a legitimate alternative.

If someone disagrees with the obvious sense of a passage, ask them, **"Do you have a reason this text should not be read in the 'ordinary' way?"** Their answer will tell you if their challenge is intellectually honest, or if they're trying to dismiss biblical claims they simply don't like.

Do I take the Bible literally? **I try to take the Bible at its plain meaning unless I have good reason to do otherwise. I read the Bible the ordinary way.** This is the basic rule we apply to everything we read: novels, newspapers, periodicals, and poems. The Bible is no different.

So that's the second key concept: Always read the Bible the ordinary way. It will save you lots of trouble.

Now to some shoals and reefs. Two troublesome biblical issues need attention: Joshua's conquest of the Canaanites and slavery in the Old Testament.[13]

When God Gets Rough

According to critics, the God of the Hebrews was patently immoral. Just read the Bible, they say. Richard Dawkins's assessment is probably the most well known: "The God of the Old Testament is . . . a vindictive, bloodthirsty ethnic cleanser; a misogynistic, homophobic, racist, infanticidal, genocidal, filicidal, pestilential, megalomaniacal, sadomasochistic, capriciously malevolent bully."[14]

As an aside, it seems ironic that an atheist who denies the existence of objective morality[15] can overflow so readily with moral indignation.[16] But that's another matter. Here's the deeper concern: this challenge needs an answer, not just for atheists like Dawkins, but because some passages in the Old Testament give even believers pause. For example:

- "When the LORD your God brings you into the land where you are entering to possess it, and clears away many nations before you . . . you shall utterly destroy them" (Deut. 7:1–2).
- "Only in the cities of these peoples that the LORD your God is giving you as an inheritance, you shall not leave alive anything that breathes. But you shall utterly destroy them" (Deut. 20:16–17).
- "Now go and strike Amalek and utterly destroy all that he has, and do not spare him; but put to death both man and woman, child and infant, ox and sheep, camel and donkey" (1 Sam. 15:3).

Strong words, and there are more passages like this these. Sounds to many like genocide and ethnic cleansing. Could these commands really come from the God of all grace and mercy? What is going on here?

Earlier, I said that reading Scripture accurately requires we be clear on the context of a text or passage, the purpose of the writing in the historical and cultural setting of its audience, and the normal conventions of language of the intended readers. Each of those is a factor in making sense of passages like the ones we looked at.

Trash Talk

First, the language. Earlier, I mentioned the habit of sportswriters, for example, to use dramatic and colorful language to press a point. The practice is not unique to our era, though. It goes back to ancient times.

Ancient Near Eastern military narrative commonly traded in hyperbole—exaggeration for the sake of emphasis—especially when it came to military conquest. The practice is evident throughout battle reports of the time. "Joshua's conventional warfare rhetoric," Paul Copan writes, "was common in many other ancient Near Eastern military accounts in the second and first millennia BC."[17]

Therefore, phrases like "utterly destroy," or "put to death both man and woman, child and infant"—as well as other obliteration language—were stock, stereotypical idioms used even when women or children were not present.[18] They decreed total victory (much like your favorite sports team "wiping out" the opposition), not complete annihilation.

Simply put, the hyperbolic language meant "thoroughly defeat." Note that after Jericho was "utterly destroyed" with the edge of the sword, "both man and woman, young and old" (Josh. 6:21), and after Joshua had "utterly destroyed all the inhabitants of Ai," "both men and women" (Josh. 8:25–26), Joshua read the law to "all the assembly of Israel with the women and the little ones and the strangers who were living among them" (Josh. 8:35). Clearly, the earlier statements implying the death of all were hyperbolic.

So, the first qualifier is that the wording regarding the conquest was not meant to be understood in a strictly literal sense. Rather, given the normal linguistic conventions of ancient Near Eastern peoples, the language was hyperbolic military metaphor common to that day—just like the practice of today's sportswriters.

"The God of the Bible ordered genocide."

    "Why do you say that?"

"He told Joshua to annihilate every man, woman, and child of the Canaanites."

    "Let me ask you a question: Do you ever read the sports page?"

"Sure."

    "Does it bother you when you read that one team completely wiped out another team?"

"Of course not. They don't mean that literally."

"Well, God didn't mean that literally, either."
"What!"

"No, it's a figure of speech, just like sportswriters use. It was common in the records of ancient Near East warfare, just like on the sports page. It's called military hyperbole."

"Are you saying there was no conquest?"

"No, there were battles, and lots of people died. But there was no command to literally annihilate everyone."

"How do you know that?"

"Because it's clear when you read the record more closely that it's not what the Israelites were commanded to do, nor was it what they did."

Hyperbole, though, like all figures of speech, is meant to make a literal point. God's clear command was that the Israelites utterly defeat the Canaanites and drive them out of the land.[19] Why? Two related issues are in play here, both tied to the historical/cultural setting.

Reaping the Whirlwind

First, a major purpose of the conquest was God's judgment on a despicable people for their wicked ways:

- "It is because of the wickedness of these nations that the LORD your God is driving them out before you" (Deut. 9:5).
- "When you enter the land which the LORD your God gives you, you shall not learn to imitate the detestable things of those nations. . . . Because of these detestable things the

LORD your God will drive them out before you" (Deut. 18:9, 12).

- "Do not defile yourselves by any of these things; for by all these the nations which I am casting out before you have become defiled" (Lev. 18:24).

God was angry. Indeed, he was furious. And with good reason. The Canaanites were unspeakably evil, their culture decadent and corrupt to its core. God did not want his own covenant people— the forebears of the world's Savior—to be morally poisoned and spiritually polluted by their wickedness.

In addition to divination, witchcraft, and female and male temple sex, Canaanite idolatry encompassed a host of morally detestable practices that mimicked the sexually perverse conduct of their Canaanite fertility gods:[20] adultery, homosexuality, transvestitism, pederasty (men sexually abusing boys), sex with all sorts of beasts,[21] and incest. Note that after the Canaanite city of Sodom was destroyed, Lot's daughters immediately seduced their drunken father, imitating one of the sexual practices of the city just annihilated (Gen. 19:30–36).

Worst of all, Canaanites practiced child sacrifice. There was a reason God commanded the Jews, "Do not give any of your children to be sacrificed to Molek" (Lev. 18:21 NIV):[22] "Molech was a Canaanite underworld deity represented as an upright, bull-headed idol with human body in whose belly a fire was stoked and in whose outstretched arms a child was placed that would be burned to death. . . . And it was not just infants; children as old as four were sacrificed."[23]

Archaeological evidence indicates that children thus burned to death numbered in the thousands.[24]

The Canaanites had been reveling in debasements like these for centuries as God patiently postponed judgment (Gen. 15:16). Here was no racist, genocidal, capriciously malevolent bully (to use Dawkins's words). Instead, here was a God willing to spare the entire Canaanite city of Sodom for the sake of just ten righteous people (Gen. 18:32), yet they were not to be found.

> God was slow to anger and fast to forgive. "If that nation against which I have spoken turns from its evil," he told Jeremiah, "I will relent concerning the calamity I planned to bring on it" (Jer. 18:8). Jonah's Nineveh is a prime example.

But is there no limit to patience? Indeed, what would we say if God perpetually sat silent in the face of such wickedness? Would we not ask, "Where was God?" Would we not question his goodness, his power, or even his existence if he didn't eventually vanquish this evil? Yet, when God finally does act, critics are quick to find fault with the "vindictive, bloodthirsty, ethnic cleanser."

The conquest was neither ethnic cleansing nor genocide. God cared nothing about skin color or national origin. Aliens shared the same legal rights in the commonwealth as Jews.[25] Foreigners like Naomi and Rahab were welcome within their ranks.

God cared only about sin. The conquest was an exercise of capital punishment on a national scale, justice for hundreds of years of idolatry and unthinkable debauchery.[26] Indeed, God brought the same sentence of destruction on his own people when they sinned in like manner.[27]

Cleaning House

The second major purpose of the conquest was a direct result of the debauched Canaanite people's defeat and their expulsion from the land. It was also critical to the larger context of God's rescue plan for the world.[28] God was cleaning house.

In the process of executing his sentence against the Canaanites,

God would be removing every vestige of their debased religion from the land. The purpose of the conquest, then, was not only judgment and expulsion—driving the inhabitants out—but also purging the country of idolatry by expunging every trace of the evil Canaanite religion from the region.[29]

"You shall tear down their altars, and smash their sacred pillars, and hew down their Asherim, and burn their graven images with fire," God told the Israelites (Deut. 7:5). By purging all trappings of the vile Canaanite religion—a kind of "spiritual surgery,"[30] as one author puts it—the Jews would ensure spiritual safety for themselves. Note God's instructions to Moses: "In the cities of these peoples that the LORD your God is giving you as an inheritance, you shall not leave alive anything that breathes. But you shall utterly destroy them [note the hyperbole] . . . *so that they may not teach you to do according to all their detestable things which they have done for their gods, so that you would sin against the LORD your God*" (Deut. 20:16–18).

God's rescue plan to save mankind depended on Abraham's offspring—the Jews. If as a nation they turned to other gods, they could not be the agency of salvation God intended. The cancer of idolatry needed to be cut out for the patient—God's plan of redemption—to survive. Syncretism with pagan religions would corrupt Israel's theological core. By purging the land of this evil, God meant to ensure that his redemptive plan—forgiveness for the evils of *any* nation—would be available in the future for people of *every* nation.

Unfortunately, instead of completing the conquest of Canaan and driving its people out as commanded, the Jews capitulated (Judg. 1:28–33). Blending in with their enemy's godless culture, they quickly were corrupted by it (Judg. 3:5–7).

Before long, the Jews had adopted all the degrading and detestable habits God had condemned Canaan for in the first place.[31] Eventually, the same judgment that had fallen on the debauched Canaanites—military destruction and expulsion from the land—fell upon the corrupted Israelites for the very same reasons.[32] The issue in both cases was not ethnic cleansing, but ethical cleansing.

In a certain sense, the lesson of the conquest is a simple one: God punishes evil. For many in our culture, though, the Canaanite offenses simply are not offensive. "Divination, sexual adventure, adultery, homosexuality, transvestitism, all evil? No way."

Virtually every crime on the Canaanite rap sheet is common in our communities or can be found one click away on the internet. Children are not being torched on church altars, of course, but thousands die daily in abortion clinics, sacrificed (literally) to the gods of choice and convenience.

There's little doubt the wording in God's commands regarding the conquest includes hyperbole. This is a common feature of narrative, both ancient and modern. But literary devices are meant to clarify meaning, not obscure it. God's clear message was that punishment was coming, and it would be poured out with a fury upon all the inhabitants of a corrupt nation that had reveled in debauchery for centuries.

> This was not carte blanche for genocide or ethnic cleansing, but rather a directive limited in time to the conquest, limited in scope to the Canaanites, and limited in location to the Promised Land.[33]

In the process of judging, God would be clearing out a safe place for truth to flourish so that Israel might rise up as a "kingdom of priests" to the nations, bringing the blessing of Abraham to all peoples—Jew and gentile alike. Paul Copan summarizes: "For a specific, relatively short, and strategic period, God sought to establish Israel in the land with a view to fulfilling this long-term, global (indeed, cosmic) plan of redemption. God would simultaneously punish a wicked people ripe for judgment. Not doing so would have erased humankind's only hope for redemption."[34]

It may turn out, though, that this explanation—or any explanation true to the text—will not satisfy the belligerent skeptic. Further, since we've all been "morally velocitized" by our own depravity, any response by God that takes sin seriously will seem inordinate to us. The temptation is strong even for Christians to sanitize the account so that God looks less extreme. "Most of our problems regarding God's ordering the destruction of the Canaanites," Clay Jones writes, "come from the fact that God hates sin but we do not."[35]

"There's another thing maybe you haven't thought about."

"What's that?"

"If you were aware that religious groups were molesting massive numbers of children and even ritualistically burning them alive, what would you think about God?"

"I'd reject the whole idea of God."

"Why?"

"Because if a good God existed, he would do something about that."

"I understand exactly. **So, if something like that actually happened, would you think God should step in?"**

"Of course."

"So now the next question. **Do you know the kinds of things the Canaanites did routinely?"**

"No."

"They sexually abused children and ritually sacrificed infants, burning them alive. You asked me, if God existed, why wouldn't he do something?"

"Yes."

"God *did* do something. After waiting patiently for hundreds of years, he finally brought judgment on those people. **Do you know what God did to the Israelites when they sacrificed their own children by fire to idols?**"

"No."

"He did the same thing to them that he did to the Canaanites. He used armies—the Assyrians and the Babylonians—to punish them and drive them out of the land."

A word of caution, though. I have little confidence the right answer to this challenge is going to placate many critics, and it may not even satisfy some Christians. Sometimes I think we have to simply let God be God and leave it at that.

"Am I Not a Man and a Brother?"

Slavery is one of the most misunderstood subjects in the Bible. There's a reason. Language, translation, and the historical/cultural context of the ancient Near East are completely foreign to twenty-first-century ears. Instead, a different historical context informs our understanding of the word *slave*.

Consider, for example, the image that comes to mind when you read a passage like this: "As for your male and female slaves whom you may have—you may acquire male and female slaves from the pagan nations that are around you. . . . You may even bequeath them to your sons after you, to receive as a possession; you can use them as permanent slaves" (Lev. 25:44, 46).

When Americans read the words "slaves" and "possession," a vivid picture comes to mind. It's an image of kidnapping, murder, rape, brutal forced servitude, utter subjugation and humiliation, disregard for basic human dignity, and complete lack of legal protection.

This was the American system. Slaves were kidnapped from their native country, chained, packed like human cordwood into filthy vessels, then shipped five thousand miles across the infamous Middle Passage, with 15–25 percent perishing along the way. Those who survived became chattel property and were beaten, raped, and murdered at will.

This wretched practice was finally abolished, due largely to Christians who committed their lives to dismantling an institution that was an offense to God and totally at odds with biblical truth.[36]

The core conviction motivating their effort as Christians was the biblical teaching that every human being is made in God's image. To communicate their creed, they used a dramatic engraving of a shackled slave bordered by the words "Am I Not a Man and a Brother?"

This doctrine is biblical bedrock when it comes to any issue related to human worth and dignity. The oldest book in the Bible contains this statement: "If I have despised the claim of my male or female slaves when they filed a complaint against me, what then could I do when God arises? And when He calls me to account, what will I answer Him? Did not He who made me in the womb make him, and the same one fashion us in the womb?" (Job 31:13–15).

Yet, there is that word again: "slave." In a moment, I will clarify the biblical/cultural meaning of the Hebrew word that has, unfortunately, been translated this way. First, though, I want you to be clear on three details in the Mosaic law that guide the biblical approach to the question of slavery.

First, kidnapping was a capital crime: "He who kidnaps a man, whether he sells him or he is found in his possession, shall surely be put to death" (Ex. 21:16).[37]

Second, murder was a capital crime: "Whoever sheds man's blood, by man his blood shall be shed, for in the image of God He made man" (Gen. 9:6). "He who strikes a man so that he dies shall surely be put to death" (Ex. 21:12). This prohibition explicitly included the killing of slaves (cf. v. 20).[38]

Third, rape was a capital crime: "If in the field the man finds the girl who is engaged, and the man forces her and lies with her, then . . . the man who lies with her shall die" (Deut. 22:25).[39]

These regulations themselves are enough to show that the so-called "slavery" regulated by Old Testament law bore no resemblance to the kind of slavery we picture when we read that word.

There is another issue, though.

Lost in Translation

Most people—Christians and critics—are not aware that in their modern translations, the words *slave* and *servant* come from the same Hebrew word most of the time: *ebed*. Curiously, rendering this single Hebrew word into two entirely different English words with radically different connotations is a recent development.[40]

In my *Young's Analytical Concordance to the Bible*—originally published in 1879 and keyed to the King James Version—there is not a single instance where *ebed* is translated "slave." Instead, the KJV renders *ebed* "bondman" 20 times, "manservant" 23 times, and "servant" 716 times.

By the middle of the twentieth century, though, the trend changed drastically. My *New American Standard Exhaustive Concordance of the Bible* published in 1981, for example, reveals 58 instances when *ebed* is translated into some form of the word "slave." Even so, in 722 instances, *ebed* is still rendered "servant" of some sort.

Why the shift? I have no idea. Regardless of this unusual trend, it's clear that the preferred meaning of *ebed* is not slave but servant. The word refers principally to work and service, not to property and ownership.

The point is this. The concept of slavery—with its obscene connotation for Western ears—is not inherent to the meaning of the Hebrew word it is translated from. Something else is going on in the Mosaic law. To discover what that is, we need to read these texts with the cultural eyes of the original audience.

The ancient Near East was a brutal world, and brutal subjugation of other human beings was common fare. The Hebrews were embedded in this culture and apt to adopt the ways of their neighboring nations. Consequently, through the Law, God placed boundaries and controls to humanize practices that were less than ideal.

> Keep in mind, though, regulating does not mean approving. Instead, God was providing for the protection of those who were vulnerable in a less than ideal situation,[41] safeguards that were virtually nonexistent in the rest of the ancient world.

The concept of slave vs. free—in the sense we understand it today—was virtually unknown in the world of the ancient Hebrews. Then, virtually everyone was an *ebed*, a servant of some sort. Workers in the fields were servants of the landowners. Landowners were servants of their king. The king was servant to his God.[42]

Help Wanted

"Hiring out" as an *ebed* was also a normal means of employment, what we would now call an "indentured servant." For those in debt or lacking personal means, leasing their labor out by pledging themselves as workers often ensured their survival. A father could even "sell" his daughter into servanthood to make provision for her long-term well-being (Ex. 21:7). In most cases, being an *ebed*, then, was for the mutual benefit of both servant and master.

> Servants in Israel were considered part of the family. Once a servant had finished his commitment, if he loved his master—as was often the case—he could stay and serve for the rest of his life (Ex. 21:5–6).

To protect the worker, though, God set down clear standards and boundaries, giving rights and protections to every *ebed* in the commonwealth.[43] In a sense, then, an *ebed* in ancient Israel had union representation: the Mosaic law.

For example, violence against an *ebed* was strictly forbidden: "If a man strikes the eye of his male [*ebed*] or female [*amah*],[44] and destroys it, he shall let him go free on account of his eye. And if he knocks out a tooth of his male [*ebed*] or female [*amah*], he shall let him go free on account of his tooth" (Ex. 21:26–27).

Under the Law, every *ebed* had a day of Sabbath rest, just like everyone else (Deut. 5:14). On the seventh year, every Israelite *ebed* was to be set free (Ex. 21:2). A runaway *ebed* who escaped his master was not to be mistreated but rather protected and allowed to live in a town that pleased him (Deut. 23:15–16).

My rather brief summary of this issue does not cover every reference to servanthood/slavery in the Old Testament, of course.[45] And clearly, some of the statutes regarding Hebrew servants did not apply in the same way to foreigners.

Nevertheless, the "slavery" under the Mosaic law in the Jewish commonwealth bore no resemblance to the brutal and obscene practice of slavery in North America. "The intent of these laws," Paul Copan points out, "was to combat potential abuses, not to institutionalize servitude."

Here's a sample dialogue:

"The Old Testament condones slavery."

"When you hear the word *slavery*, **what picture comes to mind?"**

"Africans in chains kidnapped and shipped
to plantations for forced labor, being
beaten, raped, and murdered at will."

"Is this what you think the Bible approves?"

"Absolutely."

"If that were what it meant, I'd be angry, too. **Did
you know, though, that in the Mosaic law,
kidnapping was a capital crime, punished by
execution, and so were rape and murder?**"

"I didn't know that."

"Is it possible, then, that the so-called 'slavery' in
the Old Testament was different from the slavery
you just described?"

"I hadn't thought of that."

**"Do you know the difference between the
Hebrew word translated 'slave' in our modern
translations and the Hebrew word translated
'servant'?"**

"No."

"There is no difference. It's the exact same Hebrew
word."

"Really?"

"Yes. Most of time the word appears, it's talking
about what we call indentured servants, not slaves—
people who 'sell' themselves to work for someone
else for a period of time. **By the way, did African
slaves in America have any rights?**"

"Of course not."

"Well, the 'slaves' of the Jews did. They had every
Saturday off, for example. And if you so much as
broke a tooth of a slave, you had to set him free.
One last thing."

"What's that?"

"Any idea how slavery was finally abolished in the West?"

"Not exactly."

"Christians in England and in America ended it. Here's why: they were convinced from the Bible that slavery was a terrible sin against God."

CHAPTER 14

GOD: THE SCIENCE STOPPER

When infamous atheist Christopher Hitchens debated *The Privileged Planet* author Jay Wesley Richards at Stanford on the question of God's existence, Hitchens asked Richards a pair of questions.

"Do you believe that Jesus Christ was born of a virgin?" he asked. "Do you believe he was resurrected from the dead?" Richards, the Christian, assented to both. Hitchens shrugged. "I rest my case," he said dismissively. "This is an honest guy who has just made it very clear, and plain to you, science has nothing to do with his beliefs whatever—nothing, nothing at all."[1]

It was a remarkable non sequitur from an otherwise brilliant man. What "case" did Hitchens think was vindicated? Richards affirmed his own belief in supernatural events. But this should not be surprising—or in any way damning, for that matter—since it is part of the theistic worldview Richards was defending.

Apparently for Hitchens, anything not proven by science is contrary to science, and if contrary, then irrational. Supernatural events, by definition, cannot be explained by science and thus cannot be countenanced by anyone truly committed to science. Belief in miracles, then, is ludicrous. QED, Richards is refuted.[2]

I want you to notice two things about Hitchens's dismissal of Richards.

First, notice the impulse to use science as a stick to beat up on theism. Atheists like Christopher Hitchens, Richard Dawkins, and others are convinced that the findings of science have somehow inveighed with finality against the existence of God. The intrusion of, say, intelligent design into the discussion is nothing but a "God of the gaps" science stopper.

Second, despite Hitchens's sermonizing about reason, in that moment he was guilty of a sophomoric blunder in reasoning: his own appeal was circular. The very issue on the table was whether Hitchens's materialistic view of the universe was sound. By assuming as evidence against Richards's view the very thing Hitchens was obliged to prove in the debate—atheistic materialism—he showed himself to be the irrational one, not Richards.

There is a reason Hitchens—like so many others—took this route. A philosophic shell game is afoot that you must see lest you be taken in by the sleight of hand.[3] Once you see the maneuver, you will not be fooled by the con.

In this chapter, I want to give you three pieces of evidence to show that the alleged "conflict" between science and religion is completely contrived, and that the two are not inherently at odds.

First, I want you to see it's not possible for science to disprove God—or miracles, or souls, or anything of the sort—because that task is completely beyond its capability. Second, the alleged battle between science and religion has been a not-so-subtle power play, purposefully designed to keep the God alternative off the table. Finally, belief in God was the science starter, historically, not a science stopper—and for good reason.

Weighing a Chicken with a Yardstick

Let me start by asking what might seem like an odd question: Can you weigh a chicken with a yardstick? Clearly not. Yardsticks measure length, not weight. Does it follow, then, that chickens weigh nothing? Again, clearly not. Tools meant to measure one feature tell you nothing about other features they have no capability to assess.

> This notion is so elementary, it's easy to miss its significance regarding science and the supernatural, so let me state it bluntly. Strictly speaking, science is not capable of ruling out anything, even in principle, about the immaterial realm.

The scientific enterprise, currently construed, is designed to measure physical things using empirical methods, and it fulfills that function well. It is not suited to directly measure nonphysical things. It would be a mistake, then, to take this natural limitation of science as evidence against the supernatural. Yet this kind of blunder happens habitually.

For example, years ago, *TIME* magazine made a stunning announcement. In an extensive cover story on the nature of the mind, *TIME* declared, "Despite our every instinct to the contrary, there is one thing that consciousness is not: some entity deep inside the brain that corresponds to the 'self,' some kernel of awareness that runs the show."[4]

According to *TIME*, everything about human consciousness—thoughts, desires, pains, pleasures, motives, emotions—can be explained in purely physical terms. A mother's love for her children is reduced to nerve fibers firing in her brain. The virtue of kindness is nothing more than genetic code. Our hopes for the future are simply so much chemistry. Brain and body work together as a sophisticated, biological machine with no help from a ghostly, immaterial thing called a soul.

How did they come to this conclusion? "After more than a century of looking for it, brain researchers have long since concluded that there is no conceivable place for such a self to be located in the physical brain, and that it simply doesn't exist."[5]

In other words, scientists are convinced an immaterial soul does not exist because (1) they can't find it by looking for it, and (2) there is no room in the brain for it to fit.

Let those two points sink in for a moment. This is the same as saying you don't believe in invisible men because you've never seen one. Clearly, scientists are not going to find an immaterial soul by looking for it, even if they look for one hundred years. Further, immaterial things like souls don't need physical places to fit into since, by definition, immaterial objects do not occupy three-dimensional space.

This doesn't prove souls exist, of course, but it does show that the inability of science to find one means nothing. This issue must be resolved by different means.

Though science can help us in many ways, it cannot foreclose on anything—souls, spirits, God(s), salvation, heaven, hell—outside its domain for a simple reason: it is not equipped to measure those things. It's like trying to weigh a chicken with a yardstick. This approach to defeating theism is a dead end.

Here is a sample conversation that makes this point:

"I used to believe in God, but now I believe in science."

  "Explain that to me. I'm not sure I understand what you mean." [Columbo #1]

"You know, I used to believe in all that supernatural stuff, but science has shown me none of that is real."

  "Can you help me understand exactly how science has shown the supernatural can't be real?"

"Well, ancient man used to believe lots of things were caused by gods, like the weather. Now, with science, we know

the real reason for weather, and it has
nothing to do with gods."

"I agree. There are lots of ways science has cleared
up confusion for us, but you're saying something
different, aren't you?"

"What's that?"

**"Well, you're saying science has somehow
shown that the supernatural world is not real.
I'm just asking how science can do that."**

"I guess I don't get your point."

"Science studies the physical world, right?"

"Right."

"It studies things you have access to through your
five senses, correct?"

"Correct."

"If there really were immaterial things like gods or
souls or spirits or miraculous powers, would any of
those things be physical?"

"Of course not."

**"Well, if they wouldn't be physical, how
could science have anything to say about
them? How can an empirical way of knowing
things show that nonempirical things don't
exist?"**

Science has never advanced empirical evidence to show that
supernatural events cannot happen. Instead, it has assumed—prior
to the evidence—that the material world is all there is.[6]

A Stacked Deck

One of the most popular science documentary series of all time
starts with these words: "The cosmos is all that is, or ever was, or

ever will be." The series is PBS's *Cosmos: A Personal Voyage*, hosted by legendary astronomer Carl Sagan.

Oddly, the defining concept of the series—conveyed in the opening line of the documentary—is not scientific at all. No empirical analysis can ever reveal "all that is, or ever was, or ever will be," even in principle.

No, Sagan's famous words are pure philosophy. His starting point is not a conclusion of science, but rather a philosophical presumption imposed on the scientific project meant to fix the boundaries of reality at the edge of the physical universe. It's a metaphysical doctrine, a kind of materialist doctrinal dogma. The religious "ring" to the theme line is not accidental.

In *Cosmos*, Carl Sagan offers a worldview story meant to compete with classic theism. Where the Christian story begins with the words "In the beginning, God," Carl Sagan's story begins, essentially, with the words "In the beginning, the particles."

Sagan's worldview is variously called physicalism, materialism, or naturalism since the basic concept is that reality consists of nothing but the physical, material world, governed by nothing but natural law.[7] Thus, C. S. Lewis called this the "nothing buttery" view.

Do not underestimate the power this presumption has to influence people's thinking about religion. For many you'll encounter, it's the philosophical air they breathe without realizing it. To them, the entire world is, from top to bottom, "nothing but" swirling atoms and molecules, in which "we float like a mote of dust in the morning sky," in Sagan's words from episode 1 of *Cosmos*.[8]

I am choosing my own words carefully here. For multitudes, this is a *presumed* truth. It is not a conclusion about the nature of reality, but rather the unquestioned starting point, a grand assumption imposed on science, artificially putting it at odds with religion.

Consider this statement by one atheist: "I know there was no resurrection because I know from science that dead people stay dead."[9]

Science teaches no such thing, of course. Science can tell the atheist if a body is dead or if it's alive. It cannot tell him whether a dead body can come back to life. It is not science that tells the atheist resurrections can't happen. His philosophy dictates that.

> Science has nothing to say about what can or can't take place or what is possible or impossible in the world. It's purely descriptive. Science can only tell us what *does* happen, characteristically, in the physical realm. Only philosophy can assess what can or can't happen.

The world we live in may be a purely physical place run entirely by natural law, no exceptions. Or the world may be possessed of powers beyond mere physical cause and effect. In that kind of world, resurrections are plausible.

The critical question is this: What kind of world do we live in? Science is mute on that matter. That question is one for philosophers, not scientists.

In this case, the atheist has imposed his materialistic philosophy on the question of resurrection—just as Hitchens did in his debate with Richards—then glibly labeled it a truth of science. He has confused physics with metaphysics—a common mistake.

I've already said that this philosophical move pitting science against religion is no accident but a conscious and deliberate contrivance. To verify that point, I would like you to read a striking statement made by Richard Lewontin, a Harvard geneticist and world-class scientist, who, without shame or embarrassment, admits the science game has been rigged:

> Our willingness to accept scientific claims that are against common sense is the key to an understanding of the real struggle between science and the supernatural. We take the side of science *in spite of* the patent absurdity of some of its constructs . . . because we have a prior commitment, a commitment to

materialism. . . . We are forced by our *a priori* adherence to
material causes to create an apparatus of investigation and a set
of concepts that produce material explanations, no matter how
counter-intuitive, no matter how mystifying to the uninitiated.
Moreover, that materialism is absolute, for we cannot allow a
Divine Foot in the door.[10]

Lewontin is not the only one to make this admission, but he is
undoubtedly the most brazen, which is why he is cited so frequently.[11]

Phillip Johnson, founding father of the intelligent design movement, sums up Lewontin's point well: "The reason for opposition
to scientific accounts of our origins, according to Lewontin, is not
that people are ignorant of facts, but that they have not learned to
think from the right starting point."[12]

Here is the consequence. When intelligent design of some
sort—the idea that evidence in physics and biology points to an
intelligent designer—is disqualified as being unscientific, it is
almost universally rejected not on its evidential merits—violation
of the scientific method—but on its philosophic implications—
violation of materialist philosophy.

Here is a way these points might play out in conversation:

"Intelligent design is not science. It's
religion disguised as science."

    "Really? How so?" [Columbo #1]

"Science is all about physical events,
empirically verified. Intelligent design brings
God into the picture. That's not science."

    "So, you're objecting because theists suggest that
    some agent, not some physical cause, is responsible for
    certain features of the natural world?" [Columbo #1]

"Exactly.

    "Is archaeology science?"

"Of course."

"Doesn't archaeology study the role of agents in history?"

"Sure."

"What about forensic pathology?"

"Of course, but those are different."

"Why?"

"They're human agents, not supernatural ones."

"But what if the evidence is really good that a supernatural agent is the best explanation of the physical facts?"

"It's still religion, not science."

"I have another question about that."

"Okay."

"It sounds like you're rejecting intelligent design because, strictly speaking according to your definition, it's not 'scientific.'"

"Right."

"Usually when an option is rejected, it's not because it's a certain category of answer—like 'religious'—but because it's based on bad facts or unsound thinking or some other reason people are convinced the answer is not a good one. **So, what are the specific reasons you don't think intelligent design is a good explanation for, say, the origin of life or the information on the DNA double helix?"**

God of the Gaps?

In chapter 8, I offered two general arguments for God's existence that traded heavily on scientific data—the cosmological argument based on the existence of the universe and the teleological argument based on the apparent design of the universe. For many, though, I have committed an unpardonable sin, invoking the so-called "God of the gaps fallacy." Now I'd like to answer that charge.[13]

The critic's concern is this: just because science hasn't solved some of the problems, that doesn't mean it never will. There is no need to punt to superstition. A rational (i.e., naturalistic) answer will be available eventually. Using God to arbitrarily plug holes that science has yet to fill is misguided.

Here's my response. First, this is yet another circular effort. The critic's confidence in his own "naturalism of the gaps" is dictated by the assumption that the universe runs on inviolable materialist principles, so every event *must* have a naturalistic explanation. If science hasn't discovered it yet, it will eventually.

However, the legitimacy of materialism is the very thing at stake in the discussion between theists and atheists, so implicitly invoking scientific materialism against theists is not helpful. This is the blunder Hitchens made in his debate with Richards.

> Why assume there's a "gap" in our knowledge simply because we have no explanations consistent with materialism? It's possible that some breaches remain because we've been slavishly looking for answers in the wrong place.

Second, careful appeals to a supernatural agent (God) are not based on what we don't know, but on what we do know. They are not arbitrary leaps of faith fueled by ignorance. Design can be detected empirically. Even a child knows this. If the evidence is good for intelligent design, then the gap has been filled with a real answer based on good reasons. Just because the solution is not the right *kind* of answer (a naturalistic one), that doesn't mean it's not the right answer.

Third, sometimes the very nature of a problem makes a

naturalistic explanation wildly counterintuitive. It may be theoretically possible that a man with five bullet holes in his chest died from natural causes, but is it reasonable to hold out for a naturalistic solution when evidence for agency is so decisive? What really matters is the data on hand, not facts that might be forthcoming—existing evidence, not future fantasies.

"When you appeal to a supernatural cause, that's just the God of the gaps fallacy all over again."

"What exactly is the problem here?"

"You see a gap in the scientific explanation, so you just say, 'God did it.'"

"Is that what you think I've been doing?"

"Yes."

"But what about concrete evidence that a supernatural designer is a good explanation for certain features of the world, like the origin of the universe or the origin of life or the incredible fine-tuning we see in the universe?"

"Science will eventually find the answers to those problems and fill the gap."

"Explain to me why that isn't an example of naturalism of the gaps."

"Well, science has shown it can answer the issues without any need for God."

"So, you are confident your naturalism of the gaps is okay, even though you don't have the evidence in this case, but God is not an okay answer, even though there's really good evidence for a supernatural agent?"

"Yes."

Atheists have tremendous confidence that science will continue its record of "silencing superstition." As knowledge waxes, foolishness wanes, the thinking goes. There's no need to stick God into the "gaps." Science will fill them eventually, so God is irrelevant. That's the idea.

It has not always been this way, though. Exactly how did the scientific method gain ascendancy over superstition to begin with? The historical record tells an interesting story.

God, the Science Starter

The science vs. religion warfare model is entrenched in the popular narrative, but it is a recent development.

The battle motif owes its origin to the influence of two books in the late nineteenth century that ignited the fire: *History of the Conflict between Religion and Science* by John William Draper in 1874, and *A History of the Warfare of Science with Theology in Christendom* by Andrew Dickson White in 1896. Both works fanned the flames between evolutionists and religious fundamentalists, pitting—as the authors characterized it—science and progress against superstition and repression.

Historians of science, though, give a different account of the role religion played in the birth of modern science. The philosophy of naturalism that's governed the enterprise the last 150 years was not the driving force in the early days. Rather, theological conviction was a foundational factor in the genesis of science.[14]

By Darwin's time, the basic methods of science were firmly established. They had sprouted, ironically, from the theological soil of Western civilization—Christian Europe, specifically. Other cultures—the Egyptians, the Chinese, the Romans, the Greeks— had the intellectual raw materials to initiate a scientific revolution, yet the rise of science as we know it took place in Western Europe.

Why there? Here's why: "Presuppositions derived from a

Judeo-Christian worldview helped to inspire and shape the foundation of modern science, and the founders . . . themselves perceived evidence in support of those presuppositions, including the idea that life and the universe owe their origin to the activity of 'a Being incorporeal, living, intelligent, [and] omnipresent.'"[15]

The obvious order of nature fit the conviction of these pioneers that a Divine mind had ordered it so. If a rational God fashioned the universe, then rational man—made in his image—could unlock its secrets. That was the thinking of men like astronomer Johannes Kepler (1571–1630), chemist Robert Boyle (1627–1691), and physicist Isaac Newton (1642–1727).[16]

The early thinkers used three metaphors to convey their understanding of the natural world they were exploring: a book, a clock, and a realm governed by law.

These men viewed nature as God's second "book" of revelation, displaying what the apostle Paul describes as God's "invisible attributes, His eternal power and divine nature."[17] The natural realm spoke with a "voice" that had gone out to all the earth.[18]

Clocks run mechanistically, reflecting the intelligence of a skillful clockmaker. The "clockwork universe" invited observers—if they were careful and methodical—to discover the physical mechanisms that made nature's clock "tick."

The mechanical regularity of nature coincided with the belief that some sort of governing force directed its behavior. "Law" language made perfect sense to those encountering the natural regularities. Even today, law terminology is the standard way of describing how the universe behaves.

These men also understood that, given the fall, human reason was fallible. Systematic testing, experimentation, and close observation were necessary, then, to avoid error, to accurately discern the patterns, and to quantify the regularities in the laws of nature to harness them for human use. Thus, the "scientific method" began to take shape.

> To these men, each of these metaphors—book, clock, law—reflected their conviction that a divine hand was at work. This belief was not a leap of faith, but a commonsense observation of the harmony between the world they observed and the worldview they believed in.

The uniformity of order these founding fathers of science observed in nature was a fingerprint of the intelligent Designer who made the natural world that way. The mechanisms they observed in nature perfectly coincided with their conviction that a divine clockmaker had designed them.

Here is a list of deeply committed theists—all founders of science and most of them Christians—whose religious convictions complemented rather than conflicted with their scientific efforts:

- 1473 Nicolaus Copernicus—Polish mathematician and astronomer; established the foundation of modern astronomy by proposing the heliocentric theory of planetary motion
- 1564 Galileo Galilei—Italian physicist and astronomer; empirically confirmed heliocentrism and pioneered the modern scientific method
- 1571 Johannes Kepler—German astronomer; discovered the laws of planetary motion
- 1623 Blaise Pascal—French mathematical prodigy; founded modern probability theory and hydraulics and contributed to the advance of differential calculus
- 1627 Robert Boyle—Irish developer of the modern scientific method; founded modern chemistry
- 1642 Isaac Newton—English mathematician, physicist, astronomer, and theologian; developed the principle of universal gravity
- 1707 Carolus Linnaeus—Swedish botanist; founded the

modern scientific classification of plants and animals called taxonomy

- 1769 Georges Cuvier—French naturalist; founded comparative anatomy and was the father of paleontology
- 1791 Michael Faraday—English physicist and chemist; discovered the principles of electromagnetic induction
- 1822 Gregor Mendel—Augustinian monk; father of modern genetics

One thing is clear from history. There has never been any inherent hostility between the Christian worldview and the methods or principles of science proper. Rather, Western civilization, grounded in the biblical worldview, provided the presuppositions that birthed the scientific enterprise in the first place. God was not a science stopper. He was the science starter.

Have there been genuine conflicts in the past between Christian authorities and the ideas of scientists? Of course. Galileo is a prime example. In Galileo's case—as is often the case today—some of the disagreement was on matters of scientific fact, not theology. Scientists disagree with each other all the time. Many opposed the heliocentric view on the merits, even though they were later proved wrong.

Galileo also crossed swords, however, with the reigning philosophical view of his time that seemed to comport with the biblical record: an Aristotelian, geocentric account of the solar system promoted, ironically, by the academy.

The challenge we face today is similar. Currently, though, the inquisition's boot is on the other foot, but the pattern is the same. Now the reigning scientific powers silence opposition for philosophical reasons rather than scientific ones.

The dynamic is the same one that corrupted science in the past. It makes one wonder whether the current views are sound or they're being artificially propped up, once again, by a philosophy.

Why let the reigning powers—secular or religious—dictate what *kind* of answers are acceptable instead of following the facts wherever they lead?

Christianity is not at war with science. It never has been. Cambridge physicist John Polkinghorne sums up the situation this way: "Only in the media, and in popular and polemical scientific writing, does there persist the myth of the light of pure scientific truth confronting the darkness of obscurantist religious error."[19]

Science examines the physical world, fair enough. But it need not be limited to material explanations for what it finds. When truth is at issue, our goal should be to find the best explanation, not just one that fits our philosophy.

Here is a sample dialogue that trades on these ideas:

"Religion has always been at war with science."

> "What's the conflict?" [Columbo #1]

"Religious people think faith is more important than reason."

> **"Do you know how modern science began?"**

"No."

> **"It began in Western Europe. Do you know why?"**

"I have no idea."

> **"Because they believed in a God who made an orderly world that could be discovered through careful observation."**

"I never heard that."

> **"Do you know who the founders of science were and what their beliefs were?"**

"Well, I know about people like Copernicus and Galileo. The church persecuted them because of their scientific beliefs."

"I understand that, but do you know what their *theological* beliefs were?"

"Not really."

"Those two were Christians, along with just about every other one of the founding fathers of modern science."

"No kidding?"

"No kidding. In fact, Isaac Newton wrote more on theology than he did on science. He believed that what he discovered in science would help him understand God better. There was no conflict in Newton's mind between science and religion."

"So where did all this conflict come from?"

"**It came because of the intrusion of a different religion.**"

"Really? Which one?"

"The religion of naturalism."

"Well, that's better than sticking God into the gap."

"Here's what I suggest. **Why not just follow the evidence wherever it leads?** Usually, we'll discover that causes of natural phenomena are going to be natural. No problem. Sometimes, though, the evidence points to an agent, like it does in forensic pathology. Sometimes it might even point to a *supernatural* agent. What's wrong with that?"

"Because that approach will kill science."

"**Well, that's hard to believe since, historically, religion was the science *starter*.** Let me suggest this, though. **How about if we just use the methods of science to find out the truth about our world, whatever it is**—no inquisitions on either side? What do you think?"

No discoveries of science have in any way compromised theism or belief in the supernatural. In fact, what science has discovered about the universe in the last hundred years has made the existence of a divine designer much more probable, not much less probable.[20]

Here is the real issue: Will the scientific community use its fine methodology to follow the truth wherever it leads, or will it try to replay Galileo's inquisition in reverse and use law, politics, and intimidation to silence any opposition to its own modern creation story?

CHAPTER 15

ABORTION: ONLY ONE QUESTION

On the morning of September 11, 2001, two jumbo jets slammed into New York City's World Trade Center towers, another struck the western section of the Pentagon, and a fourth plowed into a field in Pennsylvania when courageous passengers overpowered terrorist pilots.

To put the toll in perspective, on that other "day of infamy"—December 7, 1941—2,335 military personnel lost their lives at Pearl Harbor. On 9/11, though, more than that—2,977 victims—were crushed beneath one million tons of concrete and steel at the World Trade North Tower and South Tower, buried beneath the rubble of the Pentagon, or violently entombed in a meadow in Pennsylvania.

This is old news, of course, but here's something you may not know. The number of human lives snuffed out on 9/11 was less, on average, than the number of children who have died every single day, day after day, for nearly half a century through abortion on American soil.

In the United States alone, 63,459,781 abortions—3,548 a day—have been performed since the Supreme Court legalized abortion on January 22, 1973.[1] That's 21,316 consecutive 9/11 days of death.

It took Hitler twelve years to vaporize six million Jews. It took Americans six years after *Roe v. Wade* to exceed Hitler's Holocaust killing their own unborn children through abortion. That's ten holocausts back-to-back.

At least 388,000 Africans were shipped to North America over the course of two and a half centuries before abolition.[2] Abortion kills that many children—including a disproportionate number of black babies—in 109 days.

Abortion in America has killed nearly as many human beings as all the Allied soldiers, all the Axis armies, and all the civilians from both sides put together who perished in World War II.[3]

> No moral issue, no political issue, no human rights issue has greater significance in the twenty-first century than abortion.

The most dangerous place for a baby to be in the land of the free and the home of the brave is resting in her mother's womb. I want to show you how to make that location a safer place by teaching you how to use precisely placed questions to challenge the morality of the pro-choice view when you have conversations with others.

I focus on the single, decisive, defining issue in the debate when making the pro-life case, an approach I call "Only One Question." Here is how I initiate my plan in conversation.[4]

"Mommy, Can I Kill This?"

The very first set of questions I use in conversations on this issue sets the stage for my larger strategy. Make this your first move, too.

> **"Consider this analogy. Your child comes up behind you while you're working at some task**

and asks, 'Mommy, can I kill *this*?' What is the one question you must ask before you can answer their question?"

"I need to ask them, 'What is it?'"[5]

"Exactly. The reason is obvious. First we have to know what they want to kill before we know if it's okay to kill it. If it's a spider, smash it. If it's their little brother, time for a talk. Does that make sense to you?"

"Sure, so far."

"So let's apply that reasoning to the abortion question using our basic question, 'What is it?' Here's my thinking. **If the unborn is not a human being, then no justification for abortion is *necessary*.**[6] Do what you want. Remove the tissue; have the abortion. Do you agree with that?"

"Of course I do. I'm pro-choice."

"Good. Next step. **However, if the unborn *is* a human being, then no justification for abortion is *adequate*.**"[7]

"Well, I'm not sure about that one. What are you getting at?"

"Fair enough. Let me clarify with another question. Though the answer may seem obvious—and I don't mean to patronize you—play along with me for a moment. Here it is: Do you think it's okay to kill a defenseless human being for the reasons most people give for abortion: because they have a right to privacy or choice, because the human being is too expensive, because they just don't want to take care of him, because he interferes with their career, etc.?"

"Of course not. But a fetus isn't a human."

"We'll get to that in a minute. So in principle, then, you agree with those two general statements I asked you about—that if the unborn is not a human, get the abortion, but if it is a human, killing it wouldn't be right?"

"Well, I guess—so far."

There is nothing complicated or unfair about this approach. All we need to do is answer one simple question: What is the unborn? Yet this is the one question that's almost completely ignored. All the popular wordplay is about the mother: *my* choice, *my* career, *my* money, *my* time, *my* convenience, *my* rights—relativism, full tilt. What actually happens in an abortion is almost completely ignored.

> Abortion involves killing and discarding something that's alive. Whether it's right to take the life of any living thing depends upon what that thing is.

We do not kill defenseless human beings for the reasons most people give for abortion: because we have a right to privacy or choice, because they're too expensive, because we don't want them, even because they remind us of a terrible, traumatic event like rape.

Pushback

These opening questions make progress, but conversations like these do not always go smoothly. Often, there's resistance, so in the following, I've included an extended conversation as a tutorial for two reasons.

First, it provides a general model for how you might navigate resistance on this point. Second, it reinforces our conviction that answering only one question is the key to resolving the moral question of abortion. This dialogue starts with a standard pro-choice challenge:

"Abortion is a private choice between a woman and her doctor."

"Do you mind if I ask you a question? **Do we allow parents to abuse their children if done in privacy or with the consent of their doctor?**"

"Of course not, but that's not fair. Those children are real people."

"I agree. But that shows that the issue isn't really privacy at all but rather whether the unborn is a human being, right?'"

"But many poor women can't afford to raise another child."

"Yes, I understand. **But when kids get too expensive, can we kill them?**"

"Of course not, but aborting a fetus is not the same as killing a kid."

"So once again, the real question is, 'What is the unborn? Is a fetus a human just like a youngster?'"

"Why do you insist on being so simplistic? Killing defenseless human beings is one thing. Aborting a fetus is another."

"But if abortion actually killed a defenseless human being, that would be different, wouldn't it? Again, our question is, 'What is the unborn?'"

"Do you really think a woman should be forced to bring an unwanted child into the world?"

"Many homeless people are unwanted. Can we kill them?"

"But it's not the same."

"That's the issue, then, isn't it? Are they the same? **If the unborn are truly human like the homeless, then we can't just kill them to get them out of the way.** We're back to my first question, 'What is the unborn?'"

"But you still shouldn't force your morality on women."

"I get your point, but would you 'force your morality' on a mother who was physically abusing her two-year-old?"

"Sure, but that's not the same."

"Why not?"

"Because you're assuming the unborn is human, like a two-year-old."

"And you're assuming she's not. I get it. We have a genuine difference of opinion here. But what our conversation shows is that the abortion question is not ultimately about privacy, or economic hardship, or complexity, or not being wanted, or forcing morality. **The real question is, 'What is the unborn?'**"

You might think of other concerns I haven't mentioned. Each can be dispatched with a simple test question, though. Ask, "Would your point work if we were talking about a clear-case example of a human being?" This tactic has a name. We call it "Trotting Out the Toddler." For any reason a person gives to justify abortion, ask if the same reason would justify killing a toddler.

> Notice, at this point I'm not arguing yet that abortion is wrong. I'm simply clarifying—and simplifying—the issue.

I have not made the case that the unborn is a human being. That's coming up. I'm merely pointing out that there's just one issue to resolve, not many. Answering a single question, "What is the unborn?" addresses virtually all the others.

Hopefully you've been somewhat successful in helping your pro-choice friend understand the single, decisive, defining issue in this controversy. It's time for your next step. I started with the strategic foundation of our argument. Next, I want you to see the moral foundation.

Moral Logic

I want you to be crystal clear on the simple moral logic of the pro-life position.[8] It is the ethical bedrock of the view. Here it is:

> Premise 1: It's wrong to intentionally take the life of an innocent human being.
> Premise 2: Abortion intentionally takes the life of an innocent human being.
> Therefore: Abortion is wrong.

Notice a couple of things immediately. First, the form of the argument is right. The conclusion follows naturally from the first two statements. That's easy to see. This, then, is what logicians call a valid argument. So far, so good. If the premises turn out to be true, then it is also a sound argument—that is, completely reliable based on the simple force of logic. But are the premises true? That's the next step.

The first statement seems obviously correct. Few would dispute this commonsense moral notion as a general rule. If you want to be more precise to cover possible exceptions, you could add the phrase "for the reasons most people give to justify abortion." We clearly do not consider killing okay if the victim stands in the way of our careers, is a financial burden, has a physical defect, interferes with our personal freedoms, and so on.

Your initial pushback, then, is going to be about the accuracy of premise two. As we saw, you're going to encounter resistance to the claim that the unborn are bona fide human beings. Our questions, then, are designed to help your friend see that the unborn are (1) alive and growing, (2) distinct from their mothers (i.e., not the mother's body, strictly speaking), and (3) individual human beings.

Here's how that conversation might look, with the pro-choice person initiating the challenge:

"The government shouldn't tell me what I can do with my own body."

> "I think that's generally true, but **can the government say what you can do with your body concerning your two-year-old?**"

"That's different. He's outside my body. We're talking about my uterus. They can't dictate what I do with my uterus any more than they can force me to donate my kidney."

> "I agree with you,[9] but what does that have to do with the pro-life view? [Columbo #1] Do you think pro-lifers are asking you to give up your uterus?"

"No, but they want to tell me what I can do with my uterus."

> "It seems to me there's a misunderstanding here. Let me clarify. Pro-lifers are saying the government should be able to protect a separate human being growing *inside* your body just as it does a separate human being growing *outside* your body."

"But we're talking about my uterus, not a human being like an infant."

> "I thought we were talking about what was *in* your uterus."

"Okay, but that's not a human being."

> "It isn't? **Then what is it?**" [Columbo #1]

"It's just a blob of tissue."

> "Sure, but aren't we all blobs of tissue?"

"That's different."

> "How, exactly?" [Columbo #1]

"We're living people, not just tissue. Anyway, nobody knows."

> "Do you mind if I ask you a few questions about this mysterious thing inside the uterus of a pregnant woman?"

"Go ahead."

> "Is this thing alive?"

"No one really knows when life begins."

> "That wasn't quite the question. I asked if it was alive, not when life begins. So let me ask another way. **Is this unidentified thing inside a pregnant woman's uterus growing?**"

"Yes, it's growing."

> **"How can it be growing if it's not alive?"**

"Hmm . . . Okay, you've made your point. It's alive. It's living tissue, part of my own body, and the government has no say over my tissue growing in my body."

> "I'm sympathetic with that point in principle, but I don't think this tissue that is *in* your body is part of your body, strictly speaking."

"Of course it is."

> "Did you ever watch *CSI*?"

"Sure."

"When the forensic pathologist finds remains of a human body, how do they know which person the remains belong to?"

"They do a matching DNA test."

"Right. If the DNA from the tissue matches the DNA sample from a known individual, then they know the tissue was part of their body."

"Right."

"So if you were pregnant, and someone took a DNA test of the piece of tissue growing in your uterus, would its DNA match your DNA?"

"Well . . . no."

"Right. Then whatever is growing *inside* your body when you're pregnant is not part of *your* body, is it? **It has different DNA, so it must be tissue from a different body.** Does that make sense to you?"

"I guess so."

"So here's the next question: **What kind of foreign thing would be growing inside your uterus if you were pregnant.**"

"I can't say for sure."

"Well, let's go back to *CSI* again. If forensic pathologists found a piece of tissue at a crime scene, how would they know if that tissue came from a human being or from some other creature?"

"I guess they'd do another DNA test."

"Right, but this test isn't looking to identify a certain individual, but rather a certain *kind* of individual—maybe a human or maybe some other organism, right?"

"Okay."

"So if we took a piece of tissue from that living thing growing in your uterus that is not you but something else, what kind of DNA do you think it would have?"

"I don't know. I'm not a scientist."

"I don't think you need to be a scientist to know the answer to this question. Let me ask it another way. What kinds of things naturally and predictably grow inside a pregnant woman's uterus?"

"Well, offspring."

"Good. So we agree on that. **Now, if there's an 'offspring' growing in a woman's uterus, what kind of offspring do you think it is?**"

"I guess it would be a human offspring. But that doesn't mean it's a human being. After all, the unborn doesn't look like a human being."

"Sure she does. She looks exactly the way all human beings look at that stage of development. Look at your baby pictures, then look at your high school graduation pictures, then look at you now. Do you look the same?"

"Of course not."

"Right. Do you see the point? Living things never look the same at one stage of development as they do at another, do they?"

"But that's different."

"Okay, let me put it another way. If you had a cat that was pregnant, what kind of fetus would it be carrying?"

"A cat fetus, I guess."

"Right."

"But an acorn is not an oak."

"What is it, then?"

"It's a seed."

"Agreed. **What kind of seed?**"

"An oak seed."

"Right. An acorn is an oak in the seed stage, and a full-grown tree is an oak in a mature stage. But they're both oaks, right?"

"But the unborn is just a zygote, or a fetus, or whatever."

"Right, **but what *kind* of zygote, or fetus, or whatever?**"

"Human?"

"Exactly. Do living things change from one kind of being into another over time or do they stay themselves?"

"Well, I guess they stay the same thing from beginning to end."

"Right. So it looks like we know a lot about what's growing inside a pregnant woman's uterus, don't we? It's not merely her tissue, but her human offspring. Someone else—an unborn human being—is in there at varying stages of development. So now that we've solved that mystery, let me take this a step further. **Do you think the government should be allowed to protect your offspring when the child is outside your body but not when he's inside your body?**"

"Yes, I do."

"Tell me, why should the government be allowed to protect your offspring on the outside of your body—child abuse and stuff like that?"

"Because children are valuable."

"Right, I agree. But that creates a problem for you now, doesn't it?"

"How?"

"Well, if your children are valuable outside your body—say, right after they're born—why aren't those same children valuable just a couple of inches away, hidden inside your body? Why does the mere location of your child make any difference to the value of your child?"

You see how this works. Of course, those who have strong pro-choice convictions are not likely to change their minds immediately, but your tactical questions have forced them to think about the facts that matter instead of parrying with rhetoric that simply obscures the real issue.

At this point, you may encounter another dodge. Since you've clearly shown that abortion kills an actual human being (the second step of our argument), the only recourse left for the pro-choice person is to challenge the first line of our moral logic: it's wrong to intentionally take the life of an innocent human being.

The "Personhood" Shell Game

Here's the common counter: it's not really wrong to kill a human being. It's only wrong to kill a human person, and the unborn are not real persons. They're potential persons, or possible persons, or future persons, or whatever, but not the kind of humans who deserve protection.

At this point you must, without exception, ask this question: "What's the difference?"[10] What is the difference between a disposable human being and a valuable human person? Make clear to them it's absolutely essential they have an answer to this question.[11] Here's why.

Those who offer this personhood qualifier have divided the human race into two distinct categories—human persons and human nonpersons. Those in the first group have the full protection of law. Those in the second group can be killed with impunity for virtually any reason, sometimes even with government—i.e., taxpayer—financing.

> Considering the consequences of this divide, those who split humanity into persons and nonpersons must be clear on which human beings are on one side of that line and which are on the other.

Some may answer by offering a list of attributes they think are necessary to qualify as a valuable human being—certain characteristics or capabilities that distinguish the valuable people from expendable human nonpersons. These lists vary in content, of course, with different people championing different criteria.

At this point, more questions are necessary: "Where did you get the list? Who gets to decide what qualities are on the list? Who gets to decide which humans qualify for protection and which do not? What qualities are necessary to transform a mere human into a valuable, protected person? What about lists that exclude black people, or Jews, or Serb Muslims, or Gypsies, or the mentally defective, or members of the LGBTQ community—all examples of 'human nonpersons' of the past? What makes one person's list better than any other?"

You see my point. The personhood disqualifier has a dark past. It's nothing more than a crafty shell game, legal language meant to disqualify some bona fide members of the human family from being protected members of the human community. It's a convenient scheme for one group to stigmatize another group when it's in the first group's interest to disenfranchise the second.

This ruse has been tried before, and history is strewn with the wreckage—from the Dred Scott decision of 1857 declaring black slaves chattel property to the "Final Solution" when the Third Reich decreed that millions of humans had no inherent right to live and were eliminated as *lebensunwertes Leben*—"Life unworthy of life."

The SLED Test

The characteristics disqualifying the unborn's value usually fall into one of four categories: size or physical appearance (the unborn doesn't look like a person), level of development (the unborn lacks the abilities real persons have), environment (the unborn isn't located in the same place as real persons—they're inside the mother, not outside), or degree of dependency (the unborn is not "viable"—he or she is too physically dependent on others to be a person).

This list of distinctions, commonly known as the "SLED Test,"[12] is riddled with difficulties since each qualifier ends up disqualifying clear-case examples of valuable human beings.

1. Size or Physical Appearance: The Unborn Doesn't Look Like a Person. Sometimes human bodies look familiar, healthy, and normal; other times they look odd and unusual. In rare cases—and each of us has seen them—the body looks all wrong, yet the valuable human being is still there.

The movie *The Elephant Man* was a remarkable chronicle of the life of Joseph Merrick (called "John" in the film), a human being grotesquely misshapen from birth. He was caged, whipped, and treated like an animal until a compassionate doctor took him under his care.

A scene from that film is etched into my memory. One night, Merrick ventures out of the hospital on his own, cloaked and hooded to hide his disfigurement. A young child catches a glimpse of his face, however, and screams. Merrick begins to run. Men who heard the screams take up the chase. As he runs faster, weaving in and out of the throng, his hood comes off, exposing his horrible face. There are more screams, and more bystanders join the pursuit. No one knows what crime has been committed, only that a hideous creature has been put to flight.

The mob, with walking sticks and fists upraised, corners the Elephant Man, intent on destroying the monster. In a moment of desperation, Merrick faces his tormentors and cries out, "I am not an animal. I . . . am a human being."

The crowd goes silent and hovers over him for one perilous moment. Then, as his words sink in, each person turns away in shame, leaving Merrick trembling in the shadows.

Joseph Merrick, the Elephant Man, was a human being, just like you and me. So are millions of others who are odd, misshapen, and severely handicapped. So are the unborn. Humans are valuable even if their physical bodies are so distorted or so small they are unrecognizable.

Human worth transcends physical appearance—skin color, size, disfigurements, handicaps—because physical form is irrelevant to significance. Therefore, "not looking right" cannot disqualify any human being from value. Otherwise, there's no defense against racism and ethnic cleansing.

2. Level of Development: The Unborn Lacks the Abilities Real Persons Have. A powerful example of the foolishness of this criterion came from radio talk show host Dennis Prager, who had a fascinating, on-air conversation with a blind man who said he was sometimes mistreated because of his handicap.

Dennis was appalled. "Because you've lost your sight, are you any less who you are?" he asked.

"No," the caller answered.

"Of course not. Wouldn't you still be you?"

"Sure."

"It's ridiculous for anyone to think," Dennis concluded, "that a blind person is any less a person than someone who can see."[13]

Dennis could have taken his reflection further. If a person is no less himself for his loss of sight, what if he lost his ability to speak or even think clearly? Would he be any less himself? If he were smaller in stature, or weighed only a pound, or even a few ounces, like some preemies, or his body were terribly misshapen like Joseph Merrick's, would he be less valuable as a human being?

> So here is the question: How many body parts or abilities can I lose or alter and still be myself? No matter how many pieces I'm missing, as long as I'm still alive, I'll still be me.

In 1995, *Superman* actor Christopher Reeve was thrown from a horse and paralyzed. Neck broken, immobilized, unable to breathe without a machine, Reeve said to his wife, Dana, "Maybe we should let me go."

"You're still you," Dana said, "and I love you."[14] Reeve survived nine more years. When he wrote his autobiography, he titled it *Still Me.*

Do human beings become disposable simply because they can't do what others can do? Do stronger, more capable, more intelligent people have more rights than others? If a human being's value is determined by his abilities—by what he can or can't do—then all those who are handicapped are in danger. Only the physically perfect are safe.

3. Environment: The Unborn Isn't Located in the Same Place as Real Persons. I'm thinking of a little girl named Rachel. Her mother, a dear friend of mine, gave birth to baby Rachel prematurely at twenty-four weeks, in the middle of her second trimester. On the day of her birth, Rachel weighed one pound, nine ounces, but she dropped to just under a pound soon after. She was so small she could rest in the palm of her daddy's hand. She was a tiny, living, human being.

Doctors worked heroically to save Rachel's life because she was vulnerable and valuable. However, if this same little girl—the very same Rachel—had been inches away, resting inside her mother's womb, she could have been legally destroyed by the same doctors through abortion.

Here is the question: If it's homicide to kill baby Rachel resting in her mother's arms simply because she's unwanted (or for any other reason, for that matter), how can it be right to kill the same baby Rachel for the same reasons at exactly the same stage of development while resting inside her mother's womb?

If this rejoinder is sound, then minimally all mid- to late-term abortions (Rachel's birth age) are wrong because the liberty to kill the baby is based merely on her location, and changing locations is morally trivial. Clearly, our environment can't be the deciding factor. Environment—where you are—has no bearing on who you are.

4. Degree of Dependency: The Unborn Is Too Physically Dependent on Others to Be a Person. Some devalue unborn human beings because they're not "viable." They can't survive on their own outside the womb. Yet no baby is "viable" in that sense, since all depend on their mothers for feeding—whether via blood (an umbilical cord), breast, or bottle—and for protective care.

Human beings may be dependent on others for survival, but they are not dependent on others for value. Otherwise, all who rely on kidney machines, ventilators, or even full-time nursing care are disposable as nonpersons.

If degree of dependency determines worth, all people who are physically dependent on others are at risk. If reliance on an external source for survival cancels value, then no moral principle protects the weak and vulnerable from the strong and powerful.

It turns out there is no meaningful moral difference between a human being and a human person. All attempts to make this distinction end in disaster. Your probing questions press that point.

Remember our basic strategy: one, the unborn is alive; two, the unborn is not Mom, but a separate, individual being; and three, the unborn is a human being.

One Final Question

Here is your parting salvo. Ask, **"Were you ever an unborn child?"**

It doesn't seem to make sense to say anyone was once a sperm or an egg because neither by itself is a human being. Does it make sense, though, to talk about the way we were before we were born?

"Did you turn in your mother's womb or kick when you were startled by a loud noise? Did you suck your thumb? Were those your experiences or someone else's? If you were once the unborn child your mother carried, then you must accept an undeniable truth: killing that child through abortion would have killed you. Not a potential you. Not a possible you. Not a future you. Abortion would have killed *you*."

And so the moral logic stands. You have shown:

- The unborn is a living being, separate from her mother.
- The kind of being she happens to be is human.
- Humans are valuable in themselves and not for what they look like, for what they can do, for where they're located, or for lack of dependency on others.
- Abortion takes the life of a valuable, innocent human being without proper justification.
- Therefore, abortion is terribly wrong.

And you did it all with questions.

CHAPTER 16

ABORTION: BEYOND THE BASICS

Answering only one question clarifies the ethical stakes regarding abortion and, I think, reasonably dispatches any attempt to defend it morally. There is a difference, though, between answering a challenge and convincing a person. Facts alone frequently are not persuasive. The hunger for autonomy—often sanitized with noble-sounding rhetoric—overwhelms good thinking.

Since this controversy takes twists and turns in conversations on the street, in this chapter I've sketched out dialogues modeling responses to variations you'll likely encounter. I conclude with a powerful scriptural approach to answer any who identify as Bible-believing Christians yet still defend abortion.

You'll notice, by the way, that in each of these sample exchanges, my general strategy for responding to any justification for abortion is to trade on the moral logic of the pro-life view we've just covered. I also continue to emphasize—often implicitly—the single, decisive question foundational to the issue: What is the unborn?

First, though, a word about the wordplay you'll encounter.

Deadly Word Games

Solomon said, "Death and life are in the power of the tongue."[1] Another famous saying goes, "When words lose their meanings, people lose their lives." Language, carefully chosen, can make evil look good and vice seem like virtue—with drastic consequences.

Case in point. Years ago, I read Robert J. Lifton's *The Nazi Doctors: Medical Killing and the Psychology of Genocide*, which seeks to answer how doctors dedicated to saving life could be persuaded to destroy life on a massive scale. The Nazis succeeded by using language.

Lifton describes what he calls "killing as a therapeutic imperative,"[2] or, simply, killing in the name of healing. When killing is characterized as healing of any kind, Lifton argues—whether individual healing, social well-being, or cultural cleansing—then that civilization is on the threshold of indescribable evil.

In the Third Reich, that shift was abetted by a shift in language. Early on, child euthanasia was carried out by "The Children's Specialty Department."[3] Transportation shuttling toddlers to the thirty-odd killing centers was provided by "The Common Welfare Ambulance Service."[4] The elderly were dispatched via "The Reich Work Group of Sanatoriums and Nursing Homes."[5] The government referred to such measures as "healing" and "therapy." Later, the Germans called genocide on a monumental scale *die Endlösung*, the "Final Solution."

> It is risky to invoke a horrid period of human history to make a contemporary moral point. The impulse is strong to dismiss any such comparison as extreme. Nevertheless, with abortion the parallel fits.

Note the language now in play. Abortion *saves a child* from future physical abuse. Abortion *rescues a baby* with Down syndrome (for example) from an unhappy life. Abortion *protects a mother* from postpartum suicidal thoughts or from the painful recollections of rape. Abortion, killing an unborn child, is compassionate. It's an act of mercy, of love, of healing—a proper means to a noble end. Killing brings healing—in Lifton's words, killing as "therapeutic imperative."

Be alert to this trend. You will encounter this kind of rhetorical sleight of hand in virtually every conversation you have with your pro-choice friends. They're not consciously justifying vice, of course. Instead, they have been bewitched by the words. Language is the coin of the realm.

A host of examples trade on this trend of grounding the liberty to kill in a "greater good." Sometimes the attempt is subtle, however. A powerful—and therefore, persuasive—example is the simple appeal to personal autonomy. Abortion liberties are good since they secure freedom for a woman to do what she wants with her own body.

"My Body, My Choice"

Every pro-life advocate confronts the bodily autonomy argument sooner or later. The ploy is so pervasive and so inherently compelling, it's important to understand it and learn how to engage it graciously but persuasively.

Remember, our goal is not to win arguments but to change minds—and, therefore, to save lives. However, we need to know the core problems with a claim before we can convert those ideas into useful dialogues that expose the flaw, so let's start there. The problems are straightforward and reasonably obvious.

First, it's simply not true that people have the right to do whatever they want with their own bodies. The law routinely and appropriately straps all kinds of restrictions on what we can do and where we can go. This restraint on our personal liberties is so self-evidently proper, we generally comply without complaint since we understand how the social contract works.

Second—and we covered this in the last chapter—the unborn is not the mother's body. It is another body she is producing inside of her, a distinct human being who is the mother's own unborn child.

Third, no woman—or anyone, for that matter—has the right

to kill another human being because that individual interferes—even drastically—with her plans or pursuits. Human lives have value greater than any individual's right to her private projects. The basic principle of human equality dictates that no one should be deprived of the right to life for the reasons people give for abortion.

Here is a sample conversation addressing the first issue:[6]

"It's my body, so it's my choice."

> "Well, I'm committed to individual liberty, too, but I think you may be missing something. Can you give me a little more clarity on what you mean?" [Columbo #1]

"Sure. It's simple. I get to do what I want with my body. It belongs to me, not to you, and not to the government. Getting an abortion, then, is my choice and no one else's. I don't tell you what to do with your body; you shouldn't tell me what to do with mine. What's confusing about that?"

> "Got it. **But do you really think that principle *always* applies?** I mean, there are lots of laws telling both of us what to do with our bodies: traffic laws, trespassing laws, airport laws, laws against assault—stuff like that. You're not against those, are you?" [Columbo #1]

"Of course not. But abortion is different."

> "Do you mind if I ask you another question?"

"Go ahead."

> **"If you had a two-year-old daughter, and you wanted to take a vacation with your husband, could you leave your daughter at home alone while you went to Tahiti since you can do whatever you want with your own body?"**

"That's different."

"How so?"

"Because that's my baby, and she's dependent on me."

"Right. So it sounds to me like you're saying that *some* obligations you have toward others—in this case, your own child—restrict what you can do with your body. Strictly speaking, then, it's not entirely accurate to say you have a right to do whatever you want with your own body. Is that fair?"

"Yes, but like I said, abortion is different."

"I get your point, but just so I'm clear, it now looks like you *don't* think a woman can do *whatever* she wants with her own body, do you?"

"No, I guess not."

"So sometimes restrictions on a person's freedom are okay, right?"

"I see your point."

"Great. We're agreed on that. With abortion, though, you think you should be free to make your own choices without the government interfering, right?"

"Exactly."

My goal at this juncture is simple. I want the pro-choice person to admit it's completely acceptable to limit individual freedom in certain situations. That's all. Though your own conversations will vary from this example, when this basic issue comes up, shoot for the same target initially. Nothing complicated. Nothing even controversial, in most cases, once the point is clarified. Even so, you're beginning to chip away at a core complaint against the pro-life view. That's progress.

> Once you get agreement that no woman is free to do *whatever* she wants with her body, your next questions will begin to clarify the kinds of restrictions that are appropriate—restrictions even the pro-choice person will often admit are proper.

On the street, the "my body, my choice" challenge comes in two different forms, requiring two different approaches. The first form is more severe and therefore easier to deal with, since most people—even those who favor abortion—do not want to appear extreme. Both forms, however, hold that even if the unborn is a valuable human being, just like you and me, the mother's right to end her pregnancy still prevails.

The "sovereign zone" view—the more extreme option—treats personal autonomy as inviolable when it comes to pregnancy.[7] A woman has an absolute right to do whatever she wants with anything that's inside her body. No need to convince her that the child is not her body; she already knows, and it doesn't matter. No need to convince her that the child is a fully valuable human being; on this view, that doesn't matter, either.

This position is over the top, as I said, and your questions are geared to show just how extreme the view is. Here's how this approach might look:

> "So you're not against any abortion, no matter what the reason, if the woman wants it, right?" [Columbo #1]

"Right."

> "In China, women abort female children all the time because they don't want girls; they want boys. If that's what the woman wants, you're okay with that?"

"Well . . . that makes me a bit uncomfortable, but if that's what she wants, then it's her choice."

"What if a white woman discovered she had a mixed-race fetus and wanted a completely white baby? Choosing abortion for that reason would be no problem for you?"

"I never thought of that. . . ."

"Or if scientists discovered a gay gene, a woman could have an abortion so she wouldn't have a gay kid? **Is it okay with you if a mother wants to abort her child because he's gay?**"

"That's a hard one."

"But if a woman has absolute control over her pregnancy, as you said, then aborting a child because he's gay should be legal according to you, right?"

"I guess it would be."

"Some moms take drugs when they're pregnant, and that hurts their babies, sometimes even causing birth defects. You don't object to that?"

"Well, I object, but ultimately it's her right."

"Even if it harms her baby?"

"Yes."

"Okay, thanks for making your view clear."

Like I said, extreme. Notice, your questions not only make this person's view clear to you, they also make it crystal clear to her. Consequently, most who are in favor of abortion—when pressed—will not go this far. Too uncomfortable. They might defect to the human-but-not-a-person approach, and we've already covered that move. If they do, though, that's progress. Remember, we're gardening.

> Using clear counterexamples is a powerful way to show someone the logical consequences of his view—the bullet he has to bite—if he continues to press his justification for abortion.

The second form of the "my body, my choice" challenge is the "right to refuse" argument, which says that no woman should be forced to use her body as a life support system for someone else, even if it would save that person's life.

Philosopher Judith Jarvis Thompson popularized this approach with her famous "violinist" argument.[8] It would be wrong, Thompson argues, to surgically attach a woman against her will to a world-class violinist for nine months in order to keep him alive. Such coercion—a parallel to unwanted pregnancy, according to Thompson—is beyond the pale.

This basic argument has variations—including its application to rape, which is obviously nonconsensual—and the challenge has powerful intuitive appeal. It's deeply flawed in a number of ways, though,[9] and there's a fairly straightforward way to address the objections without getting overly philosophical.

First, though, an insight.

Analogies like Thompson's suggest that when a mother doesn't volunteer to be pregnant, she has no more responsibility for her child than she has for a stranger. But even though we don't choose our family members, that doesn't mean we have no obligations toward them. Courts still prosecute negligent parents, and deadbeat dads are still forced to support children they never wanted.[10]

> Pregnancy is not the thing that restrains a woman's liberty. Motherhood does that, and motherhood does not end with the baby's birth. A newborn child makes a greater demand on a woman than an unborn one. If a mother, through abortion, can deny her own child what's necessary for life *before* he's born, how can she be forced to provide the same necessities *after* he's born?

Tactically, though, the most powerful point to make with this second form of the autonomy argument is that there is a difference between the right to refuse to help another and the right to kill him.

With abortion, a mother does not merely decline to help by passively withholding aid (as in the violinist illustration). She actively kills another human being—her own child, in this case. Here's how the discussion might look for someone offering the "right to refuse" argument:

"No one should be forced to donate a kidney or even her time and energy to help someone else if she doesn't want to."

"So, if you encountered a sick patient who needed your kidney to survive, you could help if you wanted to, but you shouldn't be forced to help, right?" [Columbo #1]

"Right."

"Got it. So, if you were faced with a circumstance like that, what would your options be?"

"I could choose to help the person if I wanted or not help them, obviously. It's my choice."

"But there's another option, isn't there?"

"What's that?

"You could kill him. That would remove the problem, wouldn't it?"

"That's ridiculous!"

"Of course it is. But isn't that the option you face in abortion?"

"What do you mean?"

"Well, you could choose to help the baby in your womb by carrying it to term like you might help the person who needs your kidney."

"Right."

"But if you're pregnant, you can't choose *not* to help, can you?"

"Why not?"

"Because you can't just walk away from a pregnancy. That's not one of your options. What can you do instead?"

"I can have an abortion."

"Right, and what does abortion do?"

"Well, it kills the fetus."

"Exactly. Do you know how abortion kills a fetus?"

"Not really."

"Through dismemberment, lethal injection, or suffocation using chemicals."

"I didn't know that."

"If you choose abortion, then, you're choosing to kill the baby that way. So your options are either to carry or to kill. That's all. No walking away. No merely 'refusing' to help. Can you think of any other alternative?"

"Not at the moment."

"So, on your view, a woman has a right to refuse to help if she wants. I get that. But why should she have the right to kill someone she doesn't want to help?"

There is another path you might pursue in conversations on the issue on abortion. It's called the "equal rights argument," promoted by Steve Wagner of Justice for All[11] and Josh Brahm of the Equal Rights Institute.[12]

The pro-choice rationale is based broadly on an appeal to rights we share equally as humans. If all people possess basic rights, humans must each have some quality that entitles them to those rights—rights that cannot be denied based on superficial differences like gender, race, sexual orientation, national origin, and so on.

Here is the question for our pro-choice friends: What is that quality? What is the only thing we share equally that gives us equal human rights?[13] The one thing we all have that other creatures lack is our shared humanity. Yet, if all humans have those rights, then unborn humans do, too. Being pro-life, then, reflects a consistent commitment to universal human rights.

Here's how that conversation might look:

> **"In general, are you committed to the idea of human rights and human equality?"**

"Of course."

> **"So, you think we all have an equal right to be protected from violence, right?"**

"Absolutely."

> "Gay people, too?"

"Are you kidding?"

> "No, I'm just trying to use clear-case examples to establish a principle I think we both agree on. So, gay people. Black people? Handicapped people? Trans people? Unwanted homeless people? Noisy infants with dirty diapers?"

"Yes, on all, of course."

> "I completely agree. Now this next one may seem a little silly, but stay with me. What about opossums? Do they have the same equal right to life as all humans?"

"You mean the animal? Well, I don't think people should go around killing opossums just for fun."

> **"Neither do I, but I'm asking if they have the *same* right to life as other humans."**

"No, of course not."

"Why? **What do we all have in common that's different from an opossum—or any other creature, for that matter?**"

"We're humans, and all humans should have equal rights."

"So, all those groups I mentioned are members of what you might call the 'equal rights community.'"

"Sure."

"**Okay. What about the same human beings— black or white, gay or straight, handicapped or healthy, wanted or unwanted—*before* they're born?**"

"That's completely different. That's why I'm pro-choice."

"Maybe we can go back to that question of why you think all people have equal rights. You must think there's something we all share equally that makes us equal. What do you think that is?"

"Well, maybe it's because those who are already born are self-aware."

"So are opossums."

"I mean humans who are self-aware, not animals."

"A newborn is human, but not self-aware, yet I know you're not saying infants don't have an equal right to be protected from violence."

"Of course not."

"So, self-awareness can't be the thing that gives us equal rights. We're back to the same question, then: **What do all of us share that gives us equal rights, even though we're so different, with different abilities and physical characteristics?**"

"I can't explain it."

"Would you like to hear what I think all humans share equally that gives them an equal right to life."

"Sure, why not."

"**How about this: the one thing we share equally is our human nature. Therefore, our shared humanity is the valuable thing that gives us human rights.** That's why they call them 'human rights,' after all. Does that make sense to you?"

"I never thought of that."

"It's why racism and sexism are wrong, because these things deprive people of rights based on differences that don't matter to their value."

"I agree."

"Good. **But isn't human nature the same thing unborn humans have, too?**"

Remember, your objectives when dealing with the "my body, my choice" challenge is to use questions to show that even the pro-choice person understands (1) no one has an unlimited right to do what they want with their body, (2) the unborn is not the mother's body but her own child growing inside her body, and (3) no one should be killed—deprived of his equal right to life—in order to secure any personal, individual liberty.

Here is one more short conversation that will help you parry a common dismissal:

"You're a guy. You don't have a uterus."

"True enough, but I'm not clear what difference that makes." [Columbo #1. Have them spell out their specific concern.]

"Since you don't have to deal with an unwanted pregnancy, then what a woman does with hers is none of your business."[14]

"That confuses me. **In a sentence, why do you think I object to abortion?**"

"Well, you say it kills a baby."

"Right. So if abortion actually does kill a baby, then why would it matter if a man or a woman objected?"

"I don't get it."

"Would you object if I was abusing my wife?"

"Of course!"

"But you're not married to her. I am."

"That's irrelevant. If you're hurting someone else, that's wrong. It doesn't matter who objects."

"My point exactly."

The Bible and Abortion: Little John and Tiny Jesus

Sometimes you'll be talking with a person who is pro-choice but also self-identifies as a Christian. Though I don't usually bring the Bible up during discussions about abortion—not a compelling strategy with nonbelievers, usually—in this case, I think it's a good idea. Choosing the right passage is critical, though. Psalms aren't that helpful. They're poetry. There's a better biblical approach.

Scripture does not address abortion directly. Rather, it's subsumed under a broader biblical injunction. The sixth commandment says simply, "You shall not murder" (Ex. 20:13). It mirrors a directive going back almost to the beginning that is itself grounded in a truth found in the very first chapter of the Bible.

After the flood, God tells Noah, "Whoever sheds man's blood, by man his blood shall be shed, for in the image of God He made man" (Gen. 9:6). Twice in Genesis 1, God declares that humans bear his image (vv. 26–27). Because human beings bear God's image, any destruction of a human being deserves the severest penalty.

Here is our question regarding abortion: Are unborn human beings image bearers in the same sense God is referring to in Genesis 9:6? Are they protected under the sixth commandment, thus making abortion an act of homicide? Are the preborn the same kind of living beings as those who have already been born? Put another way, in God's eyes, are humans before birth the very same valuable individuals they are after they are born?

It does no good, by the way, to dismiss the value of preborn humans by labeling them "fetuses," or "zygotes," or "blobs of tissue." First, you and I are also "blobs of tissue," after a fashion. Second, like the word *adolescent*, the other terms are purely human inventions marking stages of biological development. Embryology—and common sense—tells us that the very same individual is present at each stage, regardless of the arbitrary terms we use to distinguish the stages.

Some will be surprised to know that Scripture itself gives a definitive answer to our question above in a passage that is clear, unambiguous, and decisive. Luke 1 records a remarkable exchange between Mary and her cousin Elizabeth, John the Baptist's mother, soon after Mary conceives Jesus by the Holy Spirit. "When Elizabeth heard Mary's greeting, *the baby* leaped in her womb; and Elizabeth was filled with the Holy Spirit. And she cried out with a loud voice and said, 'Blessed are you among women, and blessed is *the fruit of your womb*! And how has it happened to me, that *the mother of my Lord* would come to me? For behold, when the sound of your greeting reached my ears, *the baby* leaped in my womb for joy'" (vv. 41–44).

Note, this meeting took place when Elizabeth was in her late second trimester with John, and Mary was in her early first trimester with Jesus. Recall also that in Luke 1:15 we learned that John himself would be filled with the Holy Spirit while yet in his mother's womb, and this passage marks that prophecy's fulfillment.

Clearly, John the "fetus" was filled with the Holy Spirit and leaped with joy in the presence of the "embryo," Jesus the Lord.

So here is our question again, now applied specifically to the prophet and the Savior: Were John the Baptist and Jesus their same selves before they were born as they were after they were born? Clearly the biblical answer is yes. Had Mary and Elizabeth chosen abortion, they would have killed Jesus and John—not a potential or possible or future Jesus and John, but Jesus and John themselves.

The sixth commandment forbids murder. Murder is the willful killing of an innocent human being, an individual made in the image of God. Does abortion do this? According to what we learn in the Bible, yes, it does. Abortion, then—in God's eyes—is murder. No Christian should condone it. No Christian should participate in it. Every Christian should condemn it.[15]

Having a baby under any circumstance is a challenge, but especially so when the pregnancy is unplanned or the result of a traumatic experience. Even so, these complications do not change the basic biblical calculus. Abortion violates the sixth commandment.

Here is how you might make that point when talking with a Bible-believing Christian who defends abortion:

> **"Do you think God has an opinion on abortion?"**

"I don't know. I don't think the Bible ever talks about abortion."

>> "You're right. It never mentions it directly, but it doesn't mention child abuse directly, either, and I know you're convinced God doesn't approve of that."

"Of course."

>> "If I could show you clearly, then, that from God's perspective an unborn human is the very same individual before he is born as after he is born, would that change your view?"

"I don't know."

> "Let me clarify my question. For the moment, I'm just asking about your view of the Bible. **If God's Word were clear on this issue—and I'm not saying it is, at this point, but if it were— would that be enough for you to change your mind on abortion?**"

"Well, I don't think the Bible is clear."

> "I understand, but that's a different issue. My question for now is, if it were clearly against abortion, would that be enough to change your mind?"

If, at this point, your Christian friend is not committed to following God's Word, then you're facing a different problem, and it might be fair to press that issue further—using questions, of course. If they're open to the Bible's counsel, though, then move forward using Scripture so God's Word makes the point for you:

> "Do you remember early in the Gospel of Luke where Mary—who had just conceived Jesus—visits her cousin Elizabeth, who is pregnant with John the Baptist?"

"Yes, I remember a little bit about it."

> "**Good. Let's look together at that passage. Remember what we're trying to figure out here, though: Is a baby before he's born the same individual as after he's born?**"

"Got it."

> "**If so, then in God's eyes, killing the baby before birth through abortion would be no different from killing the same baby after he's born**—which means the sixth commandment,

'Do not murder,' would apply in both cases. That's what we're trying to figure out from God's Word. Okay?"

"Right."

"Would you please read this passage aloud for me so we can follow it together? [She reads Luke 1:41–44.] How would you describe, in your own words, what's happening here?"

"Well, Elizabeth hears Mary's voice, and her baby jumps for joy inside her."

"Right. I'm glad you used the word 'baby,' since that's the same word Luke uses. Who was this baby who jumped for joy in Elizabeth's womb?"

"John, I guess."

"Exactly. How far along was Elizabeth in her pregnancy?"

"Sixth months?"

"Right. **So, it looks like the Bible is clear that the second trimester unborn baby inside Elizabeth's womb was John the Baptist himself. Is that fair?**"

"I guess."

"Okay. Here's another question. According to this Bible passage, why did John jump for joy while still in his mother's womb?"

"Because Mary was there?"

"Yes, but why would that be significant to John? **How does Elizabeth describe Mary in verse 43?**"

"The mother of my Lord.'"

"Who would her 'Lord' be?"

"Jesus?"

"Exactly. So what God's Word seems to be telling us is that John the Baptist jumped with joy in the presence of Jesus when John was a fetus and Jesus was a embryo. Is that a fair reading?"[16]

"Okay."

"So if either Mary or Elizabeth had an abortion, who would they have killed?"

"They would have killed Jesus or John."

"Right, which would have violated the sixth commandment."

As you have probably noticed, these conversations often overlap in content. That's because we're using the same underlying strategy in each case—the moral logic of the pro-life position along with a focus on the central question, "What is the unborn?" Most pro-choice challenges can be addressed by using questions to weave those basic concepts into the particulars of your individual conversation.

Here is the heart of our argument: an unplanned pregnancy is really an unplanned human being. All euphemisms aside, the simple fact is that abortion kills a valuable member of the human race who has been denied full membership to the human community.

CHAPTER 17

MARRIAGE, SEX, GENDER, AND COMMON SENSE

Lately, I've been mystified and distressed by a trend I've seen with many who identify as Christian, yet who seem to effortlessly embrace ideas completely at odds with a biblical understanding of reality.

These more "progressive" Christians tend to be comfortable with gender fluidity, in favor of same-sex marriage, supportive of alternative sexualities like homosexuality or bisexuality, and sexually active themselves as single persons.

I am distressed because they have fallen into a trap Paul warns about: "See to it that no one takes you captive through philosophy and empty deception, according to the tradition of men . . . rather than according to Christ" (Col. 2:8). Instead of having their minds tutored by Jesus, these Christians have been wooed and won over by the ideas of the street.

I am mystified because there is no good biblical reason for faltering when facing any of these issues. There is no scriptural ambiguity on these matters, so there is no real cause for confusion. Why, then, are many who claim to be Christians foundering on fundamentals with such regularity? Two reasons come to mind.

First, it's clear that many Christians are untutored in the basics. To them, Christianity is simply about believing in Jesus in some vague sense, being nice, and loving people in a can't-we-all-just-get-along kind of way. That's where their theology begins, and that's where it ends. Second, many believers—especially among the younger generation, sadly—seem to care more about what their friends think of them than about what Jesus thinks of them.

Each of these failings is dangerous on its own. In combination, they are spiritually deadly.

Regarding the first, an encouragement. Getting clear on the truth is not complicated. Scripture speaks clearly on the aforementioned concerns. But what's more: no divine insight is even necessary. Common sense is all you need to figure out what's been obvious to most of the world on these topics until just recently. At the moment, of course, the world is confused. That does not mean you need to be confused.

Regarding the second, a warning. It's hard to imagine topics more emotionally charged right now than gender, marriage, and sex. Two factors fan the flames.

For one, the ethic that dominates the street like an occupying force is expressive individualism—sloganized simply as "You do you."[1] These so-called "pelvic issues" are at ground zero in the fight for unrestrained personal autonomy. The pressure to conform is intense, battering young and old alike. Cross swords on these concerns at your peril. Family relationships are on the line. Friendships are on the line. Even careers are on the line.

The struggle, though, is not just against flesh and blood (Eph. 6:11–12). A spiritual scheme is also in play,[2] a plot hatched by forces of darkness in heavenly places intent on corrupting God's good design for human flourishing—a design he established in the beginning. Gender, marriage, and sex are central to that purpose. Sabotage those, and God's image bearers suffer ruin.

> The visceral commitment to these ideas is so intense, the spiritual forces behind them so powerful, that fierce opposition awaits you if you don't toe the line. Be ready for vigorous pushback and aggressive hostility when you side with God on these issues.

Our task is simple: we speak the truth as clearly, graciously, and persuasively as possible. Then—when we have said what we're able to say and done what we're able to do—we stand. We stand firm for what is true, even in the face of hostile opposition, even when we cannot persuade otherwise.

The rest of this chapter will help you with that task.

Silent Christ

I want you to think, for a moment, about what we can learn from Jesus' teaching on homosexuality, sex, and gender. I know what you're probably thinking. *What teaching? Jesus never said anything about homosexuality, sex, and gender.* And in one sense, you'd be right.

Lots of people make this point, and it's clear what they're getting at. If Jesus didn't specifically condemn homosexuality—or same-sex marriage, or transgenderism, or abortion, or any other controversial behavior—then how can Christians condemn it? You might call this the "silent Christ" line of logic because some people attach great significance to Jesus' presumed silence on several controversial issues.[3]

I say "presumed" because it's clear the Gospels are not exhaustive records of Jesus' sentiments. The vast majority of what he said and did were left out of the record. Not enough room, as John himself admits (John 21:25). The Gospels are selective records of the words and deeds of Christ that mattered most to his immediate mission.

Notice, by the way, the tactic in play here. People try to bolster their point by enlisting Jesus as their ally. Cleary, they want Christ on their side. But why, especially if they're not Christians? Because Jesus has credibility with just about everybody. If Jesus agrees with our critics—or at least appears to—the better for them.

Now, on this point I completely agree. Letting Jesus argue for us, after a fashion, is a sound tactic I've dubbed "What a Friend We Have in Jesus."[4] When done legitimately—trading on Jesus' statements and not on his silence—it's a move we can make, too, and it's often a shrewd choice.[5]

Regarding the "silent Christ" approach in general, you have probably already figured out the problem. Actually, there are two flaws here. The first, I just hinted at. We cannot say with confidence what Jesus never said unless we have a complete record of everything he did say, which we don't. The fact that the record is silent doesn't mean Jesus was silent. We simply have no direct evidence one way or another.

Second, what if he was silent? What if in his entire ministry he never uttered a single word about, say, abortion or homosexuality or gender? What can we conclude about Jesus' view on those issues? I'll tell you. Nothing. Nothing at all. Even if Jesus did not utter a single word about a host of controversial views, his silence tells us nothing about his opinion on them.

Here's why. You cannot conclude anything about what Jesus approved of based on what he did not condemn. Even if he said nothing about abortion, for example—which is likely since it wasn't the kind of public issue it is now—it's a mistake to assume Christ would favor it since he didn't denounce it.

As far as we know, Jesus never weighed in on slavery, capital punishment, spousal abuse, sex trafficking, racism, and child sacrifice, to name a few. Do we infer from this silence that he approved of such things? Of course not. Nothing helpful follows from Jesus' apparent reticence on any issue. This is a perfect example of a flawed argument from silence.[6]

Given the problem this challenge poses, here's how it might play out tactically in a conversation, this time dealing with the "silent Christ" move to endorse homosexuality:

"Jesus never said a thing about homosexuality."

> "I'm not sure what you're getting at. **If he didn't, so what?**" [Columbo #1]

"Well, if Jesus was against homosexuality as much as you Christians are, then he would have mentioned it, but he never did."

> "I have a couple of questions about that. Do you mind if I ask them?"

"Go ahead."

> **"First, how do you know Jesus never said anything about homosexuality**? Are you a student of the teachings of Jesus?" [This question is a version of our second tactical question, "How did you come to that conclusion?"]

"Not really, but I did read the Gospels once, and I didn't see anything about homosexuality."

> **"Do you think *everything* Jesus said over three and a half years of public ministry was recorded in the four gospels?"**

"Of course not."

> "Then how can you say Jesus never said anything about homosexuality if most of what he did say wasn't written down?"

"Well, if it was really important to him,
then I think there'd be something about it
in the Gospels."

"But there's another problem with that view I think you're overlooking."

"Really? What problem?"

"Let's just say you're right that Jesus never uttered a single word about homosexuality. **Do you think that since Jesus never condemned it, he must have been okay with it?**" [Checking to make sure we've not misunderstood or misrepresented the view.]

"You got it."

"Well, that would mean Jesus was okay with slavery."

"What!"

"Well, he never mentioned anything about that, either, as far as we know, so his silence on slavery must mean approval, too."

"That's ridiculous!"

"I agree with you there, but that creates a problem for you, doesn't it? **Are you still comfortable saying that whatever Jesus didn't condemn, he approved of?**"

"I'll have to think about that."

"Okay. One last question: **If Jesus *had* said homosexuality was wrong, would you agree with him?**"

Here's the point. It's difficult to conclude anything about what Jesus did not condemn based on the limited written record of what he did condemn.

Notice I said difficult, not impossible. Sometimes we can infer

Jesus' view on something we have no record of by listening carefully to his view on a related issue that he did weigh in on, which brings me to my next point.

Not-So-Silent Christ

Even if we have no direct statements from Jesus on homosexuality, gender, or same-sex marriage, he was not silent on a closely connected issue. When asked by the Pharisees about divorce, he said, "Have you not read that He who created them from the beginning MADE THEM MALE AND FEMALE, and said, 'FOR THIS REASON A MAN SHALL LEAVE HIS FATHER AND MOTHER AND BE JOINED TO HIS WIFE, AND THE TWO SHALL BECOME ONE FLESH'? So they are no longer two, but one flesh. What therefore God has joined together, let no man separate" (Matt. 19:3–6).

Do not miss something critically important here. Jesus did not simply give his opinion on this matter. Instead, he went back to the very beginning. He went back to God's original plan for human flourishing by quoting from Genesis 2:24. Note three crucial takeaways from Jesus' teaching on divorce.

First, Jesus affirmed the commonsense observation that human gender is binary. Human beings are either male or female. God designed them that way (Gen. 1:27). That's how we reproduce (Gen. 1:28: "Be fruitful and multiply"). Some people are confused on this point nowadays, but Jesus was not confused.

Second, marriage is between a man and a woman, a male and a female. Period. Not between two males or two females (same-sex marriage) or an admixture of males and females (polygamy or polyamory). According to Jesus, what God intended from the beginning still stands today. For Christ, any deviation distorts God's original purpose.

Third, the only kind of sexuality ("one flesh") that is proper is sex between a man and a woman who are committed to each other for life in marriage. Conversely, all forms of sex expressly prohibited in the Bible—adultery, fornication, homosexuality, and bestiality—are automatically disqualified. Jesus' reasoning rules them all out.

Here's the best way I've found to sum up Jesus' view on these issues. God's original—and, according to Jesus, enduring—plan is one man, with one woman, becoming one flesh, for one lifetime. Pretty straightforward. This simple summary covers all the controversial bases.

Let's take a moment to look more closely at each area.

From the Beginning . . .

There is one thing everyone knows about the world. They know something is wrong. Things are not the way they are supposed to be. The world is broken, and multitudes suffer as a result.[7]

There was a time, though, when this was not so. Genesis, the book of beginnings, tells us the way the world was when God first made it, when "all that He had made . . . was very good" (1:31). It tells us the way the world is supposed to be, the way it was before the evil.

Here is what the book of beginnings tells us about the beginning of human beings: "God created man in His own image, in the image of God He created him; male and female He created them. God blessed them; and God said to them, 'Be fruitful and multiply, and fill the earth, and subdue it'" (1:27–28).

The image of God in man is the source of our innate and intrinsic value and our inherent dignity and nobility. I want you to notice something else, though, about the good, dignified, noble way God made humans.

From the very beginning, human beings have been either male or female, one or the other. In God's world, sex is binary, an objective reality revealed by our physical bodies. There are rare physical exceptions,[8] but that is not the way things are supposed to be. All congenital abnormalities are a result of the world being broken. It was not God's good design at the start.

> Notice that in God's order there is no hint of distinction between the sex a person is on the outside and the sex a person thinks he is on the inside. Humans were created to be unified, whole persons—the mind matching the body.

At the moment, though, this point that gender is binary and connected with one's physical sex is controversial. Some think there is no vital connection between a person's physical sex and their mental perception of their sex (often referred to as "gender"). And, indeed, there is a minuscule percent of people who are genuinely conflicted, thinking their own gender is different from their sex.[9] But that is not the way it was in the beginning.

There is a reason God made two physical sexes with their matching genders. In God's plan, men and women were made both physically and emotionally different from each other to *fit* together in a complementary way. They were created as counterparts sexually and soulishly so the woman could be what God called a suitable helpmate to the man (Gen. 2:18–25). Even after the evil came and the world was broken, this plan did not change. Indeed, without this physical and emotional fit, it would not be possible for men and women to fulfill God's command to multiply, fill the earth, and subdue it together.

Scripture is not ambiguous or unclear on this issue, and no culture—Christian or otherwise—has been confused on it for thousands of years until recently. Gender is not "fluid" in the way some have made it out to be. Imaginations may be fluid, but not gender. That is not how God made human beings.

This confusion, of course, is central to the cultural conflict and, in my opinion, the spiritual one, as well. Which brings us to the question of pronouns.

Pronouns Matter

Pronouns seem like inconsequential little things—him, her, he, she. No big deal. Why don't we just play along with "preferred pronouns"? No hassle.

If pronouns really were "inconsequential little things," then why has so much ink been spilled—and, in some cases, livelihoods lost—for not getting them right? Because getting particular pronouns right means getting a particular narrative right.

Here is what is at stake with those simple little words. We are being besieged by a worldview that is completely foreign to Jesus' view of reality. According to this view, the reality about our sex is not "out there" in God's world, but "in here" in the internal world of feelings and personal beliefs.

This outside/inside distinction is central to relativism—the primal heresy, mankind's first sin in the garden that we have already discussed. It's the error that started all other errors, and it reigns in the hearts of men and women who continue to "suppress the truth in unrighteousness" (Rom. 1:18). It's a rebellion against God's obvious truth—and also against simple common sense.

The obvious scriptural truth is that for humans, sex is binary and objective. God made that clear in the beginning, and it is clear to anyone who takes reality seriously. God made two sexes—genders, if you will (they're synonyms)—two types of bodies, for a reason. It's the way humans can "be fruitful and multiply." Again, no divine revelation is necessary to be clear on that.

In our culture, though, we are pressured to reject both God's truth and common sense to affirm a false narrative of reality. Why? Because (they say) it's the only way to be kind.

> Amazingly, the obstetrician's announcement "It's a girl!"
> is now considered child abuse by some since the doctor
> is arbitrarily "assigning" gender without the baby's
> consent.

On the pretext of being kind, the world has made pronouns the skirmish line in a broader battle of worldviews. Who defines reality, God or each one of us? This demand is not about being kind; it's about enforcing a foreign worldview. Paul warns us not to be taken captive by the empty—hollow, vacuous, void of truth—deceptions of men (Col. 2:8). This pronoun ploy is one of those empty deceptions.

So, what do we do? How do we resist the lie, live the truth, and still be kind? We take a cue from Christ and distinguish the narrative from the individual.

John says Jesus was "full of grace and truth" (John 1:14). This detail of Christ's character can help us navigate the gender minefield in the street. We protect people's feelings (show grace)—within reason—but we reject the narrative (uphold truth). Three separate circumstances require three different responses.

First, in my opinion, we should call people by the names they choose for themselves. Names are different from pronouns since names are personal preferences by nature. Refusing to call people by the names they choose just comes across as meanspirited.[10] Pronouns, though, refer to sex. One's sex is not a preference, but a fixed feature of reality.

Second, if you're required to post your "preferred" pronouns, do not simply report your accurate gender. That reinforces the lie that pronouns are mere personal preferences and yours happens to match your sex. Instead, post this: **"I don't have preferred pronouns. I have a sex. I'm male [for example]."**

This characterization is completely self-reflective. It says nothing about anyone but you. In principle, at least, it should not be a problem. You were asked for a self-assessment. You gave it. End of issue. Do not participate in the lie.

Third, if you're asked to use preferred pronouns when speaking of others, then graciously, but firmly, refuse. **Say, "This is not my view, so it would be dishonest and inauthentic to act like it was."** In most cases, pronouns are third-person references, anyway, corresponding to the sex of people not present, so their feelings are not at stake. Arm-twisting at this point is political, not ethical.

If you're a teacher, you could use students' last names for third-person references if you like or find some other workaround, but don't yield to pressure to adopt pronouns that reflect a peculiar, controversial, and divisive political view you do not hold. That's lying.

It's also not loving your neighbor. For those suffering from gender confusion, the suicide rates skyrocket. Even in Sweden—a culture completely sanguine on these matters—the suicide mortality rate for transgender people is twenty times the standard for the general population. Surgery does not improve those numbers, either.[11]

There's a reason surgery is not the answer. For one, it is biologically impossible to change one's sex. Full stop. The best one can do is mutilate a perfectly healthy body. Second, those dealing with genuine gender dysphoria are deeply broken people—even by their own admission (e.g., "I'm a woman trapped in a man's body").

The solution is not surgery, but compassionate psychological help. They need our grace and love—not our enablement of their affliction. Would we recommend liposuction to someone struggling with anorexia, or limb removal to someone with so-called "bodily integrity identity disorder"? Of course not.[12]

So, graciously hold your ground. Refuse to be bullied into affirming a lie (more on this point later). The temptation to compromise truth is intense. Don't do it. On this issue, our goal is modest. We do not demand that others abandon their views. We ask only that we be allowed to keep our views. In the long run, we may not be able to change culture, but we can keep the culture from changing us.

This is a difficult section to write a dialogue for since the issue itself defies common sense. Here are some starters, though:

"What is a woman?"[13]
"A woman is someone who feels like a woman."

"But you haven't answered my question. What exactly *is* a woman that anyone would *feel* like one?"

"I can't define it. It's something a person feels. How would *you* define a woman?"

"Someone who has the innate potential to be a mother because she has female reproductive organs. What else would a woman be?"

"Someone who *feels* like a woman."

"You mean someone who feels like they have a uterus and a vagina, even if they don't actually have them?"

"Maybe. It's hard to explain."

"So, is someone with female sexual organs a woman or not?"

"That depends. If that person feels like a woman, yes. If that person feels like a man, then he's a man."

"What is a man?"

"You should use the pronouns people want you to use."

"Why?"

"Because it's kind. It shows respect for them. It makes them feel comfortable."

"But that means I have to be dishonest about my own convictions. I'd have to affirm a lie. **Why not be nice to *me* by respecting *my* deeply held beliefs?**"

"Because you're transphobic."

"Why call me names when I don't agree with you? Is that kind or respectful?"

"People should be allowed to decide what gender they are."

"What makes you think gender is a decision?"

"Because gender is something a person believes on the inside. Babies are assigned gender at birth. That's terrible."

"I don't mean to be coarse, but no doctor can 'assign' a penis or a vagina."

Objective binary sexuality is also key to understanding God's purpose for something else the culture has been confused about: marriage.

Till Death Do Us Part

Recall that when Jesus was asked about the legitimacy of divorce, he answered by going back to the beginning. According to him, marriage was not a cultural convention based on current custom or sexual whim. Instead, God fashioned human unions according to a precise pattern for a specific purpose.

The first detail Jesus mentions about this pattern is that God made human beings male and female (Matt. 19:4). Why does Jesus begin with gender when answering a question about marriage?[14] Because God's purpose for marriage is based on gender—binary gender. "A *man* shall leave his *father* and his *mother*, and be joined to his *wife*" (Gen. 2:24). Men marry women. Women marry men. Men and women become fathers and mothers. That's God's plan.

God commanded humans to be fruitful and multiply and fill the earth (Gen. 1:28). Since children can only come from men (the fathers) physically joined with women (the mothers), being a man or a woman is determined by one's physical body. Again, no Bible verses are needed to verify this point. It's common sense.

Of course, some have argued that marriage and family are mere cultural conventions. Since they're constructed by culture (the argument goes), culture is free to alter them at will. The current definitions may have been stable for millennia, they say, yet because they're conventions, they're subject to revision.

This idea is clearly mistaken, though. Culture cannot "construct" marriage—or the families marriages create—because families must exist before culture can exist in the first place.

> Cultures are large groups of families. Families, then, construct culture, not the other way around. Bricks aren't the result of the building. The building is the result of the bricks. Since families are at the foundation of culture, cultures cannot "construct" them any more than a tree can construct its own roots.

Strictly speaking, then, marriage has never been defined by culture. Instead, it has been described by culture. Civilizations observe their parts, so to speak, and discover the components vital to their existence. Society then enacts laws, not to create marriage and families according to arbitrary convention, but to protect that which already exists, being essential to the whole.

There's a problem, though. People confuse the reason they get married with the reason for marriage. In our culture, marriage usually is motivated by love. A multitude of relationships are inspired by love, though, yet culture offers no special privileges or protections for them.[15]

Further, if love were the essence of marriage, then billions of people in the world who thought they were married are not. Most marriages have been arranged, and many today lack love, yet they're still marriages. The state doesn't care if the bride and groom love each other. No proof of passion is required. It's not on the form. Love may be the reason many get married, but it isn't the reason cultures sanction marriage.

Here is the reason: Stable families are fundamental to stable civilizations.[16] Long-term, monogamous, heterosexual unions—as a group, as a rule, and by nature—produce the next generation. No other relationship serves that vital function. That's the reason societies regulate, privilege, and protect those unique unions. Ensuring their stability is an act of self-preservation.[17]

God knows this. It was his good plan from the beginning. Most civilizations have understood this, too. Take an ax to the roots, and it won't be long before the tree topples.

According to Jesus' thinking, then, same-sex marriage—or any other variation—is not only wrong for the same reason divorce is wrong (it corrupts God's good design), it's also a contradiction in terms. The word "marriage" has no meaning when used of same-sex couples since heterosexual union is inherent to God's design of human bodies for reproduction, and also inherent to the nature and well-being of every civilization.

There is nothing ambiguous about Jesus' view.[18] Yes, the culture is currently confused, but there is no reason for you to be confused. A good answer, though, is not always an acceptable answer.[19] The world at large has no love of truth.[20] So be forewarned: it is easily deluded and often difficult to convince. Here are some sample conversations, though, that might help bring clarity:

"I think it's good that the government provides for same-sex marriage."

"Let me ask you a question. **As a rule, what comes first, marriages or families?**"

"Marriages."

"**Right. Do you think that's a good idea?**"

"Sure."

"Why?"

"Because without marriages, moms and kids can't be properly taken care of."

"Exactly. But did you notice what you just assumed?"

"What?"

"That marriages characteristically create families with children."

"Right. That's usually the way it works."

"**Do you think government should intrude on private relationships and regulate them?**"

"Of course not."

"**But there's lots of government regulations about marriage and families, right?**"

"Of course."

"But you don't object to them. Why?"

"Because of the kids."

"So, it sounds like you're saying the government can legitimately intrude in relationships that characteristically have kids, but not if they don't have kids?"

"Sounds right."

"So, if a certain type of relationship never characteristically produced children, the government should stay out?"

"Yes."

"Then I'm curious why you're in favor of same-sex marriage."

"Since you're against same-sex marriage, you don't believe in marriage equality?"

"What do you mean by 'marriage equality'?"

"Everyone has the equal right to marry whoever they love."

"Do you think children should be allowed to get married?"

"Of course not!"

"Then you don't believe everyone has the right to marry whoever they love, either."

"But that's different. Kids are too young to get married."

"And two people of the same sex are the wrong sex to get married. Neither of us believes in 'marriage equality' the way you're defining it. We both have definitions for marriage. **The real question is this: What definition makes the most sense given the reason culture cares about marriage in the first place?**"

"One Flesh"

According to Jesus, in marriage a man cleaves to—and becomes "one flesh" with—a woman, his wife. Their physical bodies are joined together in a deep, profound sexual union of body and soul, and the two become one. That is the good purpose of God.

The passage Jesus cites in Genesis 2 as the Father's perfect plan covers all of the "alternative sexualities." Indeed, every single sexual act the Bible explicitly condemns—adultery, fornication, homosexuality, and bestiality—is excluded by Jesus' simple formula.[21] The only kind of sexual behavior honorable to God is intimacy between a man and a woman in a lifelong committed relationship—marriage, in other words.

Consider homosexuality, for example. I understand that every depiction of it in popular culture is overwhelmingly positive, and those who differ are characterized as hateful bigots. This is not God's perspective, though. I want you to pay close attention to the details of a point Paul makes about homosexuality in Romans 1: "God gave them over to degrading passions; for . . . the men abandoned the natural function of the woman and burned in their desire toward one another, men with men committing indecent acts" (vv. 26–27).

The word translated "function" here, the Greek word *kreesis*, is specifically referring to the fit I mentioned earlier. Paul is talking here about sexual plumbing, so to speak. God designed men and women to function sexually together—their bodies fit together in a precise way to make sexual union possible. Since natural desires go with natural functions, the sexual passion that exchanges the natural function of sex for an unnatural function (homosexuality) is what Paul calls "degrading passions."

Notice how Paul explains the nature of this offense in God's eyes. He says, "The men abandoned the natural function of the woman." That is, they rejected the appropriate counterpart God had provided—a woman who was built by God to be man's sexual complement. That's why Scripture has nothing positive to say about homosexuality. Whenever it's mentioned in the Bible, it's condemned.[22]

Consequently, since the birth of the church, no Christian authority—no theologian, no church council, no denominational confession, no seminary—ever hinted that homosexual behavior was morally legitimate. Now, congregations across the Western world are becoming "gay affirming" at an alarming rate, convinced that for two millennia the corporate body of Christ has simply misunderstood the Bible. What have we missed?

"Not That Kind of Homosexuality"

Revisionists claim that the same-sex behavior condemned in the Bible is not what modern-day LGBTQ Christians practice. Ancient same-sex behavior was exploitive, abusive, and oppressive, they say—completely unlike the caring, committed, covenantal unions promoted by gay Christians today. Scripture, then, doesn't prohibit loyal, loving, same-sex intimacy, only abusive forms like pederasty, master-slave exploitation, promiscuity, rape, victimization, and so on.[23]

This attempt fails for a simple reason, and no insight into ancient Near Eastern sexual practices is necessary to see it. When it comes to sex, Scripture condemns the behavior, not the relationships. Take, for example, Leviticus 18:22: "You shall not lie with a male as one lies with a female; it is an abomination."

There's not the slightest hint in Leviticus that same-sex activity is only a problem when it's coercive or oppressive. Note that both participants were punished here (Lev. 20:13)—unlike rape, where only the abuser was penalized (Deut. 22:25–26).

With every passage forbidding homosexuality, the prohibition is unqualified, with no exceptions for loving, consensual, committed relationships. The Law here does not condemn perverse relationships. It condemns perverse behavior. The pattern is the same with all sinful sexual activity. Is adultery biblically acceptable if it's loving and consensual? Or fornication? Or bestiality?

Whenever a man lies with a man the way he should be lying with a woman, he is rejecting—once again—the woman who was "fit" for him, exchanging her for the man who was not. God's created order is subverted—as it is with all sexual sin—corrupting his original good purpose for sexual intimacy.[24]

My reference to the Old Testament law, though, raises another issue.

Pickin' and Choosin'?

Some think my reference to Leviticus is disingenuous and self-serving. Since New Testament Christians are not under the Law, none of the passages from the Pentateuch apply to believers today. My use of the Torah to condemn homosexuality, then, looks suspiciously like special pleading—picking and choosing verses that benefit my view while selectively dismissing others as obsolete and irrelevant to modern Christians.

It's true, the Mosaic law doesn't apply to believers today the way it applied to Jews in the theocracy. It would be a serious mistake, though, to think that none of the Law's prohibitions have any relevance for us now. Perversion is still perverse, and wickedness is still wicked, whether adultery, rape, incest, bestiality—or a host of evil acts condemned by Moses in the "old" Law.

Don't miss the larger context of Leviticus 18. The "abomination" of homosexuality is grouped with condemnation of adultery, child sacrifice, and bestiality. Keep reading, and you'll see that this grouping is no accident. These were the very behaviors that brought judgment on the Canaanites to begin with (vv. 24–26)—people who also were gentiles "not under the Law." Nevertheless, this did not exonerate them. They still were "spewed out" for their wickedness.

The point of citing Leviticus on homosexuality, then, is not to cherry-pick favorite "clobber verses" from the Law or impose Torah on New Testament believers. Rather, it's to show that any behavior twisting or maligning God's original intention for sex is evil in any era.

> God also has nothing positive to say about any other sexual behavior outside of marriage—like adultery or fornication—for the same reason: they also corrupt God's good purpose for sex.

Christians do not condone adultery, as far as I know. Nowadays, though, fornication hardly raises an eyebrow—especially among the younger crowd—yet it's just as much a violation of God's good plan as homosexuality.

God's Way

Paul offers another angle you may not have considered. Since our bodies are members of Christ, "one flesh" sexual unions outside of marriage spiritually join Christ (who is in us) in an unholy coupling, desecrating the temple of God—our own bodies. That's why instead of embracing these relationships, Paul says to flee them (1 Cor. 6:15–20).

Here is Paul's sobering summary on the status of those who engage in persistent sexual sin: "Do you not know that the unrighteous will not inherit the kingdom of God? Do not be deceived; neither fornicators . . . nor adulterers . . . nor homosexuals . . . will inherit the kingdom of God" (vv. 9–10).

God's solution for satisfying our sexual appetites is marriage: "Because of [sexual] immoralities, each man is to have his own wife, and each woman is to have her own husband" (1 Cor. 7:2).[25] Confusion on this issue, as Paul points out, is deadly deception. Do not be taken in.

God's plan for sex and marriage is built into the structure of the world he made. Since the beginning of time this has been obvious to everyone, even those without Bibles. Yes, times change, but reality does not. And God's Word does not. It abides forever, telling us the truth, protecting us from error, shielding us from harm.

Here is a sampling of dialogues you might find helpful on this issue. Please take note of an important point, though. Regarding homosexuality—or any other sexual sin—if the people you're talking with don't know Christ, their sexual habits are not the issue.

Sin—rebellion against God in a multitude and variety of ways—is the problem, not any particular sinful pattern.

"Does God hate gays?"

"Why would you think that?" [Columbo #1]

"Because you Christians think homosexuality is wrong."

"Well, to be more precise, it's the behavior that's wrong. But do you think Christians think *all* sex outside of marriage is wrong?"

"Yes."

"So, do you think God hates heterosexuals, too?"

"Maybe."

"God doesn't hate gays. He hates sin. It doesn't matter what kind it is. That means every single one of us is in trouble—me, too. We all need forgiveness, gays and nongays alike."

"The Bible doesn't condemn loving, consensual, same-sex relationships, only exploitive, abusive, and oppressive ones."

"Do you feel the same way about adultery?"

"Of course not!"

"Why not?"

"The Bible clearly says adultery is wrong."

"What if the adulterers have a loving, consensual relationship?"

"It's still wrong."

"So, Scripture condemns the *act* of adultery, even if it's a loving relationship?"

"That's right."

"Have you read what Romans 1 says about homosexuality?"

"Sure."

"Does it condemn the act itself, just like the passages that condemn adultery?"

"Yes, but Paul was condemning only abusive gay relationships, not loving ones."

"Where does it say that in the passage?"

"We know that in Paul's culture, those relationships were abusive."

"But I'm not talking about the culture. I'm talking about the Bible verse. **Does Paul make any reference to abusive relationships or any exception for loving relationships?"**

"Well, no."

"Does Leviticus condemn same-sex behavior or just abusive same-sex relationships?"

"It talks only about behavior, but Leviticus doesn't apply to us."

"Why not?"

"Because that's Old Testament, and we live under the New Testament."

"Do you feel the same way about bestiality and child sacrifice?"

"Don't be ridiculous."

"Well, those things are condemned in the very same passage. How do you explain that?"

"What's wrong with love? Love is love. Why is God against two people loving each other?"

"Why would you think God is against love?"
"Because you think loving, gay
relationships are wrong."
    "Is sex the same as love?"
"Well, no."

        "God agrees with you. They're not the same. He
wants us to love each another. That's for everybody.
God reserves sex, though, for the kind of relationship
he created it for: heterosexual marriage."

"Live Not by Lies"

In February 1974, Aleksandr Solzhenitsyn—Russian dissident,
eight-year forced-labor Soviet Gulag inmate, Nobel laureate, and
Christian—was expelled from his country and sent into exile. His
final salvo was an essay suggesting a remedy for the common citizen, the ordinary person dwarfed by the totalitarian state. He titled
it "Live Not by Lies."

Most of us are not in a position to effect any immediate change
in the culture at large. That does not mean we're powerless, though,
Solzhenitsyn argues. The lies that drive the system can be resisted
by ordinary people being faithful to truth while living lives of
simple integrity. This approach entails two things.

First, we refuse to be cowed by pressure to affirm falsehood.
Instead, we stand our ground. We live consistently with our convictions, firmly holding to truth even when we can't defend it well
or make sense of it to outsiders.

Solzhenitsyn says we should not speak, write, affirm, or dis-
tribute anything that distorts truth. Rather, walk out of meetings
where discussion is manipulated and truth is not allowed to be spoken.[26] Refuse to affirm what you do not believe. Just say no, but do
so respectfully, even when the price of fidelity is public shaming,
silencing, or canceling.

Second, we act. "The only thing necessary for the triumph of evil," the saying goes, "is for good men to do nothing." Resistance takes inner courage, of course, and courage starts with small steps. It also takes a group, a family, the body of Christ. We stand together. It takes outward virtue, too. We are careful to live with integrity in all areas of our lives.

Be direct but courteous in the face of opposition. When pressured at the office to participate in "sensitivity" seminars that would require you to act against your convictions in some way, respectfully decline. If pressed, say, **"It appears you're using your influence as my employer to get me to accept your politics. Do you think that's a proper use of your power and authority?"**

Be prudent, however. Carefully weigh the risks of resistance, counting the cost. Not all hills are worth dying on—but some are. Most importantly, carefully pass your own Christian convictions on to your children. Prepare them for the hostility they will face from culture when they are faithful to Christ.

Until now, it's cost most of us virtually nothing to be Christian. I am convinced those days are rapidly coming to a close. "A time of painful testing, even persecution, is coming," Rod Dreher warns. "Lukewarm or shallow Christians will not come through with their faith intact."[27]

> Choosing not to live by lies can change culture over time, but that is not its immediate purpose, in my view. Its purpose is not principally pragmatic, but ethical. We live not by lies because it's wrong before God to do otherwise, even if it costs us.

There is a telling passage in the passion narrative where Pilate is confronted by the mob and must decide where his loyalties lie. Mark records his decision: *"Wishing to satisfy the crowd,* Pilate released Barabbas for them, and after having Jesus scourged, he handed Him over to be crucified" (Mark 15:15).

Many in Christendom today are taking their cues from Pilate. They are more concerned with satisfying the crowd than being faithful to Jesus. They champion the criminal and turn their back on the Savior.

Culture may be confused on gender, marriage, and sex. Don't you be. On these issues, God has spoken clearly.[28]

CHAPTER 18

FINAL WORDS FOR THE STREET

That's Street Smarts—maneuvering in tough conversations by using a plan with questions meant to expose a weakness or a flaw in someone's view. It's easier than you think if you follow the steps.

First, get a clear take on your friend's view. Make sure you understand it. If there are any ambiguities, use your first Columbo question, "What do you mean by that?" (or some variation) to clarify.

Second, reflect on the challenge or do some research to zero in on its weaknesses or failings. I've provided the material here in part 2 of *Street Smarts* to help you see flaws in popular challenges to Christianity, but many other sources are available to help you.[1]

Third, chart a course for your conversation—as I have done for you in the examples in this book—using a mixture of questions (especially clarification questions) to keep your friend engaged while you move forward to expose the liabilities you've discovered. Try to have the first couple of moves clear in your mind—even memorized—so that when the challenge comes up, you'll have your first questions at the ready. This single bit of prep will save you lots of stress.

You may need to plan ahead and practice a bit, doing conversation "dry runs." As you put these principles into practice, though, the process will become almost second nature—a kind of mental "muscle memory." You'll be able to move ahead easily in conversations that used to be daunting and discomfiting, staying securely in the driver's seat on a productive route—all without speed bumps.

Before we part, though, I want to leave you with a few items of general advice: how to handle what I call "the gauntlet," four tips that will make your conversations more effective, and two secrets to increase your courage for the street.

I then want to close by encouraging you with what I learned before I was a Christian in a brief interaction with someone I never saw again, but who changed my life forever.

The Gauntlet

Running the gauntlet is no fun. Historically, it was a military punishment. Offenders were forced to run between two lines of soldiers who beat them with sticks. Like I said, not a party.

Now and then, you'll have to run a gauntlet of sorts, too. Occasionally, you'll be battered by a barrage of challenges coming at you in rapid-fire succession—sometimes from an individual and sometimes from a group ganging up on you, each one delivering his own broadside at your convictions.

Steamroller types—hostile critics who constantly interrupt, piling objections on top of objections—are clear offenders here.[2] Many who make you run the gauntlet, though, are not malicious— the contenders aren't necessarily rude or looking to draw rhetorical blood. The sheer number of their challenges, though, can still be overpowering.

You'll confront the gauntlet in face-to-face encounters with others, but you'll also confront it in print or on webcasts, in something you're reading or watching. Here's one example from an interview of a well-known quarterback who grew up Christian until his concerns about Christianity led him in a different spiritual direction: "Religion can be a crutch . . . something that people have to have to make themselves feel better. And because it's sort of binary, it's us and them. It's saved and unsaved. It's heaven and hell. It's enlightened and heathen. It's holy and righteous and sinner and filthy. . . . Like, what type of loving, sensitive, omnipresent, omnipotent being wants to condemn most of his beautiful creation to a fiery hell at the end of all this?"[3]

So, what do you do when challenges like these are piled on you all at once? Here are three simple steps to help you run that gauntlet without getting thrashed: slow down, isolate, and assess.

First, when hit with a tsunami of objections, *slow things down*, especially when facing a group. Part of the power of the gauntlet is its ability to disorient and confuse, so take a moment to collect your thoughts. I've sometimes said, "Wow. There's a lot there. Give me a moment to take it all in." Do the same when reading or watching or listening. Don't panic. Instead, take a deep breath, pause, then ponder.

What do I ponder? That's the second step. I carefully *isolate the concerns*, extracting them from the rhetorical noise. The sheer volume of piled-on charges can seem overwhelming. Isolating the claims breaks the larger challenge into parts I can deal with one at a time.

> You might say, "Let me see if I understand you. It seems to me your concerns are. . . ." Then list them as clearly, as accurately, and as fairly as you can. Don't let an aggressive group gang up on you. Calmly say, "Hold on. One at a time, please."

Some charges are explicit, and some are implied. Get them all out in the open. In this case, there are three: (1) religion can be a crutch that people need to feel better, (2) religion sets up binary "us and them" categories that seem abusive, and (3) a good, noble God wouldn't "want to" condemn people to a fiery hell.

Now, our third step: *Assess the challenges one by one*, as you're able.

What of the "crutch" claim? With this one, I move toward the objection, not away from it. I embrace it. Yes, Christ is a kind of "crutch." That's because handicapped people need crutches. Everyone has a crutch since fallen people are disabled in different ways. Here's the real question: Can the crutch they're leaning on hold them? Christ can. And yes, of course true forgiveness makes us feel better. That's a virtue of Christianity, not a vice.

Now the "binary" issue. Again, I move toward the objection. Religion *is* binary. Non-religion is, too. Virtually everything important can be clarified with binary categories. With doctors, it's "sick" and "healthy." With justice, it's "innocent" and "guilty." With religious claims, it's "true" and "false." In this complaint, it's "those who divide people into binary categories" and "those who don't," or maybe "us progressives" and "them conservatives." It can't be avoided. What's the alternative?

What of the character of God? Notice the qualities the quarterback left off his list: justice and holiness. Isn't God also good? And does a good God treat evil people the same as good people? Isn't that the complaint with the problem of evil: Why doesn't a "loving, sensitive, omnipresent, omnipotent being" do something? These are questions this challenger needs to answer.

> The assessment step is something you may need to do on your own when the pressure is off. That's okay. Most of us are not quick on our feet when facing a barrage of challenges unless we've prepared for them in advance.

So, whenever you face a gauntlet, remember these three steps. First, slow things down. Second, isolate the objections. Third, assess their significance. It's a good way to sidestep a thrashing.

Four Tips

Let's face it. Talking with others about controversial things isn't easy—and issues like God and Jesus and the Bible and morality and sin and salvation and heaven and hell are about as controversial as they come.

I know the concern. You don't want to get in over your head, you don't want to come across odd, and you don't want to get in a fight. I share these sentiments with you. These are all noble concerns, too—unless they secure our silence. If they keep us on the bench, they've gotten the best of us, and that's not good.

Over time, I've discovered some ways to make the task less troublesome. The first one is a reminder—I've already covered it in depth—but it's so important, it bears repeating.

Ask questions. Lots of them. Your first step in any encounter should be to gather as much information as possible. It's hard to know how to proceed—or even if to proceed—unless you first get the lay of the land. You need intel, and friendly queries get it for you.

When you need to buy some time to catch your wits, ask a question. When you face a challenge you're not sure how to deal with, ask a question. When the conversation bogs down and you think it best to move in a new direction, ask a question. Whenever you're in doubt about how to move forward, ask a question.

Contextualize. I always look for ways to frame my points in terms of the other person's interests, discipline, or profession. For example, once, when an attorney asked me why he needed Jesus, I used a courtroom scene to illustrate the issue. This move made my point more persuasive because he saw it in light of things he already knew or procedures he was already familiar with.

Contextualizing your points by tying your comments or explanations to relevant parts of the other person's world establishes common ground—and is an important tactical skill of an effective ambassador.

Be nice. Solomon reminds us of something we already know but still needs to be repeated: "A gentle answer turns away wrath, but a harsh word stirs up anger" (Prov. 15:1). Later, he adds, "Sweetness of speech increases persuasiveness" (16:21). Obvious stuff, but easily overlooked. Start out brash and thrashing about, and things will turn sour quickly. Start sweet, though, and they'll probably end sweet, too.

Do everything you can, then, to help friends feel comfortable with the process. Don't get mad. Don't show frustration. Don't look annoyed. Keep your cool. The more collected you are, the more confident you'll appear, and the more persuasive you'll sound.

Trust God. No matter how clever you sound, everything you say will turn to dust if God's Spirit is not in it. No matter how poorly you think you've acquitted yourself, even the most meager effort can turn to gold if God decides to move. Never presume on God either way. Be faithful in the moment, then let God do his part—which is all the rest. I'm not saying you need to "tune in" to the Spirit. Encounters on the street don't usually work that way. Rather, simply do what you can, then trust in God's sovereign control.

The very first time I ever shared Christ was less than twenty-four hours after I'd committed my life to him. It was a long conversation, I felt entirely inept (I was), my close friends were fuming, and I thought it was a complete wash. It wasn't. Four years later, out of the blue, I discovered what God had been doing that afternoon, and it was something I never would have guessed. God knows; we don't.

Courage

Sometimes opportunities present themselves, yet you can't muster the courage to face the challenge, to stand in the line of fire. I know exactly how that feels since I've been there myself. Courage doesn't come easily for us since almost nothing in our lives requires it.

We don't hunt for food. We don't fight off wild animals. We don't battle barbarians at the gate. No need for most of us to ever risk life or limb. So, how do we develop the courage we need? Two things come to mind: knowledge and action.

First, knowledge breeds courage. The more you know about an issue, the braver you'll be when it comes up. This truth applies to every daunting challenge.

Here's how to put the principle into play. Certain challenges to your Christian convictions will come up with regularity. The ones you fear the most will be the ones that demand the most courage, and you may not feel up to the task.

So, make your job easier by taking the edge off the fear. Develop a good answer to each issue—one you can deliver in a tactically sound way (with the kind of thoughtful questions included in this book, for example)—and your courage will soar. You won't fear the test because you'll know the answers in advance.

> Simply put, the more you know, the more confident you'll be—and the braver you'll feel when facing a daunting challenge. Knowledge breeds courage.

Second, action breeds courage. I've had times when I was shaking in my boots as an opportunity began to develop before me. I discovered that if I forced myself to take one small step forward to engage, I felt better. Action steadied my nerves.

I watched a western once where the good guys were outnumbered five to two as they faced off for a gunfight in the middle of town. But the pair had a plan. Once the groups had squared off in the street, the two stepped out confidently toward the line of five. It was a bold move, but it changed the outcome dramatically.

Again, using an apt question for your first step is a perfect opener. It gets you moving forward while at the same time tossing the ball in the other person's court, so the pressure is no longer on you.

Here's a bonus tip I've found helpful: small acts of courage prepare us for larger ones. Paratroopers jump from platforms before they leap from airplanes. They don't step out first at five thousand feet—too frightening. They build their nerve little by little.

When we step out on the small challenges, we increase our ability to face more difficult situations in the future. If we shrink back, we feed our fear instead of our boldness.

Whatever fears you feel, face them head on, armed with these three truths: knowledge breeds courage, action breeds courage, and small acts of courage prepare you for larger ones.

An Audience of One

Now I want to tell you about someone I met nearly half a century ago, months before I became a believer, talked with for maybe fifteen minutes, then never saw again. Yet what happened in that brief encounter changed the course of my life forever.

Her name was Adrian Thatcher, and I met her on a bus while returning from the beach in Santa Monica in the summer of 1973. I was long haired, hip, and looking for love. She had been reading her Bible, and her only interest in me was to tell me about Jesus.

I remember almost nothing about our conversation except her mention of the Wednesday night Bible study she attended in Westwood Village. My interest with her was not spiritual, though, so I dismissed it.

Months later—as an exuberant, spiritually hungry, baby Christian—I remembered Adrian's comment. Through another odd "coincidence," I stumbled upon the study—part of a vibrant "Jesus people" community and ad hoc Bible school located in a former fraternity house on the edge of the UCLA campus. Within four months, I'd moved in.

For two and a half years, I was vigorously discipled—studying the Bible under seminary-trained teachers, learning apologetics, doing street evangelism on campus, working on summer-long outreach projects in Waikiki, and going behind the Iron Curtain for Christ.

My years there fixed the trajectory of my Christian life forever—all because of a few short moments of faithfulness by a young Christian named Adrian Thatcher. And Adrian, wherever she is, has no idea how much she's influenced my life—or the many through me, by God's grace, since then.

Here is the lesson I learned from that encounter. No matter how small my audience (I was an audience of one for Adrian), I never know when my own brief effort of faithfulness will turn out to be the hinge pin, the turning point, the small event in someone else's life that changes everything for them from that day forward.

What's true for me as an individual is true for you, as well. We may prepare for each contingency in a conversation, pray through each encounter, and profess the truth with care. We may talk, engage, and cajole. We may witness with great patience, clarity, and grace, yet fail to see an immediate, measurable effect.

I have not been especially burdened by this fact, though, because long ago I decided to let faithfulness be my first focus, not results. Yes, Adrian had an audience of just one. But her most important audience wasn't me. It was the audience of the one whom she served.

That's our priority, too—yours and mine—not to hear applause from multitudes but rather approval from a single voice: the voice of one saying, "Well done, good and faithful servant."

You may be serving quietly, in the dark, often not knowing the true extent of your impact—going out in obedience, doing what is right, speaking what is true, laboring faithfully. The course of history is often changed by small things done by ordinary people at opportune times, even though they never realize it. We take what we have—our skills, our gifts, our capabilities, our opportunities—then place everything in the hands of the Savior.

So, don't be too worried about results. Leave them to God. Just be faithful with the opportunities you're given, even small ones. Outward appearances can be deceiving. A person may rebel at what you share, but if you're thoughtful in what you say and gracious in how you say it, chances are good you'll give him something to think about.

Ask a question to get things rolling, then see where it leads. Don't put yourself under pressure to go the distance. Just make the effort. Take the chance. You're gardening, after all. Then see what God will do with your small steps of trust.

Occasionally, you will get a glimpse of how God has used you in surprising ways. Sometimes, you'll learn that the person you were talking with was not the person you influenced. Instead, it was a bystander, an eavesdropper—someone sitting in the next row on the airplane, or behind you in class, or working in the adjoining cubicle—listening in on a conversation you meant for someone else that seemed to be going nowhere, yet God had other plans.

Now is not the time for fear of any kind. It's not the time to circle the wagons or to pull up the drawbridge. It's the time for ambassadors equipped with knowledge, tactical wisdom, and character to seize the moment as agents of change for the kingdom of heaven when the world needs them most.

We may not feel up to the task God gives us. That's the time to remember the loaves and the fishes. The little boy in the crowd had little to give, but he gave what he had to his audience of one. When placed in the hands of Jesus, he multiplied it to feed the multitudes.

In the same way, we take what we have and place it in the hands of the Savior. We may never see the size of the crowd he feeds through our effort. But it is enough to give what we have to him—our skills, our gifts, our capabilities, our opportunities. He will take care of the rest.

Don't ever underestimate your significance before your audience of one.

ACKNOWLEDGMENTS

Street Smarts was a challenging book to write. It wouldn't have been possible without the persistence of my wonderful agent, Mark Sweeney, the patience of my longsuffering Zondervan editor, Ryan Pazdur, and the limitless skill of my fearless colleague, Amy Hall.

I'm indebted to Nancy Ulrich for her wordsmithing skill, my longtime friend Stephen Meyer for his professional counsel and personal encouragement, and to Josh Brahm for his excellent feedback based on his own experience dealing with the abortion challenge "on the street."

My versatile team at Stand to Reason has provided consistent support, valuable feedback, and vital encouragement. They keep me balanced, centered, and productive.

Finally, I'm thankful for my wife, Steese Ann, and my daughters, Annabeth and Eva, for their patience with me as I wrestled for months with this manuscript. I love them each more than they know.

NOTES

Chapter 1: Making a Hard Job Easier

1. Acts 18:9–10.
2. Matthew 10:26–31.
3. Matthew 10:19–20.
4. Matthew 4:19.
5. Numbers 13:33.
6. 1 Corinthians 15:19.
7. 2 Corinthians 10:4–5.
8. See Gregory Koukl, *Tactics: A Game Plan for Discussing Your Christian Convictions*, 10th anniversary ed. (Grand Rapids, MI: Zondervan, 2019).
9. In addition to providing a simple, three-step plan for effective interactions with others, *Tactics* describes in detail how to graciously use a variety of maneuvers to help you discover the errors in your friends' thinking and help them see their mistakes.
10. 2 Timothy 2:26.
11. Psalm 51:6.
12. John 6:44.

Chapter 2: Harvester or Gardener?

1. 2 Timothy 4:3–4.
2. Koukl, *Tactics*, 18. This quote references Francis Schaeffer, "Pre-Evangelism Is No Soft Option," section 5 in *The God Who Is There* (1968; Downers Grove, IL: InterVarsity Press, 2020).
3. The "praying to receive Christ" practice is not part of the New Testament pattern. It entered the life of the church hundreds of years later. In Acts, people simply preached persuasively, and listeners believed. The Holy Spirit brought conviction that led to humble faith. The closest thing to an altar call in the New Testament was a baptism, but that came after faith, not before it.

4. Proverbs 20:4.

5. Romans 1:16.

6. Take note of my complete lack of religious lingo in this introduction.

7. Matthew 11:28.

8. Wallace never lost a case that went to trial.

9. Both 1 Corinthians 12 and Romans 12 make this point.

Chapter 3: How Questions Keep You Safe

1. I'll be giving you the details of that game plan in the next chapter.

2. Find this entire conversation in chapter 1 of *Tactics*.

3. Gregory Koukl, *The Story of Reality* (Grand Rapids, MI: Zondervan, 2017).

Chapter 4: The Game Plan

1. If you're new to the tactical game plan, I provide a complete tutorial—nine full chapters—on the method in *Tactics*.

2. The error is an informal fallacy known as a "straw man."

3. Precisely when the universe began is a matter of debate between Christians, but that discussion is irrelevant to my point here. If the universe *had* a beginning—which is largely established science—then the question of what the adequate cause for the universe was is a fair one.

4. Note that in conversations like these, I'm alert for anything the other person says that I can genuinely agree with. Doing so is fair-minded and evenhanded, and it also keeps the conversation amicable.

5. Incidentally, the salesperson's "you had to go and say that" comment suggested she was already aware that judgment in hell was a real possibility.

Chapter 5: The Street's Invisible Battlefield

1. Note, once again, God's vital role in rescuing captive minds and lost souls. You are not left alone to unmask the devil's deception.

2. This is the reason why defense of the truth—apologetics—needs to be a component of any church's spiritual battle strategy.

3. Jonathan Aitken, *John Newton: From Disgrace to Amazing Grace* (Wheaton, IL: Crossway, 2007), 272, emphasis added.

Chapter 6: Relativism: The Primal Heresy

1. My experiences in the Soviet Bloc were the subject of the article "Iron Curtain Diary," Stand to Reason, January 1, 2021, www.str .org/w/iron-curtain-diary.
2. "When the woman saw that the tree was good for food, and that it was a delight to the eyes, and that the tree was desirable to make one wise, she took from its fruit and ate" (Gen. 3:6).
3. Hosea 8:7.
4. C. S. Lewis authored this metaphor in *Mere Christianity*, rev. ed. (2001; New York: HarperOne, 2015), 74.
5. Philosophers call this the "correspondence" view of truth.
6. I owe this insight to my dear friend J. Warner Wallace.
7. He may have beliefs, feelings, etc., about rape, of course, but that's not what he's describing.
8. According to Darwinism, our beliefs about morality are the result of the blind "design" of natural selection. Since that kind of morality is always on the inside and tells us nothing about the outside world, Darwinian morality is relativistic.
9. Moral relativism, then, is a kind of subjectivism, since judgments of right and wrong are up to the subject—the individual person or group—to decide.
10. Carl Trueman, *The Rise and Triumph of the Modern Self: Cultural Amnesia, Expressive Individualism, and the Road to Sexual Revolution* (Wheaton, IL: Crossway, 2020), 46.
11. Rod Dreher, *Live Not by Lies: A Manual for Christian Dissidents* (New York: Sentinel, 2020), 115–16.
12. As in the activist slogan "Silence is violence."
13. Recall the right-is-wrong, up-is-down "doublethink" slogans of the Party in George Orwell's *1984*: "War Is Peace," "Freedom Is Slavery," and "Ignorance Is Strength" (New York: Signet Classics, 1961), 4.
14. Ephesians 6:14.

Chapter 7: Atheism: Distractions

1. By *morality*, I mean deep morality—objective morality as opposed to some individual or cultural make-me-up that satisfies self-interest for the moment. By *evil* I mean a true violation of morality, what people have always meant when they raise the problem of evil against God.

2. Individual atheists may push back on this characterization ("That's not what *I* believe"), but often that's because they have not carefully considered the ramifications of their view that God does not exist.

3. Bertrand Russell, *A Free Man's Worship*, repr. (1923; Portland, ME: Thomas Bird Mosher, 1927), 6–7, www.google.com/books/edition A_Free_Man_s_Worship/3FzhcduD__8C?hl=en&gbpv=0.

4. Ibid., 7.

5. Standouts include Turek and Geisler's *I Don't Have Enough Faith to Be an Atheist*, J. Warner Wallace's *God's Crime Scene*, and Timothy Keller's *The Reason for God*, to name a few.

6. This view is also called physicalism or naturalism.

7. I owe this line of thinking to my philosopher friend Douglas Geivett.

8. This is a sound answer unless he can offer a fourth option, which he can't since it doesn't exist.

9. Peter Boghossian, *A Manual for Creating Atheists* (Durham, NC: Pitchstone Publishing, 2013), 22–23.

10. Ibid., 80.

11. Ibid., 68.

12. Ibid., 23–24.

13. Ibid., 23.

14. Find my full response to Boghossian's project in "Tactics for Atheists," Stand to Reason, May 1, 2019, www.str.org/w/tactics -for-atheists.

15. Whether a critic believes the accounts or not isn't relevant to my point: since the Bible offers reasons for faith, biblical faith is not blind. A skeptic may not find those reasons persuasive, but that's a different matter.

16. In my estimation, there simply are no good arguments for atheism,

thus the distractions: pushing the burden of proof onto the theist by redefining atheism as lack of belief, and charging that theism is irrational or without evidence.

17. Arguments for God abound, and tomes have been written detailing them, including rationales based on: the origin of the universe, design of all sorts, objective morality, well-documented miracles, and Jesus' resurrection, to name just a few.

18. Richard Dawkins, *The God Delusion* (Boston: Houghton Mifflin, 2006), 53.

Chapter 8: God: The Best Explanation

1. Truth as correspondence to reality, or the correspondence view of truth, is the garden variety definition of truth, what people almost always mean when they use the word.

2. See, for example, Nancy Pearcey, *Finding Truth: Five Principles for Unmasking Atheism, Secularism, and Other God Substitutes* (Colorado Springs: Cook, 2015).

3. For an accounting of the prodigious scientific evidence for an absolute beginning of the universe, see Stephen C. Meyer, *Return of the God Hypothesis: Three Scientific Discoveries That Reveal the Mind behind the Universe* (New York: HarperCollins, 2021), chaps. 4–6.

4. I realize the big bang is controversial for many Christians because the event is generally associated with an ancient universe. The critical detail here, though, is that modern science, despite its biases, affirms a de facto creation event that fits nicely with our own story but is a mystery with materialism. Even Christians who are not convinced of the big bang can still leverage the skeptic's belief in their own favor, as we shall see.

5. Notice how my first questions, examples of Columbo #1, gather information that lays a foundation for my concluding point. I have gently enlisted the challenger as an ally to help him answer his own challenge.

6. I say "no thing" instead of "nothing" because some treat "nothing" like a kind of something. Odd, but it happens. Substituting "no thing" avoids that liability.

7. See William Lane Craig, *Reasonable Faith: Christian Truth and Apologetics*, 3rd ed. (Wheaton, IL: Crossway, 2008).

8. As it turned out, an overpumped tire inner tube had exploded.

9. Dawkins, *The God Delusion*, 143.

10. Here is what I said when Shermer raised the issue in our debate: "*You* don't believe God was created because you don't believe in God. *I* don't believe God was created because God is a self-existent, uncreated being. *No one* in this conversation believes God was created. So why are you asking who created God?"

11. Another type of fallacy where a question is based on an assumption that hasn't been established.

12. I go into more detail on the problem with the question "Who created God?" in *The Story of Reality* (Grand Rapids, MI: Zondervan, 2017), 50–51.

13. For a thorough—and compelling—treatment of this subject, see Stephen Meyer, *Signature in the Cell* (New York: HarperOne, 2009).

14. The nucleotide bases that pair to form the instructions are adenine, thymine, guanine, and cytosine.

15. For those tempted to object, "But now you're outside of science," remember: the entire *scientific* SETI project depends on our ability to recognize the signature of intelligence in encoded messages. The methodology here is the same. Anthropology and forensic pathology—both scientific enterprises—also infer intelligent agency from physical effects.

16. Michael Denton, *Evolution: A Theory in Crisis* (London: Burnett Books, 1985), 334.

17. For more details, see Guillermo Gonzales and Jay W. Richards, *The Privileged Planet* (Washington, DC: Regnery Publishing, 2004); Peter D. Ward and Donald Brownlee, *Rare Earth* (New York: Copernicus Books, 2000); and Meyer, *Return of the God Hypothesis*, chaps. 7–9.

18. See Michael Behe, *Darwin's Black Box* (New York: The Free Press, 1996).

19. Charles Darwin, *On the Origin of Species* (London: Cassell and Company, 1909), 175, www.google.com/books/edition/On_the _Origin_of_Species/d9biAAAAMAAJ?hl=en&gbpv=0. I'm aware of attempts to get around this problem by suggesting, theoretically, that evolution could have "constructed" the simpler parts of these machines for a different use, then repurposed them for the larger mechanism. First, theories are not evidence. No one has shown this actually took place. Second, the sheer number of these molecular machines combined with their staggering complexity—the smaller parts themselves are irreducibly complex—makes that alternative a *practical* impossibility.

20. See the superb Illustra Media DVDs *Living Waters* and *Metamorphosis* for details. Their *Flight* DVD is also stunning.

21. Fred Hoyle, "The Universe: Past and Present Reflection," *Annual Review of Astronomy and Astrophysics* 20 (1982): 16.

22. Quoted in Meyer, *Return of the God Hypothesis*, 108.

23. Antony Flew, *There Is a God: How the World's Most Notorious Atheist Changed His Mind* (New York: HarperOne, 2007), 155.

24. Ibid., 75, 88.

25. Robert Jastrow, *God and the Astronomers*, 2nd ed. (New York: Norton, 1992), 107.

26. Dawkins, *The God Delusion*, 145.

27. This odd circumstance we find ourselves in of pondering our unlikely existence is called the weak anthropic principle (WAP).

28. Craig, *Reasonable Faith*, 168.

29. Douglas Groothuis, *Christian Apologetics: A Comprehensive Case for Biblical Faith* (Downers Grove, IL: InterVarsity Press, 2011), 260.

30. This principle is known as "Occam's razor." It's a scientific axiom that says the simplest explanation that does the job is probably the best explanation.

31. Richard Dawkins, *The Blind Watchmaker* (New York: Norton, 1986), 1.

32. Douglas Axe, *Undeniable: How Biology Confirms Our Intuition That Life Is Designed* (New York: HarperOne, 2016), 234.

Chapter 9: Evil: Atheism's Fatal Flaw

1. See Greg Koukl, *The Story of Reality*, chap. 14, and Gregory Ganssle, "God and Evil," part 3 in *Thinking about God: First Steps in Philosophy* (Downers Grove, IL: InterVarsity Press: 2004).

2. A variation known as the inductive problem of evil is still in play. Since both the deductive and the inductive complaint rely on the existence of genuine evil—objective evil, that is—they both falter for the same reason I'll explain soon. Thus, my approach dispatches both birds with the same stone.

3. Richard Dawkins, *River out of Eden* (New York: Basic Books, 1995), 132–33.

4. A number of notable atheists have been quite candid on this point.

5. Ironically for the Christian, then, evil is an ally since it fits his worldview like a glove.

6. Koukl, *The Story of Reality*, 35.

7. This syllogism is a logically valid form of argument called *modus tollens*.

8. It's possible for atheists to avoid this dilemma by making no implicit claims about evil in the world but instead pointing to the apparent internal contradiction in theism. I've almost never heard it put this way in actual conversations, though. Atheists usually launch their complaint by implicitly affirming objective evil.

9. For a more thorough discussion of why citing evil in favor of atheism is self-defeating, see Greg Koukl, "Evil as Evidence for God," Stand to Reason, February 5, 2013, www.str.org/w/evil -as-evidence-for-god.

10. For the more philosophically inclined, there's an alternative for grounding objective morality apart from God. It's called atheistic moral Platonism, the idea that abstract moral values like goodness and mercy and love exist objectively in the immaterial world of ideals. Abstract objects, however, are—in philosophic language—causally inert; they don't do anything, so they can never impose the kind of ethical duties that lie at the heart of morality. Since obligations are held between persons, moral Platonism cannot explain what needs to be explained. For a thorough discussion of

the liabilities of atheistic moral Platonism, see William Lane Craig, *Reasonable Faith: Christian Truth and Apologetics*, 3rd ed. (Wheaton, IL: Crossway, 2008), 178–79.

11. Notice, by the way, my persistent use of clarification questions (Columbo #1) both to confirm important information and to keep the conversation moving forward in a friendly, interactive way.

12. This ancient conundrum is known as the "Euthyphro dilemma." For more detail, see Greg Koukl, "Who Says God Is Good?" Stand to Reason, February 28, 2013, www.str.org/w/who-says-god-is -good-1?p.

13. Psalm 19:7–11.

Chapter 10: Good without God?

1. For a lucid response to Hitchens's challenge, see Amy K. Hall, "Hitchens's Challenge Solved," Stand to Reason, September 8, 2008, www.str.org/w/hitchens-s-challenge-solved.

2. The other three are the cosmological, teleological (design), and ontological arguments.

3. Jeremy Rifkin, *Algeny: A New Word—A New World* (New York: Viking, 1983), 244.

4. A. J. Ayer, "Emotivism," in Louis Pojman, *Ethical Theory* (Belmont, CA: Wadsworth, 1995), 416.

5. Frankly, if God did not exist, my actions would be different in lots of ways. What those differences could not be, though, is immoral since the moral standard distinguishing good from evil wouldn't exist.

6. James Anderson, *What's Your Worldview? An Interactive Approach to Life's Big Questions* (Wheaton, IL: Crossway, 2014), 69.

7. Philosopher Michael Ruse begins his naturalistic account of morality with, "The matter of scientific fact with which I start this discussion is that evolution is true." "Naturalist Moral Nonrealism," part 2 in R. Keith Loftin, ed., *God and Morality: Four Views* (Downers Grove, IL: Intervarsity Press, 2012), 54.

8. Stephen C. Meyer, *Darwin's Doubt* (New York: HarperCollins, 2013), 292.

9. Note the distinction here between the epistemic issue—how we *know* moral truth—and the ontological issue—how we account for morality's *existence*.

10. Ruse, "Naturalist Moral Nonrealism," part 2 in Loftin, ed., *God and Morality*, 60.

11. Michael Shermer, *The Science of Good and Evil: Why People Cheat, Gossip, Care, Share, and Follow the Golden Rule* (New York: Holt, 2004), 56, emphasis added.

12. Ibid., 64, emphasis added.

13. Ibid., 19, emphasis added.

14. Curiously, these are two entirely distinct processes: an event cause (mechanistic, evolutionary forces acting on the genetic code), and an agent cause (cultural norms—a type of human design).

15. Though some evolutionists focus solely on the genetic contribution.

16. Clearly, there can be objective criteria for, say, human flourishing—as atheist Sam Harris argues—but that is not the same as objective morality. If human flourishing is itself an objective moral good, that must be established separately.

17. Michael Ruse and E. O. Wilson, "The Evolution of Morality," *New Scientist* 1478 (1985): 108–28, quoted in Ruse, "Naturalist Moral Nonrealism," part 2 in Loftin, ed., *God and Morality*, 69.

18. Ruse, "Naturalist Moral Nonrealism," part 2 in Loftin, ed., *God and Morality*, 65, emphasis added.

19. Ibid.

20. Ibid., 68.

21. C. S. Lewis, "Is Theology Poetry?" in *The Weight of Glory: And Other Addresses* (New York: HarperCollins, 1976), 139.

22. At least on the supra-atomic level.

23. Stephen Hawking and Leonard Mlodinow, *The Grand Design* (New York: Bantam, 2010), 30.

24. Ibid., emphasis added.

25. Ibid., 31–32, emphasis added.

26. Ibid., 32, emphasis added.

27. Ibid., emphasis added.

Chapter 11: Jesus, the Son

1. Ronald Nash, *The Gospel and the Greeks: Did the New Testament Borrow from Pagan Thought?* 2nd ed. (Phillipsburg, NJ: P&R Publishing, 2003).

2. Lee Strobel, *The Case for the Real Jesus: A Journalist Investigates Current Attacks on the Identity of Christ* (Grand Rapids, MI: Zondervan, 2007).

3. I go into detail on this challenge in *The Story of Reality*, chap. 16.

4. Tryggve Mettinger, *The Riddle of Resurrection: "Dying and Rising Gods" in the Ancient Near East* (Stockholm: Almqvist and Wiksell International, 2001), 221.

5. Gary Habermas, *The Verdict of History* (Nashville: Thomas Nelson, 1988), 108.

6. See Titus Kennedy, *Excavating the Evidence for Jesus: The Archaeology and History of Christ and the Gospels* (Eugene, OR: Harvest House, 2022).

7. Will Durant, *Caesar and Christ*, Story of Civilization, vol. 3 (New York: Simon and Schuster, 1972), 557.

8. Bart Ehrman, *Did Jesus Exist? The Historical Argument for Jesus of Nazareth* (New York: HarperCollins, 2012).

9. Bart D. Ehrman, "Freedom from Religion Foundation Lecture," given during the "Freedom from Religion in the Bible Belt" conference (Raleigh: Raleigh Regional Convention, May 2014), video shared August 14, 2014, on YouTube, 51:16, www.youtube.com/watch?v=VAhw2cVRVsA&ab_channel=BartD.Ehrman.

10. Ibid., 52:31, emphasis in the original video.

11. Ibid., 53:04.

12. Acts 17:18–32.

13. Arguing from effect back to probable cause, storied cold-case detective and bestselling author J. Warner Wallace chronicles the explosive impact Jesus of Nazareth had on virtually every quarter of culture—music, art, literature, science, world religion, and so forth. Fictional figures simply do not leave such an evidence trail. See J. Warner Wallace, *Person of Interest: Why Jesus Still Matters in a World That Rejects the Bible* (Grand Rapids, MI: Zondervan, 2021).

14. I realize this is not a theologically precise way of putting it, but I think it will do for the moment.

15. For our purposes here, I will not address the broader issue of the deity of the Spirit but rather focus on Jesus.

16. Richard Bauckham, *God Crucified: Monotheism and Christology in the New Testament* (Grand Rapids, MI: Eerdmans, 1999), 25.

17. C. S. Lewis, *Mere Christianity* (New York: Macmillan, 1943), 143.

18. Mark 8:31; 9:31; Luke 18:33.

19. Colossians 1:17.

20. Each of these three characteristics is true of the Holy Spirit, as well.

21. I explore the doctrine of the Trinity more thoroughly in a two-part series titled "The Trinity: A Solution, Not a Problem," Stand to Reason, October 30, 2015, www.str.org/w/the-trinity-a-solution -not-a-problem-part-1.

22. A unitarian holds there is one God, and he is a unity—that is, he is only one person.

23. This complaint is another you'll encounter, that since Jesus was God, when he prayed to God, he was only praying to himself. Note, though, that when you and I pray to God, we don't pray to his *nature*. We speak to God's person: "our *Father*." In that same sense, the person of Jesus, the Son, could pray to the person of God, the Father, without contradiction or confusion. He was not praying to himself.

24. I call this little review "narrating the debate." Find more details on this technique in *Tactics*, 93.

25. Robert G. Ingersoll, "The Foundations of Faith," in *The Works of Robert G. Ingersoll*, vol. 4, *Dresden Edition—Lectures* (New York, 1900; Project Gutenberg, 2012), www.gutenberg.org/files/38804 /38804-h/38804-h.htm#link0007.

26. Notice, I go out of my way to affirm anything I can agree with. It's tactically sound, and it's also good manners.

27. See also Mark 2:5–7 and John 5:18; 8:56–59; 19:7.

28. Leviticus 24:16.

29. John 8:58.

30. For a complete treatment of this point, see "Was Jesus Worshiped?"

Stand to Reason, June 26, 2019, https://www.str.org/search?q=was+jesus+worshiped%3F.

31. Acts 17:28–29.

32. I am not trying to establish here that Jesus is divine. That requires other evidence—like the resurrection, for example (see Rom. 1:4). I'm merely trying to show that the authoritative Christian record—the New Testament—declares him to be uniquely divine.

33. The late apologist Bob Passantino alerted me to this gem.

34. John 1:1.

Chapter 12: Christ, the Savior

1. *Cur Deus Homo*, in the original Latin, which is the title of an eleventh-century work by Saint Anselm of Canterbury explaining the reasons why God had to take on a human nature to rescue fallen man.

2. 1 Corinthians 15:17–19.

3. John's statement is also a clear testimony of the importance of evidence—apologetics—to make the case for Christ.

4. Note also that God revealed to Simeon that Jesus was *the Lord's* Christ (Luke 2:25–26).

5. For a detailed treatment of this point, see James White, "I Am He," chap. 6 in *The Forgotten Trinity: Recovering the Heart of Christian Belief* (Minneapolis: Bethany, 1998).

6. John 10:18: "No one has taken it away from Me, but I lay it down on My own."

7. This is why Jesus told the Jewish leaders, "Your father Abraham rejoiced to see My day, and he saw it and was glad" (John 8:56).

8. God reaffirms this promise during Judah's captivity in Babylon through the prophet Jeremiah (33:20–21).

9. The Jewish scholars at the time of Christ understood this passage to be messianic because the scribes cited this prophecy to Herod when the Magi visited him (Matt. 2:5–6).

10. Crucifixion was never a method of capital punishment for Jews and was only practiced under Roman jurisprudence (*Encyclopedia Americana*, vol. 8 [1960], 253).

11. Virtually every one of the thirteen times the gospel is preached in Acts by those whom Jesus personally trained to follow him, the writer focuses on guilt, impending judgment, and the need for forgiveness. Curiously, the love of God isn't mentioned a single time. For details, see Greg Koukl, "Preaching God's Love in Acts?" Stand to Reason, March 22, 2013, https://www.str.org/w /preaching-god-s-love-in-acts-?p_l.

12. I've developed this point in detail in the two-part article "One Way or Any Way?" Stand to Reason, January 1, 2019, www.str.org/w /one-way-or-any-way-part-i.

13. Clearly, Jesus was not a pluralist.

14. Find a thorough development of these points with additional supporting text references in my booklet *Jesus, the Only Way: 100 Verses* (Signal Hill, CA: Stand to Reason, 2009).

15. I call this tactic "What a Friend We Have in Jesus" and develop it in *Tactics*, chap. 18.

16. This move is an informal fallacy called ad hominem.

17. This reply is one example of how someone might respond, but there are other possible responses. No matter. Regardless of what the other person gives as criteria, the tactical approach I'm offering here applies.

18. This claim is quantifiably false, yet it's a common misunderstanding.

Chapter 13: The Bible: Ancient Words, Ever True?

1. Michael W. Smith, "Ancient Words," *Worship Again*, Provient Label Group, 2002.

2. C. S. Lewis, *Mere Christianity* (New York: Simon & Schuster, 1943), 119.

3. Genre refers to the kind or category of the writing—history, poetry, parable, etc.

4. Since these three are necessary to accurately read writings of any sort, there is nothing exotic about reading Scripture. Most of the time, we should read it the ordinary way.

5. Inerrancy *is*, however, a critical *in-house* concern, to be sure. When

churches abandon a high view of Scripture, central doctrines begin to topple, and Christianity falls into ruin.

6. Note that the New Testament Bible is not a single book, but a library of books that were circulating individually around the Mediterranean in the first century. Later—in the second century and beyond—they were bound together under one cover (a codex), creating the volume we call the Bible.

7. See Paul's statement in 1 Corinthians 15:12–19.

8. Greek *theopneustos*, literally "God-breathed," 2 Timothy 3:16.

9. I went into some detail on this point in chapter 11.

10. There may be times when you'll *quote* an individual verse, of course. I do it all the time. There's nothing wrong with that if you've taken careful stock of the context so you're reasonably confident you're not misrepresenting the author's meaning.

11. For an accessible, popular book on biblical interpretation, see Gordon Fee and Douglas Stuart, *How to Read the Bible for All Its Worth* (Grand Rapids, MI: Zondervan, 1982). For a superb, thorough treatment, see William Klein, Craig Blomberg, and Robert Hubbard Jr., *Introduction to Biblical Interpretation* (Nashville: Thomas Nelson, 1993).

12. Our first Columbo question, "What do you mean by that?" is always in order when this issue comes up. What exactly do they mean by "literally"?

13. Critics raise other issues that, for the sake of space, I cannot cover here. For an excellent, accessible treatment of other problem passages, see Dan Kimball, *How (Not) to Read the Bible: Making Sense of the Anti-Women, Anti-Science, Pro-Violence, Pro-Slavery and Other Crazy-Sounding Parts of Scripture* (Grand Rapids, MI: Zondervan, 2020).

14. Richard Dawkins, *The God Delusion* (Boston: Houghton Mifflin, 2006), 31.

15. See Dawkins's quote in chapter 9.

16. An appropriate question for the atheist raising this concern is, "Where are you getting your moral standard to judge God by?"

17. Paul Copan, *Is God a Moral Monster? Making Sense of the Old Testament God* (Grand Rapids, MI: Baker, 2011), 171.

18. Ibid., 175–77. Copan argues, "All the archaeological evidence indicates that no civilian populations existed at Jericho, Ai, and other cities mentioned in Joshua." Since attacks were directed at smaller military outposts holding soldiers, women and children probably weren't targets. Noncombatants generally lived in outlying rural areas. Rahab (Josh. 2:1) was likely an innkeeper at the outpost, and such inns were also brothels for the soldiers.

19. In Acts 7:45, Stephen refers to God driving out the nations and dispossessing them, not annihilating them.

20. Canaanite fertility religion tied eroticism of all sorts to the successful cycles of planting and harvest.

21. This may explain God's command to destroy even domestic animals, in some cases.

22. For an excellent response to the charge that God himself required child sacrifice of the Israelites, see Amy K. Hall, "God Didn't Command Child Sacrifice," Stand to Reason, October 9, 2015, www.str.org/w/god-didn-t-command-child-sacrifice.

23. Clay Jones, "We Don't Hate Sin So We Don't Understand What Happened to the Canaanites: An Addendum to 'Divine Genocide' Arguments," *Philosophia Christi* 11, no. 1 (2009): 61, ibs.cru.org /files/5214/3336/7724/We-Dont-Hate-Sin-PC-article.pdf.

24. Susanna Shelby Brown, *Late Carthaginian Child Sacrifice and Sacrificial Moments in Their Mediterranean Context* (Sheffield, England: Sheffield Academic, 1991), 75, referenced in Jones, "We Don't Hate Sin," 62n38.

25. See Leviticus 19:34 and 24:22, and Deuteronomy 10:18–19.

26. In the case of the Amalekites, God's judgment was for their unprovoked ambush of his people when en route to the land (1 Sam. 15; Deut. 25:17–19).

27. 1 Kings 9:7–9.

28. The Abrahamic covenant (Gen. 12:1–3). Recall from chapter 12 how God's rescuer would come forth from Abraham's people, bringing salvation to all the world—Canaanites included.

29. Copan, *Is God a Moral Monster?* 181, 178.

30. Kimball, *How (Not) to Read the Bible*, 285.

31. Psalm 106:34–38.
32. 2 Kings 17:16–18.
33. "All sanctioned Yahweh battles beyond the time of Joshua were defensive." Copan, *Is God a Moral Monster?* 179. The Amalekites (see preceding footnote) would be a possible exception.
34. Copan, *Is God a Moral Monster?* 191.
35. Jones, "We Don't Hate Sin," 53.
36. England's William Wilberforce comes to mind, but there were many others.
37. Note, also, 1 Timothy 1:9–10: "Law is not made for a righteous person, but for those who are lawless and rebellious, for the ungodly and sinners, for . . . kidnappers . . . and whatever else is contrary to sound teaching."
38. In context, the punishment required in verse 20 would be the penalty described in verse 12: death.
39. Recall that in ancient Israel, an engaged woman was considered married. This violence, then, would be an act of forced adultery. If a man raped a woman not engaged, the Law—to protect the woman—required he marry her and care for her the rest of her life. Otherwise, she would have been unmarriageable and destitute (Deut. 22:28–29; cf. 2 Sam. 13:11–14).
40. I was alerted to this trend by Peter J. Williams.
41. Note Jesus' comments in Matthew 19:8 on the reasons God allowed divorce.
42. Dr. Peter J. Williams, "Lecture—Peter Williams 'Does the Bible Support Slavery?'" Lanier Library Lecture Series (Houston: Lanier Theological Library Chapel House, October 30, 2015), video shared by fleetwd1, December 2, 2015, on YouTube, youtube.com/watch?v=EUOsBQYuZ9g.
43. Copan, *Is God a Moral Monster?* 127.
44. Female servant.
45. For a thorough treatment of the biblical texts on slavery, see Copan, *Is God a Moral Monster?* See also Paul Copan, *Is God a Vindictive Bully? Reconciling Portrayals of God in the Old and New Testaments* (Grand Rapids, MI: Baker Academic, 2022).

Chapter 14: God: The Science Stopper

1. Christopher Hitchens and Jay W. Richards, "Atheism vs. Theism and the Scientific Evidence of Intelligent Design," debate (Stanford, CA: Stanford University, January 27, 2008), video shared by ChristopherHitchslap, October 19, 2011, on YouTube, 42:44, www.youtube.com/watch?v=KZTzZyloR8w.

2. QED is the acronym for the Latin phrase *quod erat demonstrandum*, meaning the proof of the argument is complete.

3. A shell game is a trick used as a quick con to cheat someone using three nutshells or cups that are shuffled to disguise the location of an object under one of them.

4. Michael D. Lemonick, "Glimpses of the Mind," *TIME*, July 17, 1995, content.time.com/time/subscriber/article/0,33009,983176 -8,00.html.

5. Ibid.

6. This kind of assumption is called an *a priori* belief—one that is alleged prior to and apart from observation or experience.

7. Sagan did not describe himself as atheist, though, but agnostic since he believed no one could be certain about God's existence. He was a deeply committed naturalist, however.

8. *Cosmos: A Personal Voyage*, episode 1, "The Shores of the Cosmic Ocean," 4:27.

9. Natasha Crain, *Faithfully Different: Regaining Biblical Clarity in a Secular Culture* (Eugene, OR: Harvest House, 2022), 69.

10. Richard C. Lewontin, "Billions and Billions of Demons," *New York Review*, January 9, 1997, www.nybooks.com/articles/1997/01/09 /billions-and-billions-of-demons/, emphasis in the original.

11. I quote Lewontin myself and discuss this issue at length in *Tactics*, chap. 15.

12. Phillip E. Johnson, "The Unraveling of Scientific Materialism," *First Things*, November 1997, www.firstthings.com/article/1997 /11/the-unraveling-of-scientific-materialism.

13. For a thorough treatment of the God of the gaps question, see Stephen C. Meyer, *Return of the God Hypothesis* (New York: HarperCollins, 2021), chap. 20.

14. For a fascinating account of the birth of science in the Western world, see Meyer, *Return of the God Hypothesis*, part 1.

15. Meyer, *Return of the God Hypothesis*, 48. Meyer quotes Isaac Newton, "The Third Book of Opticks," in *Opticks: Or, A Treatise of the Reflections, Refractions, Inflexions and Colours of Light*, 2nd ed. (1718; London: The Newton Project, 2006), 345, www.newtonproject .ox.ac.uk/view/texts/normalized/NATP00051.

16. Surprisingly, Newton wrote more on theology—1.3 million words—than he did on science, according to Vincent Carroll and David Shiflett, *Christianity on Trial: Arguments against Anti-Religious Bigotry* (San Francisco: Encounter Books, 2002), 77.

17. Romans 1:20.

18. Psalm 19:4; Romans 10:18.

19. John Polkinghorne, *Belief in God in an Age of Science* (New Haven, CT: Yale University Press, 1998), 77.

20. See, for example, Meyer, *Return of the God Hypothesis*.

Chapter 15: Abortion: Only One Question

1. National Right to Life, "Reported Annual Abortions 1973–2019," January 2022, nrlc.org/uploads/factsheets/FS01AbortionintheUS .pdf. Based on numbers reported by the pro-choice Guttmacher Institute, originally founded as a research arm of Planned Parenthood.

2. "The Middle Passage," National Park Service, last updated December 2, 2021, www.nps.gov/articles/the-middle-passage.htm.

3. Mack Dean, "World War 2 Casualties," worldwar2facts.org, February 6, 2021, www.worldwar2facts.org/world-war-2 -casualties.html.

4. Some pro-lifers hold there are a number of questions in play, but I'm convinced that a single issue is foundational and key to addressing all other variations and potential pushbacks—even regarding the full humanity and full personhood of the unborn.

5. Some might say the next question is "Why? Why do you want to kill this?" If they do, remind them their back is turned, then ask, "Isn't there a more important question to ask first?"

6. I suggest that you memorize this statement.

7. Memorize this one, too.

8. I use the phrase *moral logic* because this is a logically valid syllogism with moral terms in both a premise and the conclusion.

9. Notice how, as a tactical concern, I try to agree as often as I can with legitimate points.

10. Notice how frequently I fall back on the first step of our game plan—gathering information—using various forms of our first Columbo question, "What do you mean by that?"

11. Be prepared for a blank stare when you ask this question. The response is almost never based on principle—they've never really thought about it—and is usually just a rhetorical dodge to dismiss your view.

12. The SLED Test was first introduced in Stephen Schwarz, *The Moral Question of Abortion* (Chicago: Loyola University Press, 1990).

13. Dennis Prager, KABC, Los Angeles, December 23, 1994.

14. Christopher Reeve, *Still Me* (New York: Random House, 1999), 28.

Chapter 16: Abortion: Beyond the Basics

1. Proverbs 18:21.

2. Robert Jay Lifton, *The Nazi Doctors: Medical Killing and the Psychology of Genocide* (New York: Basic Books, 1986), 15.

3. Ibid., 53.

4. Ibid., 70.

5. Ibid., 65.

6. Recall my caution from chapter 1 not to be robotic with these scripts. There's no need to follow the exchanges exactly as they appear here. Instead, use the sample questions to set your course and inform your strategy. Each conversation has its own life, and sometimes—especially with emotional issues like abortion—you'll need to stretch things out to soften the tone.

7. Both the "sovereign zone" terminology and the "right to refuse" phrase that comes later were coined by Trent Horn.

8. Judith Jarvis Thompson, "A Defense of Abortion," *Philosophy and Public Affairs* 1, no. 1 (Fall 1971): 48–49, eclass.uoa.gr/modules

/document/file.php/PPP475/Thomson%20Judith%20Jarvis
%2C%20A%20defense%20of%20abortion.pdf.

9. One variation claims the unborn child is attacking the mother, and therefore abortion is a legitimate act of self-defense. See Eileen McDonagh, *Breaking the Abortion Deadlock: From Choice to Consent* (New York: Oxford University Press, 1996). I deal with both Thompson's violinist argument and McDonagh's self-defense argument in "Unstringing the Violinist," Stand to Reason, February 4, 2013, www.str.org/w/unstringing-the-violinist.

10. Plus, no one "connected" the mother to her fetus in an artificial way. The woman is making the baby herself, a natural result of behavior she consented to, in most cases.

11. Justice for All (website), jfaweb.org.

12. Much of the material in this chapter has been informed by Josh Brahm's excellent insights found at Equal Rights Institute (website), equalrightsinstitute.com.

13. Many of the distinctions offered to disqualify unborn humans from those rights are addressed by the SLED responses we talked about in the last chapter.

14. This pushback is guilty of both a straw-man fallacy—since it doesn't take seriously the pro-lifer's case—and a genetic fallacy—since it faults the pro-life view because of the source of the complaint (a male) rather than the merits of the complaint itself.

15. I'm dealing only with the ethical status of abortion here, not the more complex policy concern of how we prosecute abortion within our legal system. That is a different question I'll leave to others more skilled in those matters. With legal judgments, facts always come first, then legislation appropriate to the facts. In the case of abortion, Scripture makes the moral facts clear.

16. Luke 1:31 indicates Jesus was himself even when he was conceived in the womb.

Chapter 17: Marriage, Sex, Gender, and Common Sense

1. Recall chapter 6, where I gave more detail on this idea.

2. Find more detail in chapter 5 about the nature of these demonic schemes.

3. It's worth noting, though, that many who hold to "silent Christ" seem to care little about those things he is not silent about when those things interfere with their personal projects—but that's another issue.

4. Alan Shlemon calls it "Letting Jesus Take the Heat." Alan Shelmon, "Let Jesus Take the Heat," Stand to Reason, September 23, 2019, www.str.org/w/let-jesus-take-the-heat.

5. In *Tactics*, chap. 18, I go into detail on how to legitimately employ this approach.

6. There are rare cases when an argument from silence is appropriate, but this is not one of them.

7. Review chapter 9 for more detail.

8. Those who, as a result of a congenital defect, are born intersex.

9. This internal conflict is known as "gender dysphoria." The apparent explosion of gender dysphoria (called "rapid onset" gender dysphoria) is a recent phenomenon and suggests that cultural pressure—what some have called a "social contagion"—is the principle driving force. In simple terms, transgenderism is a fad, though a profoundly destructive one. See Abigail Shrier, *Irreversible Damage: The Transgender Craze Seducing Our Daughters* (Washington, DC: Regnery Publishing, 2020). See also Nancy R. Pearcey, *Love Thy Body: Answering Hard Questions about Love and Sexuality* (Grand Rapids, MI: Baker, 2018).

10. With your own children, though, you may insist on a name consistent with their biology.

11. Paul McHugh, "Transgender Surgery Isn't the Solution," *Wall Street Journal*, May 13, 2016, www.wsj.com/articles/paul-mchugh -transgender-surgery-isnt-the-solution-1402615120.

12. No doubt that's coming, too, though, if the current trend continues. Parody quickly becomes reality; the absurd becomes convention. Years ago, theologian Francis Schaeffer observed that what was unthinkable yesterday is thinkable today and ordinary and commonplace tomorrow.

13. I owe this line of questioning to Matt Walsh.

14. Recall that I am using the word *gender* synonymously with *biological sex*.

15. See Gregory Koukl, "Same-Sex Marriage Challenges and Responses," Stand to Reason, May 1, 2004, www.str.org/w/same -sex-marriage-challenges-and-responses.

16. Government privileges relationships that contribute to government interests. It has no interest in stable relationships in general, only in stabilizing particular *kinds* of relationships—generally, economic relations tied to commerce (e.g., corporations) and those where the protection of children is a factor. Inheritance rights flow naturally to progeny. Tax relief for families eases the financial burden children make on paychecks. Insurance policies reflect the unique relationship between a wage earner and his or her dependents.

17. It's easy to resist any suggestion that marriage and family are fundamentally connected to children. Clearly, not all families have kids. Some marriages are barren, by choice or by circumstance. This proves nothing, though. The natural marriage/procreation connection is not nullified because in some cases children are not intended or even possible. The state protects conjugal marriage because of its institutional importance to culture. Pointing out exceptional cases doesn't nullify the general rule.

    The fact that same-sex couples can legally adopt changes nothing. This, too, subverts the purpose of marriage by robbing children of a vital ingredient: mothers or fathers. By licensing same-sex marriage, society declares by law that two men or two women are equally suited to raise a child, that mothers and fathers contribute nothing unique to healthy child-rearing. This is self-evidently false. Moms and dads are not interchangeable.

    The same is true when singles adopt, by the way, which I also oppose for the same reasons. The exception is when there is no other alternative for a child (any loving relationship is better for a child than an institution), but this is not usually the case. A mother and a father should have priority in adoption.

18. Though Jesus didn't use the word *homosexuality*, his teaching on sex and marriage apply to it.

19. I owe this insight to my STR colleague Alan Shlemon.

20. 2 Thessalonians 2:10.

21. Notice these all involve sex with someone other than a person's opposite-sex spouse.

22. For a detailed treatment of attempts by some within the church to biblically sanitize homosexuality, see Alan Shelmon, "A Reformation the Church Doesn't Need," Stand to Reason, June 30, 2015, www.str.org/w/a-reformation-the-church-doesn-t-need -part-1.

23. This rejoinder is called the "cultural distance argument."

24. For an excellent concise treatment of this issue, see Kevin DeYoung, *What Does the Bible Really Teach about Homosexuality?* (Wheaton, IL: Crossway, 2015).

25. Notice, again, the explicit reference to binary sexuality and the presumption of heterosexual marriage.

26. Aleksandr Solzhenitsyn, "Live Not by Lies," February 12, 1974, trans. Yermolai Solzhenitsyn, The Aleksandr Solzhenitsyn Center, 2006, www.solzhenitsyncenter.org/live-not-by-lies. See also Rod Dreher, *Live Not by Lies: A Manual for Christian Dissidents* (New York: Sentinel, 2020), 18.

27. Dreher, *Live Not by Lies*, 162.

28. Many are being pressured, even by other Christians, to show "gender hospitality" by using preferred pronouns to generate goodwill with those who are transgender. Rosaria Butterfield, a former lesbian activist who is now a committed Christian, argues against this practice in "Why I No Longer Use Transgender Pronouns—and Why You Shouldn't, Either," *Reformation21*, April 3, 2023, https://www.reformation21.org/blog/why-i-no -longer-use-transgender-pronouns-and-why-you-shouldnt-either.

Chapter 18: Final Words for the Street

1. *Tactics* can also be a benefit by providing a series of maneuvers— with plenty of anecdotes and illustrations—to help you be more effective on the street.

2. See *Tactics*, chap. 18 for a strategy to manage steamrollers.

3. Patrick Pinak, "Aaron Rodgers Rips Christianity, Religion in Interview: 'Religion Can Be a Crutch,'" FanBuzz, January 18, 2022, fanbuzz.com/nfl/aaron-rodgers-interview-religion/.

Also Available

Tactics provides the game plan for defending your faith and artfully communicating the truths of Christianity with confidence and grace. Study guide and video resources also available.

In **The Story of Reality**, Gregory Koukl explains the narrative backbone of the Christian story and how all the plotlines of that story are resolved in the end. Study guide and video resources also available.

Stand
to Reason

Stand to Reason offers thoughtful, relevant materials to expand your knowledge, develop your wisdom, and cultivate your character, allowing you to maneuver graciously in every situation, including:

Confidence
for every Christian
Clear Thinking
for every challenge
Courage and Grace
for every encounter

 Call-in program for answers to your questions

 MP3s, CDs, books and DVDs to help you dig deeper

 In-depth articles on today's challenging cultural issues

 Apps for helpful content on-the-go

 New monthly teaching to equip you to defend your convictions

 Blog posts addressing timely issues and challenges

We address issues you care about and need to be prepared to tackle. Whether you are searching for the truth about God and the world, are brand new to Christianity, or are a long-time follower of Christ, **we have something for you.**

SUBSCRIBE NOW ON APPLE PODCASTS

#STR*ask*
with Greg Koukl & Amy Hall

GREG AND AMY ANSWER
QUESTIONS FROM TWITTER AND
INSTAGRAM USING #STRask

Stand to Reason
with **Greg Koukl**

GREG INTERACTS WITH CALLERS
AND SHARES HIS THOUGHTS ON
RELEVANT TOPICS

1438 E 33rd St, Signal Hill CA 90755 · 1–800–2–REASON · **STR.ORG**